WHO KILLED SCIENCE FICTION?

Compleat &
Unexpurgated

JOIN

THE 18th WORLD
SCIENCE FICTION CONVENTION

c/o DIRCE S. ARCHER
1453 BARNSDALE STREET
PITTSBURGH 17, PENNSYLVANIA

YOUR BEST TWO-BUCK INVESTMENT!

MAKE ALL CHECKS PAYABLE TO
P. SCHUYLER MILLER, TREASURER

WHO KILLED SCIENCE FICTION?

Compleat &
Unexpurgated

edited by Earl Kemp
Associate Editor Earl Terry Kemp

The Merry Blacksmith Press
2011

Who Killed Science Fiction?: Compleat & Unexpurgated

For information, address:

The Merry Blacksmith Press
70 Lenox Ave.
West Warwick, RI 02893

merryblacksmith.com

Published in the USA by The Merry Blacksmith Press

ISBN—978-0-61544-103-0
0-61544-103-3

In memory of
124C41+
Hugo Gernsback

Very Best to you for a great job well done Ed Emsh —

a ◆ report . . . .

Table of Contents

Publisher's Introduction
2011

I suppose the first question is: "Why?"

As in, "Why produce a print edition of a work that has long been available for free on-line?"

Good question. I suppose one answer simply could be, "Because it's there," but that might come off as a bit smarmy and we can't have that.

A better, more accurate answer would be because it is one of my favorite books under the subject heading of "The History of Science Fiction"—a topic which I have long had a fascination for. Anyone who may recall my "not-quite-entirely-dead-but-Lordie-is-there-ever-going-to-be-an-issue-#3?" fanzine, *Sleight of Hand*, will not be surprised by this revelation. Nor should it be any surprise that one of the first books out of the gate when I started Merry Blacksmith Press was a collection of Bud Webster's "Anthopology 101" columns which explored and discussed various historically significant science fiction anthologies and anthologists.

So when I started to scout around for a new title to publish, I decided to look into reprinting a collection of fan writing, or something in the vein of science fiction history. With *Who Killed Science Fiction?* I got both.

In 1960, Earl Kemp asked science fiction authors and fans what they thought of the current state of the field. Was science fiction dead or dying? If so, why and how? What could be done about it? The answers were varied, but for the most part science fiction was doing fine, but like any living thing, it needed continued nurturing. Seventy-one people responded to Earl's questions—many names readily recognized, some perhaps less so unless you were already indoctrinated into the culture of science fiction fandom. The answers garnered from many of the most well-known and respected writers, editors and fans of day were compiled into a limited-run, one-shot fanzine, *SaFari*

i

Annual #1, which won the Hugo in 1961 for Best Fanzine. My parents had not even met at that point in time.

Twenty years later, Earl asked another round of questions. He asked questions about the success that the field enjoyed in the two decades since the original *Who Killed Science Fiction?*, and what the future held. Many of the original seventy-one contributors returned, as well as a few new and notable names. This was intended to be the second edition. In 1980 I was just entering high school, but I was already a life-long fan. I managed the science fiction section of my father's bookstore, and was an unofficial consultant for both my school library and the Westerly Public Library. If I had seen the 1980 edition, which sadly never came out, I would have been thrilled beyond belief. Those were my people talking about one of my great passions.

In 2006, Earl produced a complete and unexpurgated edition in his fanzine *eI29* (Vol. 5 No. 6) which appears, still now, online at Bill Burns' treasure-trove of a website—efanzines.com. *eI* is an incredible read. Every issue. I highly recommend it. To place myself within the timeline, by this point I had managed to publish a few pro short stories, had been making a occasional nuisance of myself in fandom, and working on the edges of the publishing world.

And now we come back to this print edition—started in 2010 and finished at the very dawn of 2011. Yes, an online edition exists, but many fans of science fiction's past, such as myself, still lean toward physical, handheld books that don't require batteries. That may seem a little contradictory given science fiction's penchant for forward-thinking and leading the curve in technology, but the tactile pleasure of holding a bound book is hard to beat. This edition does not differ greatly from the online edition, but there are a couple of things which set this printed book apart.

I've added a few more graphics: some Rotsler illos to reflect that fanzine-reader feel, and some small magazine covers in order to place some of the contributors within the context of the field. That, and it looks nice to have some graphics break up the text here and there. I've included most of the graphics from the original edition, but the originals were difficult to get a hold of and some of the *SaFari*-edition graphics and signatures look a little rough. I wish the Ed Wood graph was clearer, but I was not going to omit anything on account of some fuzzy roughness. The online version of the graph isn't much easier to read either.

Textually, I've not changed much at all. I've made sure the correct entries are with the correct names, but that's about it. Who the hell am I to edit folks like John W. Campbell or Kurt Vonnegut? Sure, there are some run-on sentences here and there. Sentence fragments A few misspelled names. But why change that? Reading *Who Killed Science Fiction?* is like listening in on an informal conversation between colleagues, friends, and family. There is a certain charm and authenticity to the occasional typo in these correspondences. But for the most part, this was all pretty clean text. These are professional writers, after all.

The index was tricky. For one, I'll be the first to admit that I am not an experienced indexer. I did the best I could in making everything consistent and accurate, but I expect some eagle-eyed readers to catch errors. Feel free to pass them on to me at john@merryblacksmith.com and I'll make sure they get fixed should there be an opportunity for a new printing. One thing I tried to preserve from the earlier edition is bolding the page numbers of responses to Earl's queries from both 1960 and 1980.

But back to that initial question of why I wanted to publish a print edition of this book. The most honest, no-bullshit answer is simply because I wanted to. This is one of the most significant and interesting works in the history of science fiction, and I wanted to be a part of it, if even in just some small way.

For that, I am grateful to Earl Kemp for allowing me to publish this. Thank you, Earl!

– John Teehan
Merry Blacksmith Press
January 11, 2011

Introduction 2006
Four Years Too Early

I lost **1980**...and it falling only four years short of George Orwell's dark fantasy. It's not something I do often, but it does happen. I was 50 at the time, old enough to know better. It was the year of significant happenings: old hero Henry Miller died and young hero John Lennon was assassinated... and the World Science Fiction Convention was held in Boston.

And, wouldn't you know it, I had just gotten around to working on one of my pet projects, the second edition of *Who Killed Science Fiction?*, scheduled for publication that year. I had done all the groundwork, gathered up an assortment of new material from a number of contributors, and it was complete with a very nice introduction by old Greenleaf pal Frank M. Robinson. It was all set, ready to go to the printers, only I was so broke I couldn't pay for the printing.

At the time, I'd been living full time in Tecate, Baja California, Mexico for a few years while pretending to be operating a graphics company in El Cajon. Already the handwriting was on the wall; PCs were rapidly putting me out of business. For the first time, any two-finger typist could become their very own writer, editor, typesetter, proofreader, and printer. They didn't need me for anything, and were quick to tell me so.

It was definitely time to find something else to do to earn a living wage. Fortunately, for a while, I had been surrounded by a group of very talented handbraiders who were making high quality tack for horses and cowboy clothing accessories. I saw an urgent need for my rare and extensive talents. With the assistance of my son Erik, we began organizing those braiders into a workforce to produce merchandise under our label of Western Gold for us to sell to the equestrian trade.

Everything worked out for the best and in no time at all we were traveling quite a bit and exhibiting our wares for sale at horse shows and major rodeos all over the USA and Mexico.

Only that's a far cry from *Who Killed Science Fiction?*

The thing is, the second edition, planned for publication in 1980, got shuffled aside, finally winding up packed away in a box that placed it firmly out of sight…and out of mind. No one even noticed that it was never published as scheduled, including me.

Throughout the copy for the 1980 edition were references to the third, or 2000 edition of *Who Killed Science Fiction?*

———

I have long ago forgotten exactly where the idea for *Who Killed Science Fiction?* originated, but it took solid hold of my thoughts with a firm determination, almost as if the scheme was running on automatic. Like everything else I did at the time, it was somehow related to the power politics the Chicago fan group was playing, drawing attention to their efforts to claim the 1962 Worldcon. I even allowed myself to fantasize about wild improbabilities like persuading a large number of prominent people to participate in the write-in symposium for *Who Killed Science Fiction?* If I worked it right, it could damn near read like *Who's Who In Science Fiction.* Then, producing the results in a manner that could best be described as deliberate attention getting. The attention I knew damn well I wanted was a Hugo.

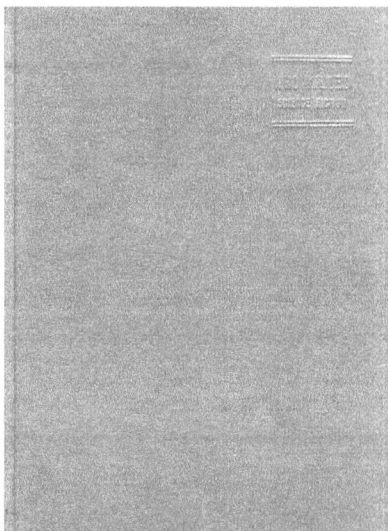

I was toying with the idea that, ridiculous as it sounded, I could create and choreograph a scenario wherein people who had never even seen a copy of my book would proclaim it the best fan effort of the year. I was so naïve in those halcyon years….

I had been a member of SAPS (The Spectator Amateur Press Society) for some time, producing my fanzine *SaFari* for the membership. I had the outlet available to me already and, because *SaFari* was approaching its first anniversary, I made the first *SaFari* Annual as *Who Killed Science Fiction?*

Thereby bringing about a persistent rumor that has plagued me ever since. There was some effort made to "change the rules" for selecting possible Hugo winners to eliminate all "one shots." However, *Who Killed Science Fiction?* was never a one shot, only another number in an existing volume of an ongoing publication.

Who Killed Science Fiction? was produced in 1960 in a very limited edition of 125 pre-assigned copies. Those copies were distributed as follows: The Spectator Amateur Press Society, 40; the contributors, 71; the Library of Congress, 2; friends of the immediate family, science fiction or otherwise, 12. And, following my dreams, it became an instant collectible and has been a popularly sought title ever since.

And, let it be told that my wildest dreams actually came true. In Seattle at the World Science Fiction Convention in September 1961, I was awarded a Hugo statuette for *Who Killed Science Fiction?* And, to pile on just a little bit more of the good stuff, I also wound up as Chairman of Chicon III, the 1962 World Science Fiction Convention.

Dreams *do* come true....

My copy of *Who Killed Science Fiction?* 1960 is bound in red buckram (see photo). I had it bound special to match the Advent: Publishers partner copies by the same binder in fact. There were a number of occasions when I found it advantageous to have them bind one-of-a-kind books for me.

The front cover of *Who Killed Science Fiction?* 1960 was designed by Emsh, and is reproduced in this publication on page two. In addition to that wonderful cover, Frank Kelly Freas also designed a two-page title page for the volume, and both of those pieces of artwork are reproduced here.

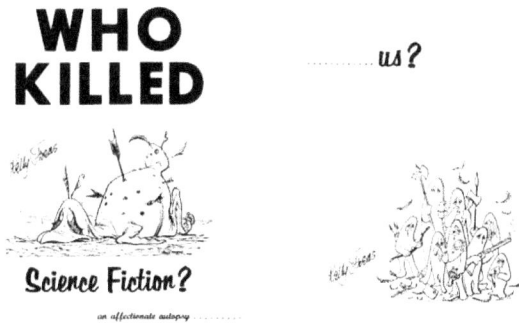

For the longest time I felt that my copy of the book was permanently attached to my hands; I seemed to cling to it so possessively. In reality, I was just taking it with me everywhere I went that there was the slightest possibility that I could get one more contributor to autograph their text. I had this foolish goal of getting every one of them to sign my book eventually. It was a commonplace sight at conventions and science fiction related parties for years.

After that, Terry took up the challenge and passed the book around for several more autographs.

Flashforward....

I lost 1980. The second edition of *Who Killed Science Fiction?* never appeared.

I lost 2000. The third edition of *Who Killed Science Fiction?* never appeared.

Hello, 2006. What are you doing out of the 20-year sequencing? Don't you have the common decency to cooperate and keep things on schedule? Well, at least you finally arrived, whatever you are…the long-delayed second edition for 1980 or the newly revirginized second edition for 2006. What difference does 46 years make anyway?

My son Terry has wanted to see the complete version of *Who Killed Science Fiction?* published for a number of years. Now and then he returns to the project, trying to get me interested in doing it again. Well, it's obvious that he finally succeeded.

With a great deal of his help, the manuscript has been digitized and reformatted for electronic publication.

With Terry's assistance, and as an extra-special Christmas bonus for our loyal readers, Bill Burns and I proudly present <*drum roll*> *The Compleat and Unexpurgated Who Killed Science Fiction?*

As a special book-length *eI* ebook, I am suspending all the regular features of *eI* until next month where they will be resumed, including the letter column. Please don't hesitate to email your comments regarding this effort to earl@earlkemp.com or snail mail them to P.O. Box 369, PMB 205, Tecate, CA 91980.

Acknowledgments

Special thanks go to the following people who helped make this book possible: John Boston, Malcolm Edwards, Edward Emshwiller, Frank Kelly Freas, Jacques Hamon, Lynn Hickman, Elaine Kemp Harris, Robert Lichtman, Jim Linwood, James O'Meara, Gregory Pickersgill, George W. Price, and Ed Wood.

Earl Kemp

Keeping the Faith!

I did it!
What's more, I know I did it. I'm the one. Don't look any further. It's high time that I come clean and confess. Is anybody out there? Are you listening? No one else can take the blame, no one the credit. One day I struck back and laid out the fatal, fateful blow. With axe in hand, I killed Science Fiction.

It took a while for the momentum to build. (Can't you feel it?) The foul, dastardly deed wasn't done in one day. It took cool planning, savage animal-like cunning, and child-like glee. Had I known the consequences at the time, I'd still have done it. The beast deserved it. For years I had heard its pained cries, howling in the night, in my nightmares, begging me…begging me to finish it off.

So I did!

Careful notes were taken at the time. Many contributed their wisdom to the plot, some their folly. In the end, in the final analysis, no one was right, we were all wrong. The *Thing* was beyond our understanding, beyond our power to control. We could not destroy it, or guide it. No fortune teller, no Delphic oracle, could have pronounced its destiny.

The Frankenstein monster that Mary Shelley created has lumbered into the pages of history and the psyche of our civilization. Even Hugo Gernsback's careful planning and desperate attempt to guide the beast into the Age of Technology wasn't enough. Praiseworthy though his efforts were, even John W. Campbell, Jr. and his magnificent genius, bringing forth the Golden Atomic Age, could not embrace the depth and breadth of this wild, untamable thing. Every attempt to codify, to describe this thing, to define its passage through time and space has been lacking.

This *Thing* has a life, a breath, and existence of its own, independent of us now. Ages from now people will still puzzle over it. Attempt to define it, measure its influence, assign responsibility and credit. Future heroes will rise up and try to conquer it, put it neatly in place, and say, "Now it's over, we can move on to something new."

It will never be over. This *Thing* is, in fact, the indefinable, inexplicable new. So long as thinking creatures exist, this medium will continue to grow and to evolve. At its core science fiction is nothing less then the compelling force of imagination at work.

And what magnificent work!

We few, we proud few, who have had our lives blessed by involvement with it, can join together and fully appreciate the momentous bounty that has enhanced our being.

It is not often given to any group of people to stand together and participate in both creating and praising the last, best effort of their generation. But here, in these few pages, passing among the thoughts of those who have loved it best, we can join together and show those yet to come that we knew the true, full value represented by the ideas contained in this field.

Who Killed Science Fiction?

We all did. Over and over again! Individually and collectively! We will all strive to do so yet again. We must because we can't help ourselves. This *Thing* begs for it, so that it can arise from the ashes…reborn.

Nothing can truly kill it. No one can alter its path. In our hands and minds we have breathed life into, fanned the flames, and released it down the corridors of time. Whether through an act of love, or through hate, whether through creation or destructive criticism, science fiction will endure.

Here among the following pages, come read the words written by those who knew it best, words written by the first who recognized it and nurtured it. Long after we have all passed into dust, these words will still remain. Generations yet to come will marvel at our times, regret that they came later, and wish in their hearts and minds that they could have lived now, in these times, and participated in this Great Conversation.

It is not to us, the living, that these words are dedicated. It is not to us to find all the meaning and place the final value. We, those who have lived these times, and read these words, can only dedicate our best, greatest effort to the future.

It is our hope. It is our reason for striving, for persisting. This is clearly the truth, for why else would we endeavor so ardently against the tides of our troubled present. Rather than succumb to the outrageous misfortunes cascading down around us perpetrated by the blind masses who have succeeded in destroying the earth, we few have gathered together knowing that our expert dreaming will light the path through any and all such troubles, in the present and in the future to come.

Science fiction is dedicated to this proposition. It is the finest of all lights guiding mankind. Without it, the lantern-lit way would be dark, impenetrable, and we would fall to the wayside.

Sometimes dimly, sometimes in darkness, we all head toward this light. It is nothing less than the light of consciousness calling us forward, bringing out the soul of our times.

So here it is, from one person to another, from one age to another, the undying light. The fiercely burning torch of imagination and creation, kindled by those dreaming dreams no one has ever dared to dream before.

It is our fondest hope, and keenest desire, that at least some small note of amusement will be kindled in those reading these words. It is my belief that some small spark of genius will pass from these pages down the long centuries and find a home and place in those yet to come. It is to those who are yet to come that these great works are dedicated. It is to those that this work is dedicated.

And when, in passing, you read these words, please remember us kindly. We have kept the faith! Our final words from now to you…do likewise!

Earl Terry Kemp

IF YOU ARE A SCIENCE FICTION PROFESSIONAL
YOU ARE AUTOMATICALLY A MEMBER OF

**THE INSTITUTE OF TWENTY-FIRST
CENTURY STUDIES**

YOUR NONOBLIGATORY SUPPORT IS REQUESTED
ALONG WITH YOUR COMMENTS ON WHO KILLED
SCIENCE FICTION?

CONTACT
THEODORE R. COGSWELL
DEPT. OF ENGLISH
BALL STATE TEACHERS COLLEGE
MUNCIE, INDIANA

SaFari

NUMBER TWO, published July 15, 1959 for SAPS #47

is edited by Earl Kemp and published with more than the normal amount of assistance on the part of Jim O'Meara and Nancy Kemp. This issue, like the first, will have the bulk of its pages duplicated on the JOE-JIM simeograph, courtesy of Joe Sarno (See cover, picture 11.) and the above mentioned Jim O'Meara who is doing the bulk of the crank turning.

SaFari is NOT for sale. Outside SAPS it serves as a letter-substitute to my long suffering friends.

ABOUT THE COVER: By now you have all heard about Robert Bloch's new novel PSYCHO (Simon & Schuster, Inner Sanctum, 185 pp, $2.95) and the fact that it has been purchased by Alfred Hitchcock (through MCA) for his next motion picture. To celebrate the occasion, and with the added event of having Bloch in Chicago anyway, we decided to have a small type party (details further on by Bloch and Tucker.) with the difference that Bloch and Tucker do the inviting in as far as possible, and we furnish the bottles. Some of the results are on the cover:

1. NO, No more autographs please! Wilson Tucker and Bob Bloch embrace a couple of old friends, Jim Beam and I. W. Harper.

2. Harlan Ellison and Wilson Tucker plus books, etc.

3. Bob Bloch, Frances Light (on SAPS WL) plus stovepipes, glasses, etc.

4. Barefoot Fern Tucker and Elsie Janda glance admiringly at Wilson, just out of camera range.

5. Bob Bloch swapping symptoms with Dr. Rosemary Becker.

6. Nancy and Charlotte Ellison discuss the pitfalls of marriage.

7. Nancy again, with her pitfall, yours truly, beard and all.

8. Harlan puts some new jazz records on the hi-fi and - -

9. Makes like a bongo on the chair-back while Wilson listens to the sound of distant drummers.

10. Harlan demonstrates a joke for Bloch with Charlotte chortling behind.

11. Wilson autographs an assembly line of books as Joe Sarno passes them along to me, who will someday restore them to their proper position on the shelves.

It WAS a swell party, at least they tell me it was!

THIS IS REALLY A SUBSTITUTE SaFari: The summer slump, plus Fran Light's big party, and the Bloch-Tucker lost weekend have pushed aside the best laid plans of Saps and men. Consequently this issue will be minus the Paperback index installment for AVON titles, as I just don't have time to cut the stencils and run them off. Also I have completely abandoned any attempt at completing IN SEARCH OF BALBOA. The details are slipping far, far away.

THE INDEX will, however, continue in the next issue.

Provided, of course, there are not too many wild parties in the meantime.

Introduction 2006
Like An Introduction

I was reading the 48th mailing of the Spectator Amateur Press Society and discovered the following quote:

"It is in some ways surprising that much of *In Search of Wonder* appeared originally in fanzines; there isn't any criticism of this quality appearing in fanzines today. As a matter of fact, there isn't any in the prozines either...."

The statement was made by Bob Leman in the fourth issue of his SAPS-zine, *Nematode*. I said to myself, "God, he's right," and kept on reading.

For about a paragraph...

Then I went back and read the quote again. "Why are there no pieces of serious constructive criticism appearing within the field?" Naturally I couldn't answer this; it presupposes a knowledge I don't possess, even if I do speak to myself with adjectives like "God." Immediately a self-imposed edict came heralding to the rescue: IF YOU WANT SOMETHING DONE, DO IT YOURSELF.

Move in fast, get the facts, hit hard, splash!
Competence, Roman candles, splash!
Blanket the field, quality, splash!
Catchy, skyrockets, splash!
Splash:
Who Killed Science Fiction?

For well over two years I had heard far too many people decrying the death of magazine science fiction, and like Bob Leman, mourning the lack of critical soul-searching from within the field.

How shall I go about it? I determined first that I would restrict this critical colossus to the magazine field only and decided on five specific points of enquiry, which were:

1. Do you feel that magazine science fiction is dead?

2. Do you feel that any single person, action, incident, etc., is responsible for the present situation? If not, what is responsible?

`3. What can we do to correct it?

4. Should we look to the original paperback as a point of salvation?

5. What additional remarks, pertinent to the study, would you like to contribute?

The next step was to prepare a letter setting forth these five points.

The original intent was to abstract the replies to this questionnaire into tabular form, write a small article about the findings and publish them in *SaFari*, extending the circulation for the issue to cover all those who had responded to the enquiry.

Who should I send the questionnaires to? It was essential that the replies come *only* from within the field, consequently a rigid control was placed on the questionnaire mailing list, restricting it to (as I said in the questionnaire) "everyone within the science fiction field who has ever expressed an intelligent critical look at the field. Since most of us have derived some measure of enjoyment, recognition, and income from the field over the past many years I feel it is up to us to make a definite step toward understanding (at least) and overcoming (if possible) the threats before us."

In order to assure a greater volume of response, realizing that the people from whom I wanted answers were accustomed to being paid for their verbiage, I said that the report would be published, which it is. I said that the report would not be for sale, and it is not. I said that circulation of the report would be restricted to the contributors and to the Spectator Amateur Press Society, and that it would be published on April 15, 1960.

That date is now!

As the first few replies to the questionnaire arrived, I knew that it would be an impossible task to abstract them and settle for a brief résumé in article form. Among the first to arrive was that of Algis Budrys; a report of such nature and quality that the entire article demanded to be included. And more followed it, of such magnitude that only by printing the entire piece could justice be done to the author. Hence, shoot the budget to hell, print everything that comes in.

And now you have it, the complete report on: *Who Killed Science Fiction?*

The title of the study itself bares little or no relationship to the actual five points under observation. It was merely to serve as splash—fuel to light the fire that would get the five questions answered. Apparently it worked, because there *were* some "whos" named.

It would have been impossible for me to answer the questions personally once I started reading the replies as they arrived because I found my opinions becoming very highly influenced by others. Reluctantly then, you will find my own answers excluded from this report (but just for the record I will answer only one, point one: I definitely believe that magazine science fiction is dead).

There will be no attempt on the part of *SaFari* to conduct a follow-up on this report. Contributors to this symposium of a professional status within the field are encouraged to send any afterthoughts directly to The Institute of Twenty-First Century Studies.* The Secretary for the Committee on Publications (Theodore R. Cogswell) has authorized me to say that a continuation of this study fits directly into the pattern of research now under way at the Institute and he joins me in encouraging you to send any further material directly to the Institute.

And now, if you please, the abstract report:

From an initial 108 questionnaire mailed, there were 71 responses. Of this number, one was unsolicited (Edmund R. Meskys; included here because he answered the five points) and one additional reply was not counted in the figure of 71 (that of Rodney Palmer, included in the report as an example of a complete outside-the-field view, but excluded from the count of 71 because he did not have a copy of the five points under study). Or, a total of 70 solicited answers from the original 108 for a 64.8 percent return, which anyone can tell you is something like a new world's record.

No attempt was made to tabulate the many references to Dianetics, psionics, quackery, saucerism, Shaverism and/or pseudo-science or references to "*Literature*," professionalism and/or "*Maturity*" (wherein the literature and maturity have respectively a capital L and a capital M, italicized).

It is perhaps significant to note that from the authors contributing to this study, four have indicated that they are no longer writing for the science fiction magazines and/or are no longer writing science fiction at all.

---

*Alas, as of 1980, the Institute of Twenty-First Century Studies is no longer functioning.

Now, let's take the specific five points under discussion and examine the results:

1.   *Do you feel that magazine science fiction is dead?*

YES: 2

NO: 55 replies, of which 38 qualified their "no" by following it with "but…," and an alarming percentage of these 38 indicated that the death struggle was already in sight.

YES: Eleven replies, stating either "yes" or definitely dying already (this figure includes my personal vote).

2.   Do you feel that any single person, action, incident, etc., is responsible for the present situation?

NO: 24 replies.

YES: Several people were specifically named, but in numbers too small to make any tabulation significant.

2a.   *If not, what is responsible?*

As contributory causes, the following were named in order of frequency: 19, dull, boring, and inferior material being published; 18, changing market and/or times and outside interests; thirteen, television; twelve, inexcusable distribution practices; eleven each, comics and paperbacks, Sputnik and/or the Race for Space; ten, incompatible word rates and a narrowing market; nine, "science fiction" movies; six, rising costs, including magazine cover prices; five, fans and/or readers and four each, "ability to read disappearing," "decay in English literature" and authors. In addition to this, fifteen contributions indicated editors as being either responsible for the present poor situation or that they should endeavor to adopt a "hands off" policy in the case or rewrites for item No. three.

3.   *What can we do to correct it?*

This is untabulatable. The most frequently appearing remedy is the last item mentioned above (at 2a) that editors should endeavor to adopt a "hands off" policy in the case of rewrites (fifteen responses). Also running, in order of frequency: nine, writers should work harder (each of these nine, a professional author), of these, one added "for less"; seven, readers and/or fans should adopt a "quality" approach with what is currently appearing within the field (reading studiously, commenting intelligently and in general taking a more active interest) and five indicated that we should purchase all the magazines published, regardless...

4. *Should we look to the original paperback as a point of salvation?*

YES: 24 replies.

NO: Sixteen replies.

5. *What additional remarks, pertinent to the study, would you like to contribute?*

This, of course, is untabulatable, but instead forms the bulk of this symposium—the entire publication that you are now holding before you.

Read on then.…

Somewhere here are the thoughts of others that confirm your own suspicions—or random thoughts that will lead you down unsuspected paths to, we hope, improvement, and most certainly profit. But above all, we sincerely hope, several hours of enjoyment and a volume of lasting significance that you will want to retain for reference.

Thus ends, or begins, the great affectionate autopsy of The Year Of Our Decline, 1960.

A work of this nature and scope cannot be conducted and delivered as a finished product without the assistance and encouragement of many people. We should then like to make our acknowledgments to the following:

To Bob Leman, for the idea
To Algis Budrys, for the line: "to slay the dragon...."
To Theodore R. Cogswell, Secretary, Committee on Publications, *The Institute of Twenty-First Century Studies,* for assistance all the way...
To Edward Emshwiller, for the burial site
To Frank Kelly Freas, for meritorious service above and beyond the call of duty
To James O'Meara, for sharing a backbreaking collation job
To Lynn Hickman, for the reproduction
and
To YOU for your personal help in working together long enough to make this a truly valuable study.

Thank you, one and all...

– Earl Kemp
Chicago, Illinois
April 15, 1960

Like Some Opinions

ANONYMOUS #1

Robert A. Heinlein

1. No, I do not feel that magazine science fiction is dead. Nor do I feel that any single person, incident, etc., is responsible for the present situation.

2. I don't know what all the bitching is about. Twenty years ago we had three leading science fiction magazines, plus several marginal ones, period. Now we have three leading science fiction magazines—whose editors are *always* screaming for copy—plus several marginal ones…plus television, movies, radio, pocket books, anthologies, trade books, book clubs, foreign rights, and a wide open market in all the general magazines. What the hell do they want? An egg in their beer?

If it is the writers who are screaming, I can't see what they have to complain about. Of course, many of them now writing have not been writing long enough to know the meaning of a dry spell, or a market with poor pickings—say back in the thirties when you either sold it to the pulps, all rights for a cent a word or a half cent a word, and if it did not sell to that market, then you might as well use it for toilet paper. So they talk about a "collapse" in the market—hell, the market hasn't collapsed; the present market is pure heaven to anyone who remembers the thirties. But some of the writers have collapsed.

Of course, the recent confusion in magazine distribution has hurt writers and publishers alike—but "this, too, shall pass." Economic dislocations come and go…and only one fraction of a writer's market was hurt by this one…and the big three still publish.

If the readers are screaming, they have more reason to. Science fiction is a branch of the entertainment business, the first axiom of which is: if the audience doesn't laugh, the clown is not funny. Tedious rehashing of elderly

In 1960, 71 rather prominent science fiction people contributed work for the first *SaFari* annual, *Who Killed Science Fiction?* Of that number only one made any unusual demands or set conditions upon their participation; that one was Robert A. Heinlein. The least most offensive of his requirements was the one forbidding me to use his name or infer that he had written the piece for me. Consequently, Heinlein's article appeared under the byline of Anonymous No. 1.

In Seattle in 1961, after I had been awarded the Hugo for *Who Killed Science Fiction?*, Robert Heinlein approached me. He had this deliberately calculated way of insulting through faint praise; his words would flow out of him effortlessly as if he had spent some time rehearsing them, perhaps saying the words aloud to himself.

"If I had of known what a good job you would do with *Who Killed Science Fiction?*" he said, "I'd have allowed you to use my name in it."

Gee, thanks, Bob? I believe that was the closest I ever came to receiving an apology from Robert Heinlein

I was holding my personal copy of the book at the time; it had been considerably annotated and autographed by the many contributors who were as proud of the volume as I was. Without me asking, Heinlein took my copy of *Who Killed Science Fiction?* from me, opened it to page 13, and wrote a big "Robert A. Heinlein" over the Anonymous No. 1 byline.

Tardy largess for the peons…

– Earl Kemp, "Heinlein Happens"

themes will not cause the readers to applaud. I suspect, from some of the crud that one sees in print, that there are "science fiction" writers who jumped in because they thought it was a gravy train, an easy way to get rich without working.

Any writer who comes along today with stories as fresh and novel as those of E.E. Smith and Stanley Weinbaum were when they were first published is certain to find a publisher and to receive ringing applause from the cash customers. But a writer who serves up the same tired old stew, simply polishing old stories, will cause the readers to sit on their hands—no matter how finished or slick their writing techniques.

ANONYMOUS #2

Philip José Farmer

There is a dianetics group still going strong in Phoenix. A man I know who does not practice dianetics but is familiar with the group has told me that there are more than a few former practitioners of dianetics who are now in mental hospitals. And they are there as a result of dianetics. I know two writers who became all fouled up through dianetics. Neither has amounted to much as a writer since then, and one of them is still goofed-up. I think that Campbell is as responsible as anyone for these people becoming institutionalized. If he had been more careful about approaching dianetics, if he had waited a reasonable period to investigate it before pushing it in *Astounding*, this fraud might have died a-borning. He owes all of us science fiction readers an apology, but he has never offered it. Instead, after being disillusioned, he has gone off the deep end on psi.

ANDERSON, POUL

Poul Anderson

…I can't give your questions the reasoned answers they call for…here are some offhand, thumbnail reactions to your questions.

1) No, though it's obviously in poor shape. But let's give credit to good (or at least acceptable) stories where they do appear; because they still do, from time to time. For my money, *F&SF* is currently maintaining the highest literary standard, which isn't saying much, I know, but accept that Bob Mills is trying his best. So, in spite of opprobrious comment, are John Campbell, Horace Gold, Bob Lowndes, and one or two others.

2) No, there is no single cause for the present sad condition of science fiction. For over a year, now, any number of pros have been arguing with great heat—and, often, great perception—in Cogswell's *Publications of the Institute of Twenty-First Century Studies*, trying to find a cause and cure; but there seem to be as many causes assigned as there are seekers. In my own opinion, the decay of science fiction is part and parcel of a general decay in English literature, traceable to the same—extremely many and complex—causes.

3) To correct it, everybody will have to do his part. Publishers will have to give the writer an economic break. Editors will have to stop imposing their own personalities on all their writers (and I am *not* thinking of any particular editor) and will have to edit more creatively: finding and developing new talent, encouraging old talent to experiment—in short, taking more of an inter-

est in their job. Writers will have to stop playing verbal games and start writing. Readers will have to develop some appreciation of quality (which, actually, rather few of them now have), offer it their moral and financial support, and be patient. You can't cure the disease overnight.

4) There are no "points of salvation." Paperback originals seldom pay well enough to justify themselves to the author: only if he also sells serial rights will he begin to approach a decent word rate. By and large, book editors are guilty of the same sins as magazine editors, plus some of their very own. Not that I'm against paperback originals, understand. They can form a very valuable supplement. I just don't see all worthwhile science fiction moving to them.

5) I don't like the idea of asking who killed science fiction? It may be sick, but it isn't dead; and particular scapegoats are merely an outlet for suppressed aggressiveness. Instead of sitting around feeling sorry for ourselves, I suggest we do something about our problems (cf. No. three) and leave to literary historians the dissection of etiologies.

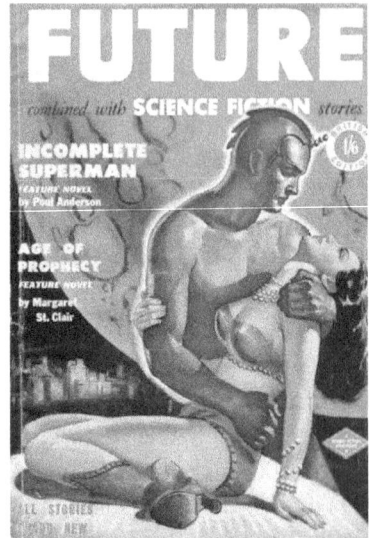

ASIMOV, ISAAC

Isaac Asimov

1) Magazine science fiction is not dead, obviously, since there are magazines still on the stands, more magazines than there were in 1948, for instance. I admit magazine science fiction seems to be declining.

2) Obviously no single person, action, incident is responsible. There is a whole complex of causes. Magazines in general are in a decline. Pulp fiction is virtually dead, killed by comic magazines and by paperbacks. The magazines as a whole suffer from rising costs, from the competition of paperbacks and from television. Science fiction, in particular, suffers from all of this and from one additional factor I have not seen anyone mention.

Beginning in 1938 (with Campbell, of course) there was increasing stress on literary quality in stories. This was accelerated from 1950 on and at present the literary standard required by the better science fiction magazines is as high (and higher) than those required by the slicks. Good! So now-a-days a science fiction writer who makes the grade finds he can write well enough to make the slicks, which pay more, so he does. Robert Silverberg came up from fandom, cut a swath in science fiction for two years, and has now graduated to the slicks. Robert Sheckley did it in four years. Others took longer but went there anyway. Meanwhile we've all gotten used to well-written science fiction and we find it difficult to go back to the kind of pulpy writing done by newcomers before they learn the ropes. (And after they learn the ropes, they'll be gone, too.)

None of this applies to me. I am interested only in writing science fiction and no other kind of fiction. I've always known that and I've always known that possible greater incomes would have no lure for me. So I did think I would be in science fiction forever. However, I did write an occasional book of science-fact. Then came Sputnik. Suddenly, books on science-fact were in great demand and I found myself deluged with offers. As it turned out, straight science was the one thing I found more fascinating than science fiction and I have written no science fiction to speak of since Sputnik. I tried to help things by giving up teaching and becoming a full-time writer, but that just means I write more non-fiction. I hope to get back to science fiction sometime but I don't know when.

3 & 4) The original paperback is no substitute for the magazine since it is heavily weighted in favor of novels which can only be turned out decently by authors who are past their apprenticeship. And without magazines where will the apprenticeship take place? Furthermore, there is a continuity about a magazine that builds up a loyal following who support science fiction and act as a reservoir for new fan-turned-pro authors. The casual on-and-off readers of the paperback novel cannot substitute for this. I don't know what we can do to correct the matter except to support the magazines. That means buying all the copies we can, whatever the price, and writing stories for them whenever we can, whatever the rates. The wheel of fortune turns and magazine science fiction may enjoy a recrudescence.

5) Obviously, Sputnik and all that followed bears a major share of responsibility for the decline of magazine science fiction. The newspapers are so science fictiony now that there is scarcely any urge to continue looking for more science fiction in the magazines. In fact, the type of science fiction in the newspapers now—all this talk of space and satellites and moonshots—is so interbound with cold war and national prestige and military brass-hats that it makes science fiction unsavory, even to me, for instance. This isn't helped by the fact that too large a proportion of science fiction stories written today are "tomorrow fiction"—that is, they deal with a situation one step ahead of the headlines so that one gets the impression that all science fiction is but a kind of "home life at Cape Canaveral" or "Look, Ma, the general is jutting his jaw and says the next satellite *will* go through carrying a *man*, Ma."

Hell, for a group of people who have been bouncing around the galaxy for 20 years, it's downright sickening to go back to trying to reach the moon with chemical rockets.

BAILEY, J.O., PROF.

I have read with interest your "Who Killed Science Fiction?" Here are the best answers to your questions that occur to me:

1) No, I do not feel that magazine science fiction is dead. So far as I know, any really good, original story may still find a publisher.

2) Since it is not entirely clear to me what is meant by "the present situation" (for magazines carrying science fiction are still on the newsstands), I do not have any idea who or what may be responsible for this situation.

3) First, I should say, define with particulars and details what needs correction.

4) I am not sure what is meant by "salvation." I have the general idea that publishers of paperback books will publish whatever they think they can sell to enough people to make a profit.

5) No additional remarks occur to me.

BARRETT, C.L., M.D.

C. L. Barrett M.D.

[Doctor Barrett starts by including a copy of Stephen Takacs's speech "Alas, What Boom?" delivered at the Cleveland World Science Fiction Convention and pointing out that "as you can see, practically all of his predictions have come true."—E.K.]

1) However, some of the situations Steve mentions are only part of the story. One of the factors which he did not mention which I think Hans Santesson mentioned in Detroit, was the fact that when science fiction apparently became popular, is that everybody got on the bandwagon and put out some 20-plus magazines. Hans, and some of the other editors there, stated that whole magazines appeared on the newsstands with stories by good authors, but material rejected by most magazines in existence before the boom.

Whole magazines were published of second-rate material from good authors. People buying this stuff, if they read that crud would have choked, which they did, and they didn't buy again. The end of it was that we are down now to five or six magazines.

That is not the whole story as to why they quit. Another factor is the pocketbooks. I find that the itinerant or casual reader would much rather have a long complete story in a pocketbook and read that than read a magazine. So that is why I say the original paperback may be *a* point of salvation (item No. four on the questionnaire). It will keep a certain number reading but it will not help the fan field at all. No, magazine science fiction is not dead, despite everything.

2) I do not feel that any single person, act, or incident is responsible. One of the facts that you failed to bring in is outside interest. I have been corresponding with Ted Carnell for years, and he is behind in correspondence. The reason now is that he is so interested in forming a new Masonic Lodge that he is spending a lot of time with that. He has given up all except his professional activities. He expects to come back in again but it will probably take him two or three years to get his Lodge going right.

The same thing has happened with me in Shrine; I have a Funster Unit of some 40 clowns and developing that has and is taking a lot of time.

Man is not given to being satisfied with any one activity. Over a period of time he may (watch particularly the doctors) get into farming and have cows, sheep, or something, then change to motorboat racing and then to airplane flying. And they go through a cycle, it may be the same series, it may be a different series, but their interests vary from time to time and that is true of any group of people.

There is only so much time that a person has to use and when you find yourself in an activity like this where the individuals that I work with, I like so well that we go to dances eight or ten times a year, there is less time to read science fiction than previously. Now another factor is those who have children. I would say that Kemp and Hickman are the only ones who have a larger number of children that have been able to keep active in science fiction. They have, in spite of their broods, been able to continue.

Now, with most of those, such as our friend Milton Rothman in Philadelphia (I have been corresponding with him and been trying to get him back in) it is children, work, and degrees that is keeping them busy now. Eventually they will filter back into fandom after their children get older.

I found that we were unable to indulge in social activities when our children were young. The number of dances per year dropped to one or two until the youngest child got to be eight or ten and the older children were old enough to take care of that one. Of course we were stymied some by the fact that my mother-in-law had a stroke and for some five years was bedfast with nurses. Others are having, not exactly the same, but similar circumstances.

Each of us must have a group that we run around with, a local group, etc. The fortunate ones find themselves in a science fiction group (Cincinnati) and all their friends are in that same group and they can continue to have more activity in fandom. Those of us who are isolated are bound to acquire friends that have no interest in science fiction, and live and play with them.

Another factor which has entered into the situation is the rising cost of food, clothing, and everything, consequently there is less money to spend on magazines. One reason the magazine field collapsed (that is the general field) was that the percentage of money spent for advertising stayed the same. The newspapers still kept their 76% but the other 24% made a very marked shift from magazines to television. Some $4.5 billion, I think, that the television industry picked up in a year was the year *Bluebook* collapsed and other magazines. That meant that the magazines that had the lesser circulation and lesser general appeal lost out. That is why today *Life* is selling at 19 cents. They were losing out. The advertising people were channeling their dollars into television rather than into the magazine field and, of course, the magazines of a particular field of lesser circulations were forced out.

As far as books are concerned, a science fiction fan goes through a period of time where he is not married, and all of his spare money goes on science fiction. Then he begins to take up bowling or tennis, swimming or skin diving, or chasing women or something. He may join the Elks, Masons, or Eagles and he has less money to spend so he becomes more selective in what he spends his money for. If they want to spend their money and get as many books as possible for say $25 or $35 a year, quite naturally they turn to the book clubs which collapsed all of our friends who had gone into the publishing of science fiction for the love of it. I find now that the book reviewers don't list the better science fiction books as science fiction, but as imaginative literature or extrapolations of the possibilities of future development.

What we also forget is that from 1922 to '23, the time I can remember, I knew everything that was being published and read everything up until the 1940s. Since that time, it has been impossible for any one person to read all of it. There has been so much in the book as well as magazine field that after you get it, you wish you had never seen it at all, you couldn't even read it…There are only a few completionist fools like myself and Dr. J. Lloyd Eaton who will even attempt to do this. I find that it is totally impossible for me to obtain all the books that are published each year, financially as well as otherwise. I am more interested now in obtaining some of the old classics that I know are good, than I am in obtaining everything that is published today.

3) I don't think that we can do a whole lot to correct it. I do think that one of the important things is for all science fiction fans to subscribe to *Galaxy, Astounding,* and *F&SF,* which seem to be the only ones that will survive, although *Amazing* has an astounding ability to come back. The fans are such a small part of the buying public that we could do very little except stabilize it a few places. My idea of permanent subscriptions to the major magazines to keep them going is about the only contribution that I think we can make.

With the magazine or book publisher, everything is purely money. He is only in the business to make money (fan publishers excluded). This is a part of a trend that may be good. After it is all cleared up and some of these have lost their shirts in the market, they will quit publishing and leave it to the ones that can put out better literature which will keep the quality of the magazine up and maybe eventually build up a greater number of readers outside of the fan circle.

The thing that we are not doing is increasing our fan groups this way. All we can hope to do is get in touch with them through the letter columns and by advertising the conventions, attempt to gain back what few we can, or get an increase of changing readers-to-fans insofar as possible. Only one or two percent of the readers probably are of that peculiar mental quirk or abnormality that could make fans of them. Our plan should be to try to get, and get as many of these as we can, into the fan field. However, somebody else may have better ideas than myself on that. It is a possibility that eventually the fans may have to put out the type of science fiction they want to read in privately circulated fan magazines devoted entirely to fiction.

BARTLETT, LANDELL

1) I certainly *don't* feel that magazine science fiction is dead! The big-name magazines (with their big-name writers) are still going strong—in fact, getting better all the time. Notable are *F&SF, Astounding, Amazing, Galaxy, Fantastic*—to mention a few. *Star* and *Vanguard* were fine, but died a-borning. The plethora of titles attempting to ride the boom in science fiction following World War II deservedly faded away, for they offered only second-rate fare at the best, and there just wasn't room for so many—or—demand. Parenthetically, shouldn't it be "what" killed science fiction, rather than "who"? (Besides, I'm trying to say science fiction *hasn't* been killed!)

2) Just what is the present situation? Why is the status "deplorable"? (There I go—answering a question with questions!) Admittedly, there has been more sex than science, more bug-eyed monsters than betatrons, than many would care to see, including myself. Perhaps Gernsback's rigid insistence on *science* in science fiction is the answer, with a soft-pedaling of fantasy. In other words, not enough of the former, and too much of the latter, perhaps, in current offerings? Many adult readers are revolted at clumsily contrived fairy stories palmed off as science fiction. I would say, then, let them take the trouble to be selective, and read only the best, if science fiction really interests them.

3) I presume "we" refers to the writers in the genre. Personally, I prefer those who follow the H.G. Wells, A. Conan Doyle, and Olaf Stapledon pattern—practitioners with great literary skill and imaginative originality. Dia-

logue a la Hemingway may be all right, but usually is mangled. "We" should stick to a strong story, plausible, catching the desirable sense of wonder—thus classics are spawned, and if they are good enough, will never become dated.

4) The original paperback need not be "a point of salvation." More and more they are shouldering their way into the picture, and more power to them. They, alone, are evidence that science fiction has not been dealt a deathblow. As for magazine science fiction, I still believe that it will survive, if only to meet the competition of the paperbacks.

5) To sum up, I believe that magazine science fiction will pull through because the best editors know that what they select must have a pretty high standard of excellence. The shakedown of fly-by-night, gaudy, childish, low-level magazine is about over, don't you think? The only threat facing "us," as I see it, is mediocrity.

BESTER, ALFRED

Alfred Bester

Here are my answers to your questions. I hope they can help. I also hope that you will not take them too seriously. They are only the opinion of a writer who most emphatically does not regard himself as a sage and elder statesman of our fascinating and infuriating science fiction.

I don't feel that magazine science fiction is dead, but I do believe that the public interest in science fiction, as we know it, is dwindling. The inexorable progress of life is responsible for this. The tremendous strides that science has made in the past decade fill the public with so much wonder and amazement that the headlines of the daily newspaper now provide what science fiction used to offer. Fiction has been supplanted by fact.

What do you mean when you ask: "What can we do to correct it?" We must move with the times. We should be delighted with the change. There is nothing to correct unless you mean the diminishing magazine market for science fiction. The answer to that is the fact that the situation is correcting itself. The more popular entertainment media are becoming aware of the fascination of science fiction. Television and movies are hungry for it. Even the more popular, and better-paying magazines (who themselves are rapidly dying out) are becoming interested. The market isn't dead, it's merely changing, and writers must adapt themselves to this change…either by satisfying the demands of the existing market, or by creating a new one with a new science fiction.

There will always be a market for paperback science fiction, just as there are markets for detective fiction and westerns. There are other markets, too, as I mentioned above, but there is no market for the limited writer. The writer who has devoted himself exclusively to science fiction is himself the only source of his woes. He has been living in a dream world for the past 30 years, imagining that this tiny, specialized area in the vast field of literature and entertainment, can be a self-sustaining world in itself which will go on forever.

Sensible people have always known that science fiction is a luxury for the writer, and sensible writers have always made sure of their bread and butter in other, less esoteric fields of literature and entertainment. The man who dedicates himself exclusively to science fiction today has my sympathy, because he's fallen upon hard times, but he doesn't have my respect. There are too many other branches of literature and entertainment that offer a living, there is too great a demand for talent, and there are too many opportunities.

To my mind, the crux of the situation is this: Are you a modern writer, in tune with your times, or are you trying to remain an old-fashioned science fiction writer, still exploiting an aspect of literature that is rapidly becoming out-moded? Science fiction isn't dying; it's changing. We must change with it, or become extinct.

BLISH, JAMES

My own views on all the questions you ask appear in issue No. 131 of Ted Cogswell's *Publications of the Institute of Twenty-First Century Studies.**

…Nor do I think that a writers' strike against the science fiction magazines would have to work out the way Bob Lowndes predicts. It never has been tried, on a formal scale. If Horace Gold's tally of inactive writers is even vaguely correct, there is an informal strike going on right now, and Horace is hurt by it and says so. That the slump in the field might be due at least in part to a wildcat writers' strike had never occurred to me until I saw Horace's figures quoted in *PITFCS*;* up until then, I suppose I had thought I was the only striker. But it makes sense. Contrariwise, there is no slump in the market for paperback science fiction books, and hence no strike; they pay well, they sell well, and everybody seems to be churning them out like mad.

Poor pay and a narrowing market seem to me to be adequate explanations of the strike itself. While I agree with A.J. Budrys that persistent editorial meddling can become so annoying as to cause a writer to go out of his

---

*Publications of the Institute of Twenty-First Century Studies, abbreviated PITFCS, are known affectionately as "pitfucks" by one and all.-E.K.

way to avoid it, I think he does not make it clear enough that this complaint applies primarily to Horace Gold, with whom it used to be a habit (I have no recent experience to draw on); none of the other editors in the field, in my experience, have asked for changes except infrequently and on a small scale and, like Poul Anderson, I've found that John Campbell's relatively rare suggestions have mostly been helpful. Editors differ. Horace also used to write rejection letters of such remarkable viciousness that I could hardly blame a writer who never wanted to read another of them. Tony Boucher sat on manuscripts, unless they were by women, for months and even years and refused either to answer queries about them or return them; I gave up submitting to *F&SF* for this reason alone, and I wonder if I was the only writer to do so. Even price may not be a deterrent—that too depends a great deal on the editor: I hate Lowndes' rates but he has taste and puts up a gallant battle to put out a good magazine all the same you would need three hands to count all the gifted newcomers he has spotted—and I for one had a wholly uneconomical leaning toward taking his 1 cent rather than *Super Science*'s 2 cents.

I gather from Ray Russell's letter that there's also been some complaint about psionics in this context; all right, I dislike the stuff myself and could draw my philosophic objections to it out some distance. But as far as the market is concerned, psionics narrows it only in that it cuts down the number of pages available for other kinds of copy, in the top-paying market. Campbell also buys stories on other themes and does not put a gun to anybody's head; people who want to push his psionics button do so of their own free choice.

...I am quite in agreement that it would be impossible to put together a readable magazine from the slush pile. During the five months that I was reading for *Vanguard*, I got a hell of a lot of slush, especially after the first issue appeared, and out of all that material I was very fortunate to find one printable story by a brand-new writer (H.M. Sycamore's "Success Story," which Bob Mills recently printed). Most of the rest of it was downright awful; for that matter, even much of the material I got from agents ranged from mediocre to poor. (Naturally, I do not count submissions by good writers who have no agents, like Dick Wilson, as part of the slush pile.)

I was interested, too, in your [Ted Cogswell's] reply to Dean McLaughlin, particularly by your remark that "the stories we write...have little or nothing to do with Literature." While I don't want to anticipate Dr. DeWitt's forthcoming article, I have a few comments; I'm not sure of your meaning. In the scientific sense of the word, everything we write is part of "the literature," in that it is in print and can be run down and consulted. As producers of Literature which is accepted as being a necessary part of an educated man's cultural furniture, and which gets talked about in survey courses, etc., we have no standing; but this rarely happens to a practitioner in any way during his lifetime anyway, numerous though the exceptions are.

But if you will accept into your definition of Literature any work of art undertaken with serious intentions and which realizes those intentions reasonably well, regardless of whether the public or the Establishment recognizes it as such, then it seems to me that there are a number of science fiction stories and novels you will have to allow. What you said to Dean certainly needed to be said, but I don't want to see *More Than Human*, for example, written off for the sake of a forensic point.

The fact that much of what we write is not literature even in that sense of the word is mostly simply a reflection of the fact that science fiction is commercial fiction, and shares with all the other kinds of commercial fiction the flaws of haste, inattention, perpetuation of clichés and adoption of made-to-order values consequent on working in an art as though the products were link sausages. What is more important is Poul Anderson's point that "science fiction is not the whole of literature." As he says, there are things that it cannot do. Still worse, there are things that it can do but that most of the readers don't want to see done; perhaps this was the point Dean was shooting around. Most of the science fiction I have ever read, including most of what I would classify as good science fiction, has little or no emotional content—and I can see no evidence that improving this situation, which is certainly remediable, would be welcomed by the readers. The career of Ted Sturgeon is a glaring example of this; though Ted is held in relatively high esteem, I don't recall anybody' ever hanging any medals on him for being the finest and most thoroughly conscious artist this field has ever had; he ought to be covered with medals by now, but now it seems to me that most readers prefer such writers as Heinlein, Asimov, and Arthur Clarke who, regardless of many other strengths as writers, generally produce work where the emotional content is shallow or even absent. For a writer who believes that human emotions make up the primary raw material in this and every other art, science fiction has indicated pretty plainly that the rewards are just plain not there. Second, most of the science fiction, good and bad, that I have ever read has been weak on intellection. That may seem to be a peculiar statement but I think it is true. One of the rewards of fiction lies in the

FUTURE

combined with SCIENCE FICTION *stories*

NOV.
20¢

WORLD-MOVER
FEATURE NOVEL
by George O. Smith

THE
SECRET PEOPLE
FEATURE NOVELET
by James Blish
& Damon Knight

chances it gives the writer to tackle a large philosophical question; he may not supply the answer but at least he has the chance to illuminate it from all sides in terms of its implications in human life, an opportunity denied to the nonfiction writer. Very few science fiction writers do this or even seem to be aware that it can be done; and here again I am not at all sure that it would be welcomed by the fans. On the other hand, every science fiction novel by an "outsider" which has gained a large public following does this very thing, and it doesn't have to be a big-name outsider, either: look at Bernard Wolfe's *Limbo*. Meanwhile the pros sit around groaning because their much more professional work doesn't seem to gain any status by these occasional successes, oblivious to the fact that the difference between a pro like, say, George O. Smith and an "outsider" like Kurt Vonnegut, is that Vonnegut can plainly be seen to be thinking about something.

Originality in the invention and elaboration of fantastic ideas and scientific rationales is, of course, a form of thinking, and more of that kind goes on in science fiction than in any other kind of fiction, but it will never command a large audience and there's no point in wishing that it could. The kind of thinking I am talking about is fundamental to good fiction of any kind (is there anybody in the audience who thinks *Moby Dick* is primarily about whaling?) and in science fiction it is usually 100% absent.

…Currently I am doing just as much science fiction as I ever did, and perhaps a little more, but it is almost entirely novels. Whether Horace can use them or not, that is where the money lies; it is uneconomical to write magazine short stories when with the same expenditure of time you can produce a chapter of a novel for two or three times the expectable income. Anybody who has been doing this for long soon finds that the difference is substantial, particularly as the small checks for subsidiary rights pile up; for the past three years, I have made more money on subsidiary rights than I have on first sales of new work, and I am *not* complaining.

I have also come to share…[the]…feeling that science fiction is far from the whole of literature and that in certain specific respects it is a cramped and unrewarding genre. I am not moving out of the field, which certainly would be financial suicide for me—and besides, science fiction *is* fun, but I am expanding to cover more territory where the restrictions don't apply, and I will be well satisfied if I can eventually reduce my science fiction writing to an occasional *jeu d'esprit*. I hope I have found something to do which will not only engage my full attention and allow me to do things that science fiction doesn't allow, but which also will enable me to use as much as three-fourths of the special skills a science fiction writer develops, but every writer has to solve this problem in his own way, and there's no reason to attempt a solution even a second in advance of the time that you yourself really come to think of it as a problem.

BLOCH, ROBERT

Your questionnaire…is a good idea, I think….

1) No, I don't feel that magazine science fiction is "dead" although it might well be moribund…due to the same factors which adversely affect all other types of magazine fiction. Said factors, in my opinion, being price increases, which bring magazines into direct competition with full-length novels in pocketbook form, and the continuing influence of television on reading…and on the *ability* to read, which seems to be diminishing rapidly among the adolescents.

2) No single villain is responsible for the present situation, in my opinion. The above factors play a part…and there are at least two others which I would mention. (1) the bad "advertisement" for the field provided by so-called science fiction movies, which misrepresent the quality of science fiction to the general public. (2) Atrociously low word rates, which do not encourage writers to spend an inordinate amount of time, thought, and effort upon their output—unless they write as a hobby and earn the major portion of their income through such illegitimate channels as teaching, projecting science fiction movies, or fronting for the Syndicate.

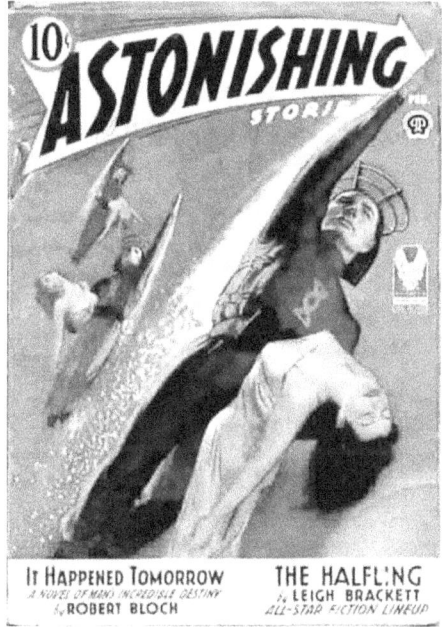

It Happened Tomorrow
A NOVEL OF MAN'S INCREDIBLE DESTINY
by ROBERT BLOCH

THE HALFLING
by LEIGH BRACKETT
ALL-STAR FICTION LINEUP

3) I believe individual effort and individual proselytizing are the only practical avenues of correction available to us. We cannot "organize" any "movement," nor do complaints seem efficacious. But we can, each of us, do our best to sell science fiction to friends as a source of entertainment. And we can do our best to correct erroneous impressions, produced by the worst possible examples of what is mislabeled science fiction, by recommending the best.

4) Should we look to the original paperback as a point of salvation? For an answer to this one, I suggest you just look *at* the *original* paperbacks which have been published. When you stop vomiting, then rephrase your

question. Do not pass Go, do not collect $200. Just hope and pray that some-day there will be some new paperback publishers who will open a market for decent work instead of the crud now offered.

5) Undoubtedly, amongst the answers you receive to the above questions, you will find many which infer or directly state that magazine science fiction is in a bad way because of editorial decisions. While there is a case to be made for this viewpoint (and a host of enthusiastic hatchetmen to splinter the kindling and construct said case), I feel that editors, by and large, do a conscientious job within an area which is horribly constricted. It is the *publishers* who peg the low rates, who insist on the stinking luridities, who often dictate choice of material, who stick their noses into policy, who botch up distribution arrangements and circulation deals.

BOK, HANNES

Lost your letter anent who what why when and how science fiction was killed, so can't perhaps answer all the queries therein, but here's one man's opinion (cribbed by the way from Wylie's *Generation of Vipers*, which I've been rereading, and which I noticed was very applicable in this instance):

Who killed science fiction?

The editors, naturally. A writer can write the superbest yarn of all time, but it won't do him any good if editors don't feel like publishing it. Hence it's editors and editorial policies that have run science fiction into the ground.

How?

By printing only what they, the editors, think that the public should (or might wish to) read. Since people can purchase only what's on the market or else not purchase anything, either they had to "make do" with the unreadable garbage in print, or else switch to other forms of literature. Both of which they've done.

WHY?

Science fiction was okay in the early days when it was IMAG-INATIVE LITERATURE, with no

Afterthoughts...

I HATE YOU! YOU RUINED MY WHOLE DAY! *Who Killed Science Fiction?* came this ayem and I should have done work, but instead read the damn thing kivver-to...would you much mind if I lent it out to various stf-readers (who are not fans) whom I know? I pity the un-Kemp-ed fans who won't get to read it.

– Hannes Bok, May 1960

holds barred, but then the "scientific attitude" came into domination. Stories could be written ONLY extrapolating known facts. Now, I've always maintained that NEW facts are bound to be discovered time and again in the future, many of which may negate today's "facts"—hence "visions of the future" which are based strictly on today's principles are bound to be wrong. (And, oh boy, are they DULL!) As Wylie says (except that I apply it to today's editors), "He is…unable even to conceive of the possibility of knowledge that is broader, other, or different."

For instance, science has ignored a lot of subjects (astrology, witchcraft, etc.) which DO work (I've plenty of proof). I've always wanted to write a story in which the future United States is run by witchcraft (after all, think of the 50 pentagrams on the flag, and the Pentagon Building wherein "evil forces are summoned" all too darned often. And what about that Fifth Amendment, h'mm?) But it wouldn't stand a chance in today's magazines. Science "knows" that witchcraft can't work (just as 100 years ago it "knew" that heavier-than-air craft was impossible).

To quote Wylie: "The result is not science but 'scientism'—authority set above free inquiry [Bok: substitute "imagination" for "inquiry"] and while almost any sane scientist will admit that science has much truth to learn, almost every [editor behaves] intellectually as if nobody had a right to question the finality of his concepts in his chosen field." Yeah, man. Yeah…

BOUCHER, ANTHONY

The one thing I'm fairly certain of is that science fiction is in a bad way. I should suspect that it was just me—that I've lost my taste or gone stale—if it weren't that I hear so many other reactions similar to mine.

I haven't even tried to keep up with magazine science fiction in the past year, but as a book reviewer I am plain bored. Everything that comes in is a retelling (sometimes competent) of a dozen earlier stories. I have to flog myself to read science fiction books, and half the time (at least) I see no reason to finish them or to publish a review.

(Note: This is emphatically not true in the much older field of the mystery novel. To be sure, there's always a fair amount of repetitive crap, but there's always enough fresh, creative work to keep a reviewer stimulated and happy even in his 18th year of professional reading.)

This quality of boredom prevails even in the work of (onceuponatime) very good writers. Let's not mention names, but keep it clean. I felt the same way in my last year or so as an editor. Manuscripts would come in from authors whom I used to feel I could damn near buy sight unseen—and the manuscripts wouldn't even be worth finishing.

The very existence of your survey reassures me that the fault is not (entirely) in me. Something is wrong, and the only thing I can think of is that science fiction needs some kind of a new breakthrough.

Which apparently it should have every ten or twelve years. In 1926 there was Gernsback. In 1938-9 Campbell brought the field to life with better science and far better fiction. In 1949-50, first J. Francis McComas and I, and then Gold, tried to expand the horizons and place more stress on literary and psychological values. And each time, the result was vigorous, exciting, creative work, for five years or so.

It's time for yet another fresh new revitalizing approach…and if I knew what it was, I'd probably get back into the field and do it.

As to the questions:

1) Of course science fiction is not dead. It's always been a small part of (particularly Anglo-American) literature, and doubtless it always will be. Whether we've succeeded in creating an economically satisfactory market for it as a specialized labeled category (comparable to the mystery or the western or the historical) is another question. The necessary converting of new readers once looked like a hopeful project; I doubt if much conversion is going on right now.

2) Responsibility? I don't know. Certainly not any single factor. I do not believe that science fiction has been "killed" by psionics or psychology or literary self-consciousness or any of the other frequently heard assertions; the bad effects (if any) of each of these affected only a portion of the field. And the weariness is everywhere—in psionic stories, in sheer space opera, in "novels of character"…

3) To correct it? I only wish I knew.

4) "The original paperback as a point of salvation?" Well, economically it's been a help to writers, but the standards of editing have been so low as to encourage writers to turn out crap for a fast sale. The trend does seem to be away from magazines and toward the paperback book, on the part of both readers and writers. This could possibly be all right (for everybody but magazine publishers), but not at today's standards.

5) Additional remarks: or I suppose this should really have been under Number four: I was interested in a recent remark of Poul Anderson's—that he's now writing mostly novels rather than shorts and novelettes, because the eventual total income on a novel (which means principally the paperback money) makes it a more profitable procedure.

Novels used to be the rare and welcome plums in science fiction—infrequent and usually something special and exciting. An author didn't embark on the financial risk (in those days) of a novel unless he had a story he strongly wanted to tell, an idea that demanded extensive development. Now...

BRADBURY, RAY

Ray Bradbury (signature)

1) A bit dormant, perhaps, but soon science fiction will spread through all the other types of magazines.

2) I believe we're in a period of transition, when science fiction, under that label, may vanish, to reappear in the guise of realistic fiction everywhere, as indicated above. I believe the Space Age itself, the beginning of it, might be responsible for this period of uncertainty we're going through. But once we've assessed our goals, set up some ways to get where we want to go, established values, I see an influx of talent into science fiction from all sides. We need more good writers and writing. Ten writers, and there are about ten really excellent writers in the field, cannot do all the work. They need help. There are only eight or nine good western writers, eight or nine good mystery writers. Eight or nine good practicing novelists in the broad general field. But I would like to see more people, like Robert Frost, for a wild example, coming our way.

3) We can do our part, by writing as well as possible when each of us, as writers, sits down to do a science fiction story.

4) The original paperback will help, in some ways, yes.

5) I have some ideas I want to try myself, in order to move science fiction into new fields. I have already finished two science fiction one-act plays. I am starting work on a science fiction one-act opera, have already finished another chamber opera, and two others, based on my works, are in existence done by young U.S. composers. We should stimulate more of this in order to prepare a climate of acceptance, not for science fiction per se, but for the Space Age itself, which should be the end-all and be-all of this hullabaloo.

BRADBURY, WALTER I.

I am really at a loss to offer anything intelligent on the points of inquiry.

I not only have not been able to keep up with science fiction magazines, but have unfortunately been removed from even the book publishing end of it. I'm afraid my opinions and knowledge would be from a time so far back that it would do you no good.

BRADLEY, MARION ZIMMER

And then the corpse sat up and demanded to know why in the hell they were holding a funeral over him?

And they, who professed to love him, quickly pushed him back and screwed down the coffin lid, muffling his cries.

That is how I feel when I hear all this talk about "Who killed science fiction?"

Science fiction is not dead, even in the magazines. It is being read, even the poor stuff which is passed out today. But it is perilously sick from malnutrition. Who is keeping it on this starvation diet?

The writers. And a worse damned bunch of incompetents never lived. All of us…and I include myself in this indictment…are directly responsible for the state of science fiction; and if we want science fiction to boom again (and the time is ripe for such a boom as you never heard) it is going to be up to us.

What sparked the previous booms? The first big boom was the Golden Age of *Astounding*, and I think we have to give John Campbell's forethought in envisioning a fascinating magazine, without gadgets ("grant your gadgets and start from there") the credit. Unfortunately, he has now abandoned this notion—of printing wonderfully readable stories—in favor of using his pages as a crusade to save the world through psi, and this is as dreary as such crusades usually are. BUT THE WRITERS ARE TO BLAME: they played along, writing this dreary claptrap, to soak up those fat *Astounding* checks.

The second boom came with the great explosion of magazines in 1953; through sheer quantity, *some* of these stories had to be good, some of the new writers who were able to break through the clique of "big names" had to be good ones.

And then we got careless and complacent. For a while, there were so many magazines around that editors would buy almost any piece of writing which was halfway literate. This gave new writers a chance, sure. But it also gave good writers, who should have known better, a chance to write (and, worse, to SELL) the kind of thing they secretly wanted to write but that nobody really wants to read at all, except a very small percentage of "literary" writers. The editors, starved for stories, printed everything with a "Big Name" on it…including those "writer's darling" stories which the writer loves and his friends love and which bore HELL out of the readers.

We forgot the main thing, that pulp magazines exist, not to create works of art, not to develop great writers who are too good for the pulp magazines, but to ENTERTAIN A VAST, NOT TOO INTELLIGENT AUDIENCE. I'm not saying we should write down to this audience; I say that we should write enjoyable stories…not write "literary pieces" and say, when they complain, "Of course you don't understand it. Man, this is literature, nobody understands it, but you clods keep on reading it and someday you'll be IN."

Now we come to a common alibi offered by writers: "Sputnik killed off science fiction. Now they can read it in their daily papers."

My answer to that is terse and unprintable, but the general gist is "Oh, shut up, who are you kidding?"

Did the atom bomb kill off science fiction? Heck, no; it spurred the biggest boom in science fiction we've ever had. Sputnik could easily have done the same, but the current crop of writers, instead of challenging this wonderful new era, immediately flocked to change their spots. They started pluming themselves and preening; "Now we, the science fiction writers, are the writers of TODAY!" Instead of writing for new vistas of tomorrow, new worlds to conquer, more escape from the grim realities of Russian satellites overhead, they tried to amalgamate science fiction into "realistic *timely* stories"—and the bastard product was as unhappy as all illegitimate offspring.

Science fiction, by its very nature, dares not be TIMELY. It must exit outside time and space.

So what kind of science fiction have we been getting? Well, we got some "gutsy" stuff about how it feels to be one girl in a ship full of spacemen (shades of *True Confessions!*) or pale little emotional vignettes about the emotions of a spaceman taking off on a rocket. Plot? Heavens, no; that's old stuff from the pulp magazines, and have you forgotten? (so they swagger,) *We* are creating *Literature* now! *We* are the current Big Men!

The few people who stuck to the escape fiction have often, grossly and culpably, gone to the other extreme and written sheer spoof stuff. Space op-

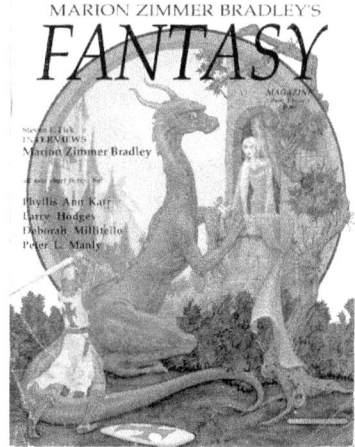

era? Oh, no, that's old stuff, so let's write a nice subtle (or blatant) little *parody* on space opera!

And how does this affect the kids, the garage mechanics and policemen and college students who want to relax their brains after an evening wrestling with the problems of the world, the boss, and the devil? I only know how it affects some old readers and nonfans I've been talking to lately. "Science fiction used to be fun to read," they say, almost in the same words. "Nowadays I pick it up and I might just as well read the newspaper or some-pin'. Either it sounds like somepin' out of the men's mags or else I can't make sense of it, it's like a private sort of joke."

Their reaction? The magazine goes into the corner and on goes the television set, and next time they buy a copy of *Rogue*. Which may suit Harlan Ellison just fine, but it jolly well doesn't suit ME.

People who read science fiction are, by definition, people who are bored with today and they are looking for tomorrow.

Another common argument says "People are scared of space, what with Sputnik and all." Well, back in 1946 they were scared of the atom bomb. But it is the function of science fiction to look beyond the immediate dooms to the bright or bitter tomorrows. (Or beyond the immediate delights to the bitter tomorrows.)

People go to science fiction, by and large, because todayish fiction has failed them somehow. Some writers still say science fiction ought to be timely and realistic. I say timeliness and realism are killing science fiction, and between the television and the men's magazines, if it ever gets screwed down in that coffin…well, coffins are harder to get out of than to get into.

I don't believe the paperback novels offer any solution. Writers love to *write* novels, but I am sadly conscious that a lot of people today don't want to read them. The average novel used to be 100,000 words long. The magazine's "book-length novel" was about 50,000. Now the "paperback novel" runs about 60,000 words and the magazine novel about half that…and what they print as book-length novels in some magazines would hardly be called a novelette in the old magazines, but they are still complained about by people who want something to pick up and read quickly. Oh, yes, inveterate readers buy novels, but the backbone of readership must always be the people who read with some difficulty (even college students show reading deficiencies, and the mass of the population wants something short; if we don't give it to him he will buy *Rogue* and *Reader's Digest*, not a pocketbook. Of course, once we have gotten him firmly snared, and as he reads more, THEN he will read novels, but the new readers must be snared by short stories, and for that we need MAGAZINES).

Will science fiction die or boom? I think the only hope is for the *writers* to change their spots, and to think less about their goddamn "artistic development" than about writing stories which the average reader will flip over.

And if they don't—well, we will have all our leisure time to write artistic stories for our own delight and read them aloud to one another in our garrets where we slowly starve.

BRINEY, ROBERT E.

Robert E. Briney

1) Not necessarily dead, but science fiction magazines are now on their last legs.

Science fiction is still in the process of reverting to its status as a specialty field, catering to a limited audience, and able to support only one or two small magazines entirely within its borders. (And this specialty field will never again reach even its modest popularity of the mid-1930s, let alone the "boom" periods of ca. 1940 and ca. 1950…) As the reading audience falls away, existing magazines turn in different directions to widen their appeal; all of these directions lead away from science fiction proper, none of them will do any good for the field, and at least two of them may even hasten "the end."

One direction, being taken by *Analog: Science Fact & Fiction* (formerly *Astounding*) is implicit in its title. Symptoms are the large, slick, illustrated fact articles, and the emphasis on twists in *old ideas* for the stories. Within a year, I'll bet *Analog* will scarcely be distinguishable from *Popular Mechanics.…*

Another direction, that adopted by *Fantastic Universe*, is toward the cult-occult borderline; this is heralded by increasing prominence given to ("fact") articles, most of them on spiritualism, UFOlogy, and other topics calculated to appeal to readers of *GalacTicks…* Even in the stories, this increased emphasis on spiritualism and mental powers is evident. (And in more concrete terms, it is worth noting that most of the lead stories are *reprints* from British magazines; this seems to hint at a lack of original material, or at least at word-rates too low to encourage original material.)

A third direction, and (at present) by far the most successful, is the appeal toward the general adventure story market: in science fiction terms, an emphasis on space opera and reworking of old ideas—BUT, at least as evidenced in the Ziff-Davis magazines *Amazing* and *Fantastic*, it is good space opera, and the "old" ideas are old only to science fiction enthusiasts, but still fresh and (I hope) exciting to the general reader. These two magazines seem to have a monopoly on the best current American science fiction, at least in the longer stories, and they represent one of the few markets for *new* writers in the field. (Jack Sharkey may turn out to be another Sheckley—little ideas, highly polished—but at least his is a fresh voice in the field.)

As for other directions—well, *Galaxy* has always marched to its own music, seemingly unaffected either by the economic troubles in the field or by the fact that it publishes trash, and now *If* is going along with it. And the Columbia magazines seem to exist on a shoestring, which is becoming more and more frayed... And as for *F&SF*—the Boucher magic has worn away, Robert Mills seems to have run out of ideas, and heaven knows how long it will take for Ferdinand Feghoot to kill the magazine completely.

The biggest problem faced by the field (and the one that will eventually deliver the *coup de grace*) is the economic vicious circle: dwindling readership leads to dwindling rates, which cause the full-time writers (the ones who write for a living, not for fun) in the field to look elsewhere for markets; as the authors desert the field, the editors find it more and more difficult to fill their issues with readable material, thus their circulations drop even more, and... In addition, the low rates and the general unexciting atmosphere of current science fiction combine to keep new writers from entering the field. There are just no paying markets for any except the most prolific and well-known authors, and most of these can get far higher rates in other fields.

Sudden thought, from another angle: the science fiction magazines are about the only fiction magazines left on the stands. Even the mystery magazines are down to two regular titles, and everything else except the "true confessions" variety has all but disappeared. With the wealth of reading material available in paperbacks, people just don't read fiction magazines any more. This will also be a large contributing factor in the death of science fiction, and means that even the appeal to a general adventure audience, which seems now to be working well for *Amazing* and *Fantastic*, will sooner or later fail (and probably sooner).

In spite of all this, there would probably always be enough people willing to buy and read (and hence others to publish) science fiction to support a small publication. But there is a further factor, nibbling at the very roots of science fiction growth: *science fiction just isn't very interesting any more!* It has none of that particular excitement which should differentiate it in an essential way from other types of fiction. Character study, psychological probings, emotional and physical conflict, suspense, adventure—all these are available in many other areas, so why get excited over finding them (however well done) in a "science fiction" story, especially when that story offers nothing more to the reader. It isn't the gadgetry that's missing or rather, that isn't what really counts, since gadgets are not exciting any more but the type of *thinking* that used to mark a good science fiction story—philosophical, historical, or scientific speculation and extrapolation, looking at things in a new light, from an odd angle....

Afterthoughts...

Received *Who Killed Science Fiction?...have been reading* and re-reading them. As usual, I am nigh speechless at the amount of work you put in on it—though I shouldn't be, having seen ample evidence before of the energy you put in on science fictional activities...I think the *Who Killed* symposium comes out as evidence of some good solid thinking on the part of a majority of the contributors, and the halfassed burbling of a couple of the minority was in its own way just as revealing and entertaining (are you listening, John?). Perhaps the greatest surprise, however, was in the shallowness and lack of perception shown by a few of those who should have had more significant things to say—notably deCamp, Bradbury, and damon...was amused by *Flesh* Farmers references to "good meaty stories with valid science fiction backgrounds" which are apparently going begging...could be possibly have been referring to a certain recent novel of his own??? Boy, fascinating to read the MCs—like coming in on the middle of a one-way phone conversation.

– Robert E. Briney, May 1960

Part of the difficulty may be that science fiction settled too far into a fixed mold in the "boom" periods: editors found out what sold copies, and began insisting on getting exactly that. No experimentation, no deviation from the norm that makes us money—and now, firmly settled in the rut, with the authors who would have welcomed the chance to experiment, try out wild ideas and new writing styles—with these authors turning away, science fiction is suffocating in the old, used-up, oxygen-starved atmosphere of conformity.

Thus:

(a) Authors turning away because of low pay and lack of opportunity to experiment; and no new authors coming, for the same reasons.

(b) Diminishing market for fiction magazines of any kind.

(c) Diminishing interest on the part of science fiction readers or potential science fiction readers, due to general lack of quality and/or excitement in present day material. These factors are killing science fiction magazines (and #c is helping to do away with science fiction in *any* medium).

4) Not for science fiction as such; the paperback originals (except for certain ill-fated experiments which the publishers did not repeat—Jack Vance's *Dying Earth* for example) have been mostly of a "pro-integrationist" variety (in P. Schuyler Miller's phrasing)—combining science fiction with straight

adventure, with mystery and suspense, or just with sex, and depending on the wider appeal of these other areas to sell the books.

Maybe, as Miller says, science fiction is being integrated; but even if it is, this will contribute to its demise as a special field. The "integrated" commodity must appeal to a wide class of readers, hence will have lost the special appeal that good science fiction should have.

BUDRYS, A.J.

Well, yes, I feel magazine science fiction is dead—in the sense that the great days of the magazine science fiction form *as we recognize* it are gone, never to return. This statement holds true, I think, no matter what particular days in what particular magazine are the "great days" to your mind. I, personally, have become reconciled to the fact that the 1940's *Astounding* is past all resurrection. At the moment, there seems to be a paucity of magazine editorial policies capable of exciting and attracting large audiences; even "large" in science fiction magazine terms. Whether this is because science fiction has become exhausted as a reservoir of exciting editorial ideas, or whether this is because the world's English-speaking population has exhausted its capacity to be excited by science fiction among other things, remains to be decided, if it can be decided at any point between these particular two extremes.

I do not think a specific cause for this effect can be pinpointed. I am of the opinion that the first people to see this current lethargy coming were the editors—who have been roundly excoriated for espousing strange, unorthodox policies which, it is true, *may* be *one* of the causes of today's difficulties, but at least represented an attempt to *do* something. Since we cannot see the actual causes—or at least, for the life of me, I cannot—I hesitate to advocate remedies, for fear that we might wind up in an alley equally as blind as the attempt to make *Galaxy* metamorphose into *The Saturday Evening Post*, of to make *Astounding* the standard around which the partisans of some worthy cause might rally.

The original paperback, by definition, cannot save magazine science fiction. The original paperback is the mortal enemy of the magazine, and, furthermore, occupying the newsstands in its present position, an enemy who has won. But this is not the same as saying that the paperbacks—particularly but not entirely the original paperbacks—killed the magazine market. They may have—though the evidence for this fails at a few crucial points—or they may simply have moved in and occupied a vacuum. Phil Klass, Bob Sheckley, and I did some arithmetic on this a few months ago, and came to the conclusion that original paperback wordage just about equals the difference between magazine wordage today and magazine wordage before the advent of Ballantine Books and the start, in reaction, of the extensive general science fiction paperback publishing program. But what this means, exactly, is something we can't tell. I offer it to you for what it's worth. As for whether the original paperback can "save" science fiction—science fiction as something larger than magazine science fiction—the evidence quoted above does seem to indicate that it represents only a metamorphosis in form, and has little effect in either increasing or decreasing the amount of science fiction published. It does, of course, circumscribe the length, and so to some extent, the *kind* of science fiction for which a ready market is available. This may very well lead to a sharp division, on criteria of length, between paperback science fiction (I think we can forget about hardcovers except as library items in editions of 2,500 copies) and the magazine science fiction of the future. Because some of the technical effects of writing to given lengths are not completely understood, it would be an invitation to error for anyone to predict what the science fiction magazines would be like under this hypothesis, but they would not much resemble anything in the market today.

Attempting to answer these questions leads, I find, to larger questions. For example: What is there about magazine science fiction that makes it worthy of special concern more intense than any concern for science fiction as a whole? When I attempt to answer that question for myself, I find myself forcibly flattening my nose against the unkind fact that my concern for the magazines is either sentimental or provincial, but not rational. The science fiction I liked best, as an adolescent, was magazine science fiction—furthermore, as published in a particular magazine. And even by my objective standards— that is, my subjective standards dressed up in stiff collars—the flowering of the science fiction form occurred in the magazines. But magazine publication represents an eyeblink in the span of science fiction's existence, and there is really no reason to suppose that simply because it was there when we were children, and was acknowledged chief, it will still be there for our children. There *have* after all, been other presidents since Franklin Roosevelt, though you could have gotten large bets against it at one time.

Then, again, one is brought to ask: Since there are still well over 60 issues of science fiction magazines published every year, representing, at rough count, at the very least some three million annual words, how does this square with the notion that the field is dead? It is true this represents an enormous come-down—magazine science fiction has now sunk to a volume comparable to that of the crime fiction magazine—but the next question fairly leaps to mind: Are three million words of readable *anything* publishable every year?

We tend to forget that even in the 1940s, when, for my money, the marks were being set, every issue of *Astounding* was matched by four or five issues of incredible crap turned out by men who have, some of them, become leading lights in the market today, but who were in those days interesting only to students of literary evolution and who were, in any case, swamped by the hackwork of literary plumbers trained to conform rigidly to standards low enough to make a subway platform guard disdain them. We hear a lot of folklore nowadays about roses that bloomed forlorn in the pages of *Stirring Science*. Examination of the work in question undeniably leads to pleasant surprises in the form of a well-turned phrase here, an unconventional character there, or a curious plot twist elsewhere, mostly at the hands of one man. But as a whole, even the best of these pieces are, as I've said, only the yearling stumbles of men who did not walk tall until much later, and the folklore stems from the same nostalgic phenomenon that leads 40-year-old businessmen to ascribe importance to the interfraternity politics of their college days. In the 1940s, magazine science fiction had an abysmal average standard of excellence; the memorable stories, which men like Healy and McComas, Groff Conklin, and others have skimmed off for all our enjoyment, come largely from *Astounding*, and come largely from a handful of men—run your eye down the contents page of the Healy/McComas anthology* and see how many individuals are represented—who, *in their contemporary setting*, were buried under a swale of John Russell Fearn. And who, furthermore, had no idea whatsoever that they would someday be referred to as standards.

We see the 1940s from a viewpoint created by the good writers of the 1940s, and the standards by which measurement of their excellence is made are the highest standards which *they* set. We are the convinced audience they created—"we" meaning I and anyone who thinks as I do—and it's no wonder we cannot find others to equal them, or magazines as satisfactory as the one that published them. But when we decry the magazine science fiction of today, and concern ourselves with its deterioration, we're missing the point of the old saying that the winners write the history books. We miss it because the proper word should be not "winners," but "survivors." Those people who survive as magazine readers, should the magazines survive in any form, may well find excellences, in the contemporary magazines, that you and I are totally unaware of; they may well idolize writers we ignore, just as a Polton Cross enthusiast of 1940 would have said: "Who?" to the mention of Robert Heinlein's name. Ted Sturgeon

has said that 90% of everything is crap. Maybe so—it seems unarguable to me that three million words of anything must be largely crap, which might be concealing almost *anything* from our eyes, but not to the eyes of those who, ten years from now, will be looking back from another viewpoint.

So I honestly think that much of the rife dissatisfaction with today's magazines stems from a hopeless nostalgia as inevitable, and as inconsolable, as Sam Moskowitz's yearning for the Gernsback *Amazing*. And I think also that whatever the causes of the deflated science fiction boom might be, they are only the latest causes of a condition permanent to science fiction and all other evolutionary organisms—the shedding of dead skin and the generation of new organs and functions. I think we expected the boom to last, and I think we feel cheated that it didn't because we feel that science fiction *deserves* to boom. But by what rational thinking can it be said that it does? Simply because it is "better" than the crimezines? By whose standards? When you come down to it, what service does science fiction perform for the average magazine reader that is not performed as well by a dozen competing specialties?

———

In looking over this essay, I realize that I haven't done what I, as a convinced fan, desperately hoped I would do—assign some simple cause to the current (unfair) decline of magazine science fiction, and having done so, recommended a straightforward and obvious (if somehow up-to-now overlooked) remedy. But though I could snipe at editors and publishers—and, were I an editor or publisher, snipe at writers and readers—I would only be adding to the surf of backbiting that surrounds the rock of our mutual affection for science fiction as a whole. I have, God knows, done enough of that in the past to see its futility.

I think it quite likely that the frustration many of us feel at our failure to slay the dragon is that, as so often is the case, there is no dragon and we know, deep inside, that the broadsword we hold poised is only going to give us one hell of a case of bursitis. I am sorry I haven't done what I'd like to have done, just as I would be pleased to see that despite my best rationalization here, someone else *has* found the dragon I overlooked, and slain it. But so many people have gone over the ground—cries of a lack of soul-searching are, to be kind about it, based on a misapprehension so ludicrous as to be past laughter—that I cannot for the life of me imagine where the beast might be, that it should have evaded such persistent detection.

I think science fiction will continue, in one form or another, slowly increasing its readership in direct proportion to population growth, despite our best efforts to lead fresh horses to water or to express our discomfort when the stream changes channels. Science fiction is, I think, a literary form that springs inevitably from the mind of a certain kind of person, and appeals to a certain kind of person. That's the only certainty I have on this point—I couldn't begin to define what I mean by "a certain kind," except negatively: Fans are NOT Slans...nor are they Ted Sturgeon's only non-telepath in the world. But matters of form are only matters of form, and while an inquiry of this nature will inevitably bring a number of valuable small things to light, the large decisions will, it seems to me, be made by the surviving readers of perhaps a decade from now.

BUSBY, ELINOR

(A postscript.)

I think that science fiction needs some new ideas, or new approaches, or an entire new crop of readers.

BUSBY, F.M.

1) No. Things are poor, but they've been worse (1946-48, for instance). In that period the science fiction field consisted of 28 readable issues per year: twelve *Astounding*s, six each *Startling*s and *Thrilling Wonder Stories* and four *Planet*s. Even with this scarcity, I found *Amazing* (monthly) and *Fantastic* (bi-monthly then, I think) mostly not worth buying. There were also several strictly fantasyzines: *Weird, Famous Fantastic Mysteries, Fantastic Novels,* and several short-lived digest-sized zines, but I'm not much of a fantasy buff except for the *Unknown* sort of thing.

We now have twelve each *Astounding, F&SF,* and *Fantastic Universe,* plus six each *Science Fiction Stories, Future, Galaxy, If,* from United States sources only, for a total of 60 issues per year. Further, *Amazing* (monthly) and *Fantastic* (what is that one, monthly or bi-?) have become quite readable indeed since Cele Goldsmith got rid of Paul Fairman's backlog, so that makes either 78 or 84 readable US issues, each and every year. Also, the UKzines are available with a little effort: twelve *New Worlds* and six each *Science Fantasy* and *Science Fiction Adventures.*

Titlewise, we had four readable and two cruddy science fiction magazines in the United States in 1946-48. Today we have nine United States and three UK titles available, though there is some reprint-overlap on the latter. Which brings us to:

Distribution, and high-handed tactics of distributors, appear to be a major factor. Distribution is in horrible shape today. So now somebody tell me of any extended period during which distribution has *not* been horrible except for one or two stands in any given town. 1953 was probably the high point, but knight's* *Worlds Beyond* and the attempted resurrection of *Marvel* were killed by indifferent distribution just two years previously. Today's distribution trouble is made worse by the recent advent of several new kinds of crud in volume: the "men's" zines (both the sadistic and the *Playboy* imitator types), the Dirtzines (*Confidential* et al.), and the straight semi-nude picture-zines, are all relatively new and are taking up a greater share of the shelf space all the time, along with the perennial *True Confessions*, movie magazines, teen-zines (TV idols), true crime, etc. And going to less offensive things, the flood of hobbyzines (cars, hi-fi, photography, etc.) is growing rapidly, too. These are all large-size zines and take a lot of shelf space. Science fiction is relegated to the back shelves with the "peekaboo" zines full of saaad jokes and cartoons of girls with big teats saying something stupid. As a small-circulation deal, science fiction has it tough against large circulation crud.

3) What can we do? Bitch in all directions, probably, but I'm not much of a crusader. There'll probably be all sorts of things suggested that would be of some help if done consistently by a great number of science fiction readers. However, I do *not* advise a gross rearrangement of the zines at your favorite newsstand, to give the science fiction magazines a featured display—not unless you want a clop over the ear from your favorite newsdealer. He wants to find things the way he put them, next time he has a box of assorted zines to lay out.

4) Yes, as a last resort, maybe we should look to the original paperback—but as a poor substitute. Certainly we'll fall back on whatever medium is printing original science fiction. I buy most, if not all, of the original sci-

---

*The lower-case "k" is not a typographical error; it is a reference to a fannish-days affectation of Damon Knight of lowercasing his own name.—E.K.

ence fiction paperbacks, and sometimes even rewrites and one-side—new double—backs, but I wouldn't buy anthologies with one new story for bait, except about one in ten. The paperback is not really a good substitute for the magazine, because it has no personality, and let's face it, we who are hooked on the stuff go for the personality of a zine every bit as much as we do for the stories therein, in most cases.

5) The people who bug me are the ones who bemoan the "death of the prozines" but mention in the same breath that they, "don't buy them much, any more." Somebody is going to holler about Quality and Sense of Wonder in connection with my quantitative remarks under item No. one. But I think that if you face a relatively new reader (three to four years, say) with the 1946 output and the 1959 output, and ask him to list the Really Good stuff, he'll list much more 1959 than 1946 material. The same greater quantity, though, insures that we get a surfeit. Not only a surfeit of crud, but a plain old surfeit. I wouldn't bet you on the *percentage* of Good Stuff in the two years cited, and I am definitely not the guy to make the assessments, since I was thirteen years fresher when I read the 1946zines, and we all know about nostalgia. That's why I specified a reader who (1) had not previously read the 1946 crop, (2) had not been worn out by the 1953 boom, and (3) has been reading long enough to recognize a few of the standard plots and not go all goshwow over trite items. 1946 is a good comparison, because Campbell was just as overboard then on Atomic Doom as he is now on Psi, and on Strong Men. 1944 or 1945 would have been even rougher for quantity; everyone went quarterly except Campbell, I think. And the war years have all too many tired war-propaganda bits in with the good stuff. Anyhow, I don't agree that magazine science fiction is dead today. In trouble, surely, and for reasons that are hard to cope with at the fan level. All we can do is buy the stuff, and maybe write some encouraging letters and do a bit of missionary work, unrewarding though that usually is.

CALKINS, GREGG

1) No, I don't feel that magazine science fiction is dead, although at the moment things are in a very precarious position, largely due to the fact that *Astounding* has recently changed publishers after a number of years and nobody seems to know what their attitude will be toward a monthly science fiction magazine in the future. I believe the future of magazine science fiction rests largely, if indirectly, on what happens to *Astounding* in the next several

years. Another recent blow to magazine science fiction was the loss of Anthony Boucher from the editorial helm of *F&SF*.

As for the death of the other science fiction magazines, with the exception of the complete disappearance of the true pulp magazine, I can't help but feel it's a good thing. The market was overstocked—and with poor quality science fiction to boot!—and eventually supply exceeded demand with the characteristic drastic results as far as the suppliers were concerned. It is my opinion that the magazine science fiction field is at its most stable configuration with one or two monthly magazines complemented by two to three times as many bimonthly or quarterly magazines.

In short, if the magazine science fiction field is trimmed to a more reasonable size, I believe it will continue to exist in spite of the increasing encroachment of pocketbook science fiction…*unless* the major standard-bearer since 1930, *Astounding*, either folds or changes to paperback format itself. I do not think magazine science fiction can withstand *this* assault. Even if this disaster should occur, however, I am not convinced it would kill off magazine science fiction completely. Temporarily, perhaps, but a certain number of science fiction magazines would reappear after the hiatus, I believe.

2) Not any *single* action of any *single* person, no, although of course some people had more influence cause-and-effect-wise than others. Editors are a bit more to blame than authors, as a group, boo… Campbell for letting his hobbies run away with his science fiction magazine; Gold for his policy of presenting the type of fiction *most* readers want, regardless of whether or not it is very good science fiction (and I defend this accusation by pointing out that *most* people have very poor taste, on the whole, than does any select group, whether they be science fiction fans, music lovers (witness Presley versus the classics), persons with college educations versus the other 90% of humanity, readers of good books versus readers of sexy pocketbooks), and the other editors for their apparent policy of making money while the boom boomed and to hell with science fiction. Too many stories were hastily written, shoddily conceived, and uncritically accepted to be very good science fiction. True, the authors are at fault here to some extent, but an author is out to make money and he'll sell as much as he can with as little effort as he can and it is up to the editorial staff to see that the authors produce quality instead of crud. I think the editors have failed us miserably in this respect.

3) Complain first and then stop buying the magazines so they'll know we mean it. For instance, Horace Gold knows, I think, that I haven't bought an issue of *Galaxy* in several years and he also knows why. At the present time he thinks I'm just wrong or spiteful or something, but at least he understands my opinions. If other sales drop far enough, perhaps he'll remember my complaints and reconsider. Maybe not, but there's a limit to what a reader can accomplish against an editor. The ultimate weapon of the consumer is

the refusal to consume. If the producer cannot sell his product he has two alternatives: (1) redesign the product until it will sell, or (2) get out of business. Since either way I fail to get good quality science fiction, I do not care which end I accomplish by my boycott—that is, either way if he continues at present or folds rather than modify his magazine. If he redesigns to suit me this is, naturally, the best result I could wish for.

4) What is the "original paperback?" If you mean will paperbacks take over the field and bring us science fiction even though the magazines fold, I'd say yes. The paperback field has increased astronomically in recent years and I think it will continue to do so, regardless of how the magazines fare. In other words, we—the reading public—are going to be able to get good science fiction in the future no matter what. *We* can't lose...but the magazine publishers can...and will, if they don't change their ways.

5) To tell the truth, I've been so windy thus far that I can hardly add more without repeating myself. If you want me to do that, I will.

Namely: the science fiction field is not dead but it sure isn't healthy, either. Conditions are not impossible, but a lot depends on the immediate future of *Astounding* under its new publishers. I'd like to see the field cut down still a bit more than it is at present...at least the magazine part of it. Pocketbooks are doing a wonderful job, especially in the development and preparation of the science fiction *novel*, and the quality of material they present (with the possible exception of the recent Ace offerings) is consistently high. I'd like to see more and better pocketbooks.

Editors and authors are both to blame for the present sad state of affairs—and I suppose we could include a substantial percentage of fandom, too, for their lack of disapproving noises via letters to the editors—but editors more than authors. Personally, I hope the bad editors fail to make it through the next couple of years...harsh, perhaps, but survival of the fittest environments always breed the best genetic types, and science fiction could use a few hardy souls in editorial circles.

CAMPBELL, JOHN W., JR.

1) Dead?! We're going better than ever before!
2) First establish that the alleged situation exists! I haven't found it!
3) Why correct it? What would be more correct than it is?
4) Not for me, thanks!
5) It isn't *science* fiction that's in trouble—it's *fantasy* fiction!

CARNELL, E.J.

1) No, I do not feel that magazine science fiction is dead. Basically, the science fiction short story will *always* be the backbone of the genre. At the moment, however, it is going through one of its periodic transition periods—the curve being forced lower than usual by the vast strides astronautics has made during the past few years.

2) It would be unfair for me to say what I think is wrong with *American* science fiction, as this is purely a domestic problem. Obviously editors are looking for some new trend which will give an indication that the waning interest of their regular readers is being revived.

As a British editor with an *international* readership, I probably have a better insight into what is happening to science fiction in the three main centers of interest—Europe, America, and Australasia. None are exactly the same, but all follow in each other's footsteps; the cycle seems a closed one, but there are deviations on each continent.

Basically, however, I agree with John Campbell's feelings that one of the main contributions to the present low in science fiction is the mess that Hollywood movies have made by labeling weird and horror films as science fiction. Potential new readers of the genre, appetites whetted by both American and Russian space probe successes, must receive a severe jolt when viewing a movie labeled "science fiction" which, apart from the appallingly poor dialogue and mediocre acting, is based mainly upon some monstrosity from

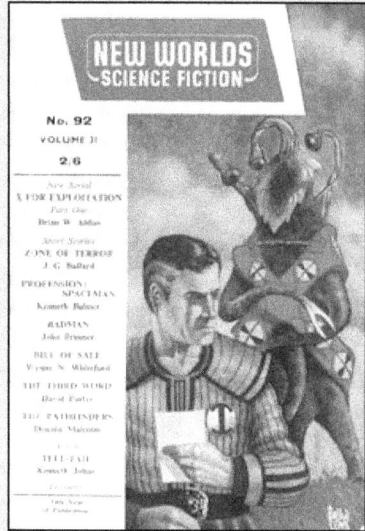

Meanwhile, some deep soul-searching has been going on amongst some sections of the sf community, which give pause for thought. A recent questionnaire sent out to leading amateurs and professionals in America and Great Britain by bibliophile Earl Kemp, of Chicago, posed some pertinent questions, the general answers to which Mr. Kemp proposes publishing privately for those who took part. Bearing in mind that this particular questionnaire was designed *primarily for the American field*, the relevant questions are still worth passing on in view of the change taking place in our own market. With Import [sic] restrictions lifted we shall soon see original U.S. editions of magazines and pocketbooks on sale in Great

Britain and this added competition will certainly have some effect on our own market, small though the percentage of sf titles will be.

Headed "Who Killed Science Fiction?" Mr. Kemp's questions were:

1. Do you feel that magazine science fiction is dead?
2. Do you feel that any single person, action, incident, etc., is responsible for the present situation? If not, what is responsible?
3. What can we do to correct it?
4. Should we look to the original paperback as a salvation?
5. What additional remarks, pertinent to the study, would you like to contribute?

"Mr. Kemp's deadline for replies is now long past, but if any of you feel that you want to answer these questions from the British viewpoint, the pages of "Postmortem" are wide open for an airing of pet ideas and theories.

– E.J. Carnell, *New Worlds*, March 1960

[Text courtesy John Boston Collection. Cover scan courtesy Gregory Pickersgill Collection.]

outer space or the depths of the ocean. The sight of the words "science fiction" on a magazine cover must be sufficient for these people to shy a long way away from it.

Unfortunately, while fat profits can be made in the movie industry for a modest outlay of about $10,000 per picture, there will be little change of heart. The fat profits come from the vicarious thrill teenagers get from this type of junk. And the teenager who goes to see a horror movie is *not* the type who will eventually become a regular science fiction reader.

Another contributing factor, I believe, is the vast upswing in pocketbook exploitation and sales. We know that there is a constant transition of science fiction readership—old readers drop out (temporarily in many cases, permanently in others) through some changing pattern in their life: change of job, location of business, illness, marriage, a growing family, loss of job, increasing overheads. In the past, when there were a surfeit of magazines (and no horror movies), it seems to me that there was always a progression of new readers coming in at the lower levels and graduating upward to the adult magazines. At the moment, new readers (apparently) are just not coming in.

In America, I believe that a greater part of the loss of sales of the magazines to the pocketbook market is due largely to the chaotic system of distribution—in fact, the science fiction depression stems largely from the collapse of the American News Company. This was the straw that broke the camel's back and had repercussions throughout the American trade. However, *any* commodity that works on 25 to 50% wastage to effect a profit cannot be operating at maximum efficiency. To be allowed to operate in the land of Time and Motion Study seems fantastic to me!

3) If any of us (professionals) could answer this one accurately we would be assured of a place in the Hall of Fame. I guess that every editor, past and present, has done his damnedest to improve the lot of science fiction, in sales and storywise. Making science fiction "respectable" has been a major ambition of both professional and amateur, assuming that respectability also carried increased sales. By book reviews, radio, television, even the better quality films, plenty of people have tried to improve science fiction's lot. Sometimes it seems to no avail. In the long run I think it will prove worthwhile, but that doesn't answer what can be done about things *now*.

4) No, except for salvation of the novel. Outside the United States, the anthology and short story collection is practically dead (there are exceptions, of course). To project the science fiction short story into pocketbook form does not appear to be the answer, mainly because there appears to be increased resistance to reading collections in book form (paper or boards) by the *general reading public*. Such anthologies or collections are mere collectors' items.

5) Most of the foregoing remarks cover the questionnaire but one additional aspect does present itself to my mind.

Afterthoughts....

Congratulations on your monumental opus *[Who Killed Science Fiction?]*...my deepest thanks for the copy you sent... It will take many days to read and many weeks to digest (and doubtless will trigger off various inspirations for further editorials in *New Worlds*)...

– Ted Carnell, private correspondence, May 1960

———

Following his editorial in *New Worlds* 92 March 1960, Ted Carnell followed up with another editorial in the April 1960 *New Worlds* 93. This one focused on the topic of "Soul Searching" that was in reality an extension of his March editorial about *Who Killed Science Fiction?* however it was done without mentioning *WKSF?* That editorial is followed by the "Postmortem" letter column wherein John Brunner takes up the discussion for a bit.

In *New Worlds* 95 June 1960, the "Postmortem" discussion continues with letters from Robert J. Tilley, William Aitken, and Donald Malcolm.

In *New Worlds* 96 July 1960, Carnell again takes up his editorial typewriter and continues the *Who Killed Science Fiction?* story.

– Earl Kemp

Final Summary...

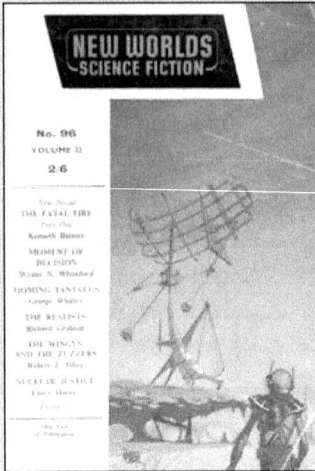

Having started the "Soul Searching" debate with the March Editorial (which has developed into one of the most interesting discussions this magazine has ever had) I must report that Earl Kemp of Chicago has now finalized the replies to his questionnaire in a magnificently duplicated 1101-page book. Space does not allow me to do justice to this monumental work but as a substitute I am publishing my own reply herewith. Many professionals agree with my own feelings— but bear in mind these questions primarily applied to the American market.

At this point, Carnell reprints with only minor revisions, his entire contribution to *Who Killed Science Fiction?*, ending with this statement:

Our "Postmorten" column will remain open for anyone who wishes to continue the discussion.

– John Carnell, *New Worlds* 96 July 1960

[Text and data courtesy John Boston Collection. Cover scan courtesy Gregory Pickersgill Collection.]

It does seem to me that magazines *in general* are in a period of moral regression, especially those where the short story is dominant: 1959 saw mergers of some of the largest British magazine publishing houses. The same "takeover" system was also applied in the Unites States. Out of the ruck of reorganization, many regular titles are merged with competing titles with, presumably, some boost to circulation, but the falloff in advertising revenue continues, at least in Great Britain, where the small land area is now adequately covered by commercial television.

I follow the biyearly statistics of all British newspapers and periodicals very closely and the last two years have shown that, apart from the phenomenal rise of women's' magazines, all other publications have been steadily dropping. Television cannot be entirely blamed for this, although it must contribute something. After the seven-week printing strike here, when all publishers expected to lose some circulation, sales in fact increased over 10% and have remained up *despite* a 5 to 10% increase in cover prices! This seemed to me to be proof that after a surfeit of watching television, the general public found that reading was, by and large, a more interesting pastime.

In view of this apparent regression—a general shrinking in numbers of all forms of magazines—the number of magazines now devoted to science fiction are still in proportion to the number in the general field. Being mainly (or solely) concerned with the science fiction field, we have been inclined to assume that the "depression" was only hitting us. If the regression is general, as I suspect (and American readers of this will be able to check statistics in their own country which are not immediately available to myself—Sam Moskowitz, for instance), then science fiction has only been taking part in the present phase of redistributed leisure time.

Both the movies *and* magazines have lost part of their regular audiences to TV, but, in general, the masses are spreading their spare time over a far wider range of outlets, due primarily to increased wealth.

CLIFTON, MARK

1) No, I do not quite feel that magazine science fiction is dead. But how long it can continue to survive its present treatment is anybody's guess.

2) I see a process taking place resulting from certain points of view, rather than any particular person, action, or incident as responsible for the enfeebling of science fiction.

There has been the tendency to freeze the concept of science fiction into a static mold. Perhaps some of this may be due to the timidity of pro editors who found a formula which was financially successful and feared to change lest they lose position and money. Some of it due to highly vocal pressure groups of fans who oppose anything new lest the traditional flavor of science fiction be lost. Both fail to take into account that by definition, by its very nature, science fiction must be ever changing, ever exploring, ever experimenting, else it cease to be.

John Campbell put his finger on it some years ago when he turned down a story of mine which was too much like the previous one I'd written: "You said this in you other story," he wrote. "Our readers are bright. They get the idea the first time."

But editors have not applied this admonition to themselves, for there is nothing new in science fiction, it has all been said before, many times. I can well understand and sympathize with the pro editor in his attitude toward his magazine. He feels it is his own creation, his responsibility, and so it is; but this exacts some penalties when carried too far. In recent years the pro editors seem to have adopted a kind of orchestra who must play each note of their stories in time with the beat of the leader's baton, and with the interpretation he demands. But performers and composers are two different breeds of musicians. When we know that we must confine ourselves to certain themes, written in a certain way, with a certain interpretation, we cease to be creative authors and become ghost writers for the editor's ideas. This produces a monotonous effect after a time. No matter how unique the flavor at first, it becomes monotonous with repetition, the miasma of sameness lays over it all, as if a cheap brown gravy in a greasy-spoon restaurant were spread over everything served regardless of the dish. Not only does each issue read as if it were all written by one person, but issue after issue, year after year.

In any field of human activity, where a leader grows so dominant that only his view is permitted, that activity cannot grow beyond his own personal limitations; and this has happened to science fiction. But the readers are bright, they get it the first time, and want something new.

But ah, do they? Then what of these highly vocal groups of fans who bitterly oppose any new theme, idea, or treatment? I never thought to see the day when science fictionists would become traditionalists to oppose any change from what has been done in the past. Yet, on every hand, I see this among the fans.

For a quarter century science fiction was a literature of material gadgetry. This was fine. Around the turn of the century when the science emphasis was on new concepts of the nature and behavior of the material universe, some wondrous new concepts came into being, and science fiction from about 1925 to about 1950 rightly explored the potentials of these concepts. But science emphasis changed from theorizing to implementing those theories, pure research gave way to engineering exploitation, and advancing new theories fell out of fashion. Consequently the new material available to science fiction began to diminish, dwindle away. We'd speculated on everything, in our extrapolation we'd explored to the limits of the material universe. What could possibly be said that hadn't been said before?

But there was a new field opening up to us. Although we have libraries full of writings about the nature and behavior of man, now we began to realize that these were nonscience and often nonsense opinions about him, no more valid than the middle ages opinions about energy and matter. We began to realize that no really scientific work had been done about the nature and behavior of man, that we had been so busy stating our opinions of what we thought he was and how he ought to behave we'd never actually taken a good look at what he really is and how he really does behave.

We began to explore the nature and behavior of man in science fiction, as we had explored the nature and behavior of the material universe. And a howl of outrage went up from the fans and is still howling. "Psychological junk!" they cry. "No scientific basis—" they cry again.

Well now, there are a great many concepts in the old, traditional litera-ture, accepted by everybody with no trouble, for which there is no scientific basis. Such as space-warp, hyper-space, contra-terrene, super-time, anti-gravity, laminated dimensions, time travel, etc., etc., etc. Why then the re-fusal to consider mental speculation? Anybody who can swallow time travel ought to be able to contemplate poltergeist effects, particularly since there's a great deal more evidence supporting the latter than the former.

Have we lost the power to use our imaginations, to speculate on the pos-sibilities of something? Have we grown too timid in our thought processes? It would seem so.

You can't have it both ways. You can't have new stories if you won't per-mit new ideas and new themes to be introduced.

The twin effect of these two points of view (1) the editor's refusal to print a story which doesn't conform to his direction and (2) the refusal of the fans to permit exploration not confirmed by tradition, these two things have stopped the growth and expansion of science fiction, made it as formularized and limited as a western story.

3) What to do about it? I think the first move must come from the fans. I think they will need to give first aid to their imagination, pump the breath of life into it again. Then letters to editors saying, "The story in the November issue is a repetition of the story in the May issue. What goes on here?" I think we may legitimately attack the *theory* as much as we please, so long as we have an alternative solution to offer, but the trend of attacking the theorizer for daring to advance a possible explanation, or attacking the editor for print-ing it, this seems to me to be anti-science fiction in every sense of intent and performance. Let us then pull the theory to pieces if we will, but encourage the theorizing.

I think we should demand that some science be used in the writing of science fiction. We have gone so far in the other direction that we are solely concerned with exploiting outré effects and seldom permit any discussion of *causes*. This ceases to be science fiction and becomes pure fantasy. In our let-ters to editors we need to demand some substantiation of causes to account for the effects.

Yes, I know, editors say the vocal fan makes up only some 2 to 5% of their readership, and they print what the total readership wants, but I believe they will, nonetheless, respond to letters from fans.

4) The original paperback can be a partial solution, but it won't solve anything if it duplicates the same errors we are now making in the pro mags. If anything, the editors of mainstream publishing houses are even less hep to what makes vital, strong, alive science fiction than the magazine editors, and will be more inclined to select fantasy. We went through this back in the late 1920s, when the Gernsback magazines were making money. A host of imita-

tors arose, and the various adventure magazines started playing up the outré theme. But they didn't get the idea, and their selections were not satisfactory. They were like opera stars trying to sing rock and roll; they just didn't have it. There's no guarantee that they've got it now.

5) I think I've made the essence of my remarks.

COGSWELL, THEODORE R.

1) I do not feel that magazine science fiction as such will ever die. However, I have an unhappy feeling that magazines devoted exclusively to it do not have too bright a future. If three years from now only *Fantasy and Science Fiction* and *Astounding* (or whatever its new name is) are the only survivors, I will be unhappy but not surprised.

2) It does not seem to me that any single person, action, incident, etc., could have a pronounced effect upon an entire field. What has happened, I think, is that the general intellectual climate has so changed that the particular type of romantic escape which science fiction represents is no longer palatable. I see popular science fiction as growing out of the economic conflict and chaos of the late 1930s and early 1940s. For both writers and readers, it reflected a then-acceptable escape into an exciting sort of dreamworld. I believe that the basic thesis of much successful science fiction was that something was wrong with the here and now and that something should be done about it. Current complacency has no place for such questioning.

3) Nothing. Individuals cannot change climate, at least not immediately.

4) The original paperback may save the novelist but it offers scant salvation for the short story writer.

5) What seems especially significant to me is that new, young, and creative writers are conspicuous by their absence in the field. The few younger people that are coming in, with the exception of a few who don't belong there in the first place, seem to be con-

PITFCS

Proceedings of the Institute for Twenty-First Century Studies

Edited by
Theodore R. Cogswell

tent with turning out tired imitations of the work of their elders. I believe I am safe in saying that the average science fiction writer is now definitely middle aged. He may have acquired more technical skill than he had 20 years ago, but he has lost the ability to believe in his own dreams. What impresses me especially is that now the age of space is finally with us with tremendously exciting and dramatic things happening every day, both science fiction writers and ardent fans have turned their backs on the very age whose advent they spent so many years proclaiming. They are no longer a brave little group who can obtain emotional satisfaction from feeling that they are the wave of the future. The future has become the now and the prophets have been left behind in a stagnant little backwater in which all they can do is to imitate their earlier selves. There are obviously a number of exceptions to this blanket indictment, but still, generally I cannot overlook the complete lack of interest of the field in the startling technical advances of the past few years.

COLEMAN, SIDNEY

Although magazine science fiction may not die, it will never grow back to the size it had in the recent past, not even to a state of 150 magazines a year. Although this sad state of affairs is probably the result of things done by science fiction people, in the sense that if all the editors in the field had paid 6 cents a word, all the writers consistently turned in copy as good as Heinlein, and all the distributors treated every science fiction pulp as if it were *Life*, the field would undoubtedly be considerably healthier now, still I do not believe that what has happened is John Campbell's or Horace Gold's or Ray Palmer's fault, nor do I believe that any dozen decisions or policies done differently would have had any large-scale effect. I do not think there is anything we can do to help the magazines. I think that if there is another boom like that of the 1950s, it will come to the paperbacks rather than to the magazines, and that in any case, the paperbacks will grow to overwhelming domination of the magazines.

Now there are two points I would like to make at some length, explanations of possible mechanisms that have contributed to the processes we have observed. I don't think they are the only causes of what has happened by any means, but the other causes have already been analyzed, and these have not. Please understand that I do not think these are *the causes* or even *the major causes*; I have no desire to see myself damned as a dirty Aristotelian or a pig-like Scene-Agency thinker (both of these are rather mechanistic explanations), at least when I am not one.

FIRST, about Booms and Busts. It has been my experience, in high school and college, that there is a large group of young people who are potential science fiction readers. Sometime between the ages of ten and 17 they come across science fiction, and are enchanted by it, but for the wrong reasons. They are enchanted by what they take to be its freshness and originality, its store of new ideas. What they think are new ideas may be new to the non-science fiction reading world, but they are really the clichés of science fiction. I don't only mean gimmicks like time-travel and robots, I mean plots like the one about the bucolic peasant-like aliens who turn out to be really so much superior to us, and moods like end-of-the-empire *weltschmerz*, and characters like…etc., ad nauseam.

When these young people see their supposed new ideas and fresh insights turning up again and again, they become bored with science fiction and go read something else. Often they do not realize what has happened; if queried as to why they dropped science fiction, they will say "They don't write stories like they used to" or "I guess I just outgrew it; it doesn't seem to interest me any more." The whole process, from first discovery to total disenchantment, seems to take a year or two.

In normal times, these people are entering and leaving the science fiction world at equal rates. However, when a boom comes along, there is an enormous amount of publicity about science fiction. All of these potential short-term science fiction readers, some of whom would not, in normal times, come to science fiction until four or five years later, learn about science fiction at once. They all enter the field at once (i.e. in a year or so). A year or two later, they all leave, and the number of science fiction readers is depressed not only by those who left, but by those who, in normal times, would have been passing through the field, and now have already done so during the boom. I am not so foolish to claim that this mechanism is a major cause of booms and busts, but it does undeniably act to make the booms bigger and the busts more depressing. How powerfully it acts I do not know, and cannot tell from the facts available.

SECONDLY, about the advantages of pocketbooks over magazines. In large part, I think, it is homogeneity. Magazines are heterogeneous, they contain many different kinds of stories. Pocketbooks are homogeneous; every part of a novel is of the same quality and tone as every other part.

Much science fiction is bought by people who do not read all the science fiction published, not even all the science fiction published that meets their taste. They may read three or four magazines and pocketbooks a month. Let us take as a case a man I know, an experimental physicist, whom I will call Joe Brain. Joe likes Heinlein. In days of old, when he felt the desire for some science fiction, Joe would amble down to the corner drug store and look through the magazines. The one that had the installment of a Heinlein serial, or an Asimov novelette (Joe also likes Asimov) would be the one Joe would buy. But now, when Joe comes down to the newsstand, that magazine has got to compete not only with magazines that contain no Heinlein or Asimov, but with pocketbooks, some of which are solid Asimov or Heinlein. Joe, no fool, plunks down his 35 cents for the pocketbook, getting his full 70,000 words of the desired product, instead of only 20,000 words of Heinlein and 50,000 words of some junk he doesn't like.

Somewhere, although I have never met him, there exits Joe's counterpart, Sam Clod. Sam can't stand Asimov—all that fancy talk is too much for him—but he likes Real Science Fiction Adventure, like, you know, Jerry Sohl. Sam must exist because Ace Books, which is not in business for its health (or for that matter Bantam Books, which is also not in business for its health, and is in much better health besides), finds it profitable to publish Jerry Sohl. When it comes to taste, Sam is far from Joe. But when it comes to the drug store, he rejects the magazine as surely.

There is no way magazines can duplicate this advantage of pocketbooks without publishing all-one-author issues, i.e., becoming pocketbooks. (I wonder how the all-Leiber *Fantastic* sold?) And likewise, publications that share every advantage of pocketbooks

Afterthoughts...

I had several pleasant hours of reading *Who Killed Science Fiction?*, and even had time to spend five or ten minutes on other people's contributions... masterful. Idea, design, quality of contributions, level of illustrations, layout... Advent should publish such books. Your writing in the introduction and the explanatory material scattered throughout is admirable. It is clear, precise, grammatical (except for the usual misplaced semi-colons) and to the point. If you think this is weak-tea praise, or that this sort of stuff is easy to write, pick up a technical book or a newspaper some day, or read the instruction manual that comes with your hi-fi, or try and visualize what the characters are really doing in the descriptive passages in a typical sf story. To write clear descriptive prose requires nothing but clear thinking, patience, and discipline. Neither energy nor talent are needed. But you have always had energy and talent, and your expository prose has always been a formless blotch (I mean, until now)...

– Sidney Coleman, May 1960

except homogeneity, such as the *Star* sequence, will not sell as well as pocket novels.

One footnote on the above: I have heard it argued against my opinions (most recently by Bob Silverberg) that the real advantages of the pocketbook are the better display it gets and the longer period it spends on the stand. This may be true at bookstores and magazine stores (universally known as cigar stores), but it is far from the case at the place where most science fiction is sold, the corner drug store. I have been timing the science fiction pocketbooks at local drug stores, and rarely do I find one that stays on the stands for a time as long as *Galaxy*'s two months. And in addition, the druggists have no scruples about placing a book on the racks, behind newer books, sometimes only a week after it arrives, so it can only be found by assiduously searching. (I am talking about science fiction books, not *Lady Chatterley's Lover.*) I hardly ever see this done to magazines; *Astounding* has at least its spine showing, and often its face, for all the time it's in the store.

COULSON, ROBERT

Robert Coulson

1) No. I won't admit that magazine science fiction is dead until the last magazine (probably *Astounding*) ceases publication. But I do think that it's in bad shape.

2) No single person, action, incident, etc. is ever responsible for anything. I think the cause of the science fiction slump is three distinct trends in the nation's reading habits, which may or may not be interrelated. First, there has been an overall slump in magazine sales. Hans Santesson says so, and the folding of non-science fiction magazines and the price-juggling of such stalwarts as *Reader's Digest* and *Life* bears him out. In fact, the handwriting was on the wall when the *Digest* accepted advertising. *Life* and *Reader's Digest* can experiment all they like; science fiction magazines don't have the capital for more than one or two attempts; if they don't guess right the first time, they likely will fold. Second, there is a specific trend away from *fiction* magazines. I've been intending to take a survey of the number of titles on a reasonably good newsstand which contain the word "true." What's the present ratio of love pulps to confession-type magazines, and of detective fiction magazines to "true detective" types? Look at the adventure field…a good 30 magazines featuring "true" adventures, and *Short Stories* couldn't survive as the lone adventure fiction magazine. (Not that I think that *Scientific American* is drawing any readers away from *Amazing Stories*,

but I do think that all the men's adventure magazines—*True Men, Savage, Virile, Raw, Guts,* etc.—are draining a large part of the casual readers who were interested in science fiction primarily for the adventure it provided.) Never mind if the stories in these "true" magazines are really true or not; the label is all that counts. Third, science has become a dirty word, associated with intellectuals and eggheads, and everyone knows that intellectuals and eggheads are nasty sorts who pretend to be better than their neighbors and take money on fixed quiz shows. Science, in short, is a rather dull affair with test tubes, without any of the earthy realism of *True Crime* or *Savage Adventures.* And, combining items two and three, a magazine with the title "science fiction" has two strikes against it to start with, which are too many to allow it to buck the magazine slump. The fact that any magazines at all are surviving is due, I think, to the fact that they've attracted *regular* readers who know and like them; they aren't attracting the casual newsstand browser any more.

3) We (I assume you mean science fiction fans) can't do a damned thing about it.

4) I think a few magazines will survive, but the bulk of future science fiction will come out in either original paperbacks or paperback reprints of original hardcover novels (the latter mostly in the case of established writers in and out of the field). They will provide little salvation for fandom, but should assure that some science fiction continues to see print.

5) I don't know if it's pertinent or not, but at the Detroit World Science Fiction Convention someone mentioned that paperback publishers should be better informed about science fiction and cited Donald A. Wollheim of Ace Books as one publisher who really knew his business. If that's true, I'd like to know why Ace publishes such crud and the only paperback publisher which regularly puts out above-average material is Ballantine Books. Incidentally, in answer to item No. two, I gave no causes for the trends cited. I don't know the causes…or at least I have no idea as to the cause of the general magazine slump. Paperback competition may be responsible; I don't think that television is too much of a villain. People who watch television regularly never read much anyway…if they didn't have television they'd listen to the radio, go to the movies, or play cards, but they wouldn't read. As for the antifiction trend—I know it's there because I can see it operating, but as for the cause…I guess people are just more interested in gossip than they are in literature. And the antiscience trend has been with us quite a while and been documented fairly thoroughly. (What was television's most successful fantasy-type show last year? "Alcoa Presents"…*true* stories of the weird and supernatural.)

DAVENPORT, BASIL

The following is an answer to your questionnaire, to the best of my ability.

1) I do not feel that magazine science fiction is dead. I subscribe to and read the *Magazine of Fantasy and Science Fiction* and I generally buy and read *Galaxy*. I used to read *Astounding*, and still occasionally sample a copy, but a few years ago it got generally over my head. This is not intended as an adverse criticism of *Astounding*; I myself have very little scientific background, and not much scientific interest; the latter owes a good deal to my reading of science fiction. It is an excellent thing that there should be a magazine like *Astounding* to appeal to readers with more scientific background than I. But I am straying from the point. These three magazines seem to be flourishing, and perhaps three magazines are all that can be expected to survive, in so comparatively narrow a field. However, science fiction is now appearing off and on in other magazines, the *Saturday Evening Post, Playboy*, and others.

2) I do not feel that any one person or action is responsible for the decline in the number of science fiction magazines. I think the boom started with the atomic bomb, which let the genie out of the bottle. A lot of people then sampled science fiction; some of them liked it enough to keep on, and others simply got enough of it.

3) I do not know what can be done to correct the situation.

4) I don't know enough about the economics of the situation to speak very definitely about the original paperback, but I think it might help. I see reviews of many science fiction books which I should be glad to read, and would go out of my way to get, if I could either buy them in paperbacks for 35 cents, or could rent them at a lending library, but which I frankly do not want to spend $3 for. It is in my experience a very rare science fiction story that can be reread with pleasure, which is one of the things I consider when putting out money for a hardcover book.

5) I am sorry to have to confess that my own interest in science fiction is not so strong as it was ten years ago. This may be simply because I have read too much of it for a balanced diet, but it seems to me that the good ideas have all been used. I very rarely encounter a new idea in a science fiction story. I think there is here some hope to be found in the exploration (which is, of course, going on) of such inexact fields as sociology (utopias and reverse utopias) and the paranormal.

DAVIDSON, AVRAM

*All hail, Earl and Countess! Liege-man,
Avram Davidson*

1) I do not feel that magazine science fiction is dead, but it sure is sickly. I think it will survive, though.

2) It would be unrealistic to hold "any single person, action, incident, etc....responsible for the present situation." Sputnik may have lost us readers who can now get their fill of space-satellite talk in factual publications, but is magazine science fiction confined to space satellite stories? Damon Knight* may have scared off a few untalented writers and even improved a few semi-talented ones, but aren't stories as bad as those he tore into still being published? Campbell has been in a rut for years and years, but the rut must suit his readers—look at his circulation. And if the rut doesn't suit everybody who writes or has written for him, I wonder why it suited them five years ago. I see no difference. Bob Mills may not be Anthony Boucher—in fact, Bob Mills is *not* Anthony Boucher—but I suppose fantasy is outside your query's scope; and anyway, I think *F&SF* is showing definite improvement very recently. *Amazing Stories* I don't read, but understand it's been buying some material of a better sort than it usually used to. So we come to Horace Gold. I agree *Galaxy* isn't what it was. Gold says it's because it doesn't get the stories that it used to. Others say Gold doesn't have the critical judgment that he used to. I don't know. I have gotten out of the field because rates haven't kept up with the rise in general prices (including the prices of science fiction magazines! How about that? Printers and papermakers now get more, but writers get the same, sometimes less) and I can make more writing for other fields—well, this is one reason I got out. Another is that I don't want to be confined to any one field. And the falling market was a factor, too, i.e. fewer magazines, etc.

3) I be damned if I know what we can do to correct it. Raising rates might help; most of the science fiction writers I know are writing non-science fiction now in addition and most of them indicate they'd like to get out altogether. But they are used to this field and if they could remain in it economically...

4) Salvation of what? Merely of a type of literature [sic] called "science fiction," no matter how rotten it is? Does anyone claim that original paperback science fiction is *better* science fiction? (I don't say it's worse.)

If you mean, salvation of science fiction writers, I can't answer. I never wrote any science fiction novels and attempts to sell my collected science

---

*Damon Knight's criticism of the field first appeared in book form as *In Search of Wonder*. – E.K.

fiction short stories to either hard- or soft-cover houses has been unsuccessful; as has, also, my attempt to sell an anthology of science fiction shorts of a particular kind. Publishers say that collections don't sell. Of course, collections continue to be published, anyway—some of them pretty grim. In fact, to return to my remarks about original paperback science fiction novels, I think the general level is much below the general level of magazine science fiction *as published in the three top science fiction magazines*—and in many cases, below that of the lower-grade magazines. When one considers the time involved and the effort in turning out a novel, compared to comparable wordage in short stories, I'm not sure the fiscal returns are worth it. I doubt if the literary returns are, either.

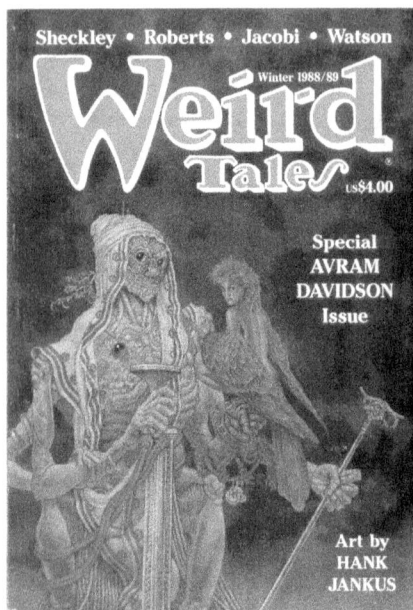

5) I observe, in a letter just off to Cogswell's *PITFICS*, that "the freshness seems to have departed from science fiction." Perhaps it's just that the freshness seems to have departed from me. Like most, I now read more factual than fictive books. I seem to think that the level of fiction in general is either not what it was or that it has stayed the same while my standards have risen or my taste become more jaded. When I was a kid in the '30s there was something to be found in science fiction magazines simply not to be found anywhere else—a heady atmosphere of Out To The Stars! and On To The Future! Rarely indeed was anything of this sort found in a newspaper or a general magazine. Since the war, increasingly, it is found everywhere; and the question of space travel is now a commonplace before it has more than barely gotten started. Civilization has caught up with the pioneers and the pioneers have failed to move on to newer, more distant, frontiers. As long as fifteen years ago it seemed to me that science fiction was becoming repetitive, writers simply mining or cannibalizing other writers. It never seemed to me that this trend was reversed or slowed down. From a nest of singing birds we have become a coop of clucking fowls. I'm told that in times past a science fiction convention was a swarm with kid fans. Last year, in Detroit, there were exactly two (2), count them, two. Why should they bother reading dull science fiction when they can read similar stuff, not fiction, and not dull? The kid who may well expect to visit the moon before he fathers his first child isn't interested in space opera; nor should he be. Look at your fanzines (if you can bear to): 19 out of 20 never even mention science fiction!

Of course, I cannot really say I was ever a science fiction writer. My stuff was either outright fantasy or damned close to it. Fantasy, mark you my words, doesn't date the way science fiction does. Yet the market isn't there for fantasy, bad as the market may be for science fiction. Sometime you must make an inquiry into fantasy!

DE CAMP, L. SPRAGUE

©1960 by L. Sprague de Camp. All Rights Reserved.
Manufactured in the United States of America.

[signature: L. Sprague de Camp]

Here are the best answers I can give:

1) No, I do not feel that magazine science fiction is dead, but it is in a gradual decline from a peak in the 1930s and 1940s.

2) I think this decline is the result of social forces and not of any individual actions. A genre of literature attains popularity when it has technically equipped publishers, qualified authors, and an eager audience.

(a) Science fiction, in the first half of this century, had technically equipped publishers. The techniques of magazine printing and distribution could take care of any such demand. If, for example, there had been a vogue for agricultural, bucolic stories, they could have handled it as well. On the other hand, a science fiction vogue wouldn't have gotten far in ancient Babylonia, because the technique of writing in cuneiform on clay tablets would not have supported any large secular literature.

(b) There were enough authors who had the smattering of science to enable them to write the stories. For those who hadn't, there was a body of popular science and speculative writing by which they could make up their deficiencies.

(c) There was a receptive audience, because the scientific revolution had progressed to the point where scientific speculation afforded a *point d'appui* for stories of romantic adventure in exotic surroundings. Such romances have always been popular and perhaps always will be, but their nature changes with the times. Formerly the author could grip his audience either by laying his story in an unknown

Afterthoughts...

I never for a moment doubted that L. Sprague deCamp was copyright 1960 by L. Sprague de-Camp, and manufactured in the United States of America...

– Dean McLaughlin,
May 1960

earthly land (*vide* the *Odyssey*) or by dealing with the supernatural (*vide* Aupleius' *Metamorphoses*). Exploration, however, has eliminated the unknown earthly lands, and the spread of scientific materialism has made it harder for most readers to believe, or even to pretend to believe, in the supernatural. Hence the decline of fantasy, which has been much more marked than that of science fiction.

These changes left the past, the future, and other planets as subjects for such stories. Historical novels, exploiting the past, have flourished ever since Sir Walter Scott put them on a sound basis 150 years ago, and show no sign of decline.

Science fiction, no the other hand, exploits the romantic possibilities of the future and of other worlds. Now, within the last decade, something has happened both to science fiction's authors and to its audience. A general growth of the publishing business and an opening up of new fields (popular science writing, juvenile writing, technical writing for advertising agencies, etc.) have lured away some of the abler science fiction authors by higher rates of pay.

Likewise, the audience has dwindled, mainly, I think, not because of anything wrong with the stories, but as a natural result of scientific progress. Stories of pure science fiction (that is, of things that *might* happen in the future) inevitably date as science catches up with them. Sixty years ago, the flying machine was an obvious subject for science fiction and was well exploited. Now it is no longer available. Space travel is on the verge of doing the same thing, and some of us may live to see immortality realized in the same way.

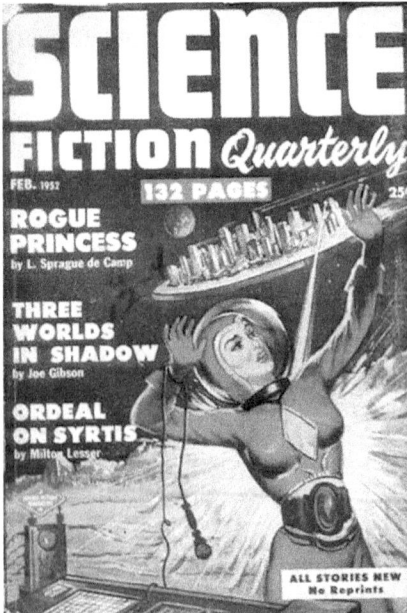

SCIENCE FICTION *Quarterly*

FEB. 1957   132 PAGES   25¢

ROGUE PRINCESS
by L. Sprague de Camp

THREE WORLDS IN SHADOW
by Joe Gibson

ORDEAL ON SYRTIS
by Milton Lesser

ALL STORIES NEW
No Reprints

As scientific predictions are realized, they become less and less attractive as subjects for stories of romantic adventures in exotic settings. For one thing, the settings cease to be exotic, just as the opening up and taming of Africa have turned H. Rider Haggard's stories into period pieces. For another, the prosaic facts, as they become known, kill off the romance. John Carter could get to Mars by simply wishing hard; nowadays he would need a million-megabuck project passed through a myriad of overlapping governmental space agencies, and the story would be swamped in technical and administrative detail.

3) I don't think that anything can be done to "correct" this situation.

4) Paperback publication is a good thing in many ways, but I don't think it will save any genre of fiction whose necessary economic basis of audience interest has been destroyed by the march of events.

5) I don't think our knowledge of social forces is good enough yet to enable us accurately to prophesy what will happen. However, I think science fiction will go on being published for a long time, *diminuendo*. I suspect that it will split into two branches. One is pure science fiction, based upon realistic possibilities. This will tend to disappear as factual knowledge catches up with it, though the development of science into new and fictionally unexploited directions may long provide it with new subjects and stimulation.

The other is the story based on unrealistic or impossible assumptions, such as the story of time travel, alternative universes, or (if I judge aright) extrasensory powers. Stories of this group will tend to merge with the story of supernaturalistic fantasy, with which they will share a common fate. That is, they will continue to be written, but more and more as labors of love, as fantasies like Tolkien's *Ring* trilogy are written nowadays.

Exceptional works of these types will be published, mainly as book-length novels, in cloth or paperback form, and may sometimes even return a modest profit. But it will not be possible to make a living by writing such stories, just as you can't make a living writing ghost or weird stories today. There aren't enough readers, willing to pay enough money regularly enough, to make a magazine specializing in the genre an attractive investment for the publisher's dollar or the author's hour.

DE LA REE, GERRY

If I had a cure-all for the ailments of the science fiction field I wouldn't be wasting my time contributing to a nonprofit survey. Rather, I'd be in New York City selling my ideas to the publishers of one or more science fiction magazines.

Still, a problem does seem to exist and batting a few ideas around certainly won't hurt things. And if someone does come up with a few sound suggestions, perhaps the field which we enjoyed these many years will in some small way profit.

In answer to the questions asked:

1) Do you feel that magazine science fiction is dead? Obviously it is not. There are still a steady trickle of magazines appearing on monthly and bimonthly schedules. But while the magazines appear far from dead, there is little doubt that they have enjoyed healthier days.

2) Do you feel that any single person, action, incident, etc., is respon-

sible for the present situation? If not, what is responsible? Well, I'd hardly blame it on any one individual or small group of individuals. I would, however, suggest these as possible reasons for the slump:
(a) Lack of competent writers in the field, resulting in:
(b) Poor stories.
(c) The spate of pocketbooks published in the last decade.
(d) Overexposure of science fiction during the same period.
(e) Man's race into space, which has not accelerated or enhanced the popularity of science fiction to the degree anticipated by many persons, but rather has opened up a new generation of readers primarily interested in factual science.

3) What can we do to correct it? If by we, you mean those of us contributing to this survey, I'm afraid I must confess there is little we can accomplish. I've read fanzines and attended conferences and conventions for more than 20 years. I've watched members of fandom's hard core attempt to dictate policies to the editors of professional magazines, and in the early days of my teens I was as guilty as the rest. But somewhere in the late 1940s I awoke to the realization that fandom is a drop in the bucket. An editor who is foolish enough to follow the dictates of a fan is just asking for trouble. There are perhaps 300 fans who regularly turn up at these conventions or who have at one time or another taken a fling at fanzine publishing. If these 300 fans tomorrow stopped buying a particular science fiction magazine, say *F&SF*, the loss would be infinitesimal to the publisher.

Fans, I believe, have accomplished quite a bit considering the fact they could just as easily have been told to "get lost" by the professional publishers. More than one pro magazine, I feel, has suffered because of the editor's having leaned too far in an attempt to pacify the fans.

So, in summing up my answer to question No. three, I'd say that we, as fans, can do nothing to correct any slump that may exist in the field.

4) Should we look to the original paperback as a point of salvation? Well, certainly the pocketbook field has produced *some* of the better original work in recent years. Perhaps the rates are superior to those paid by the science fiction magazines. I hate to use the word salvation, but I do feel that pocketbooks are to be encouraged and not frowned upon.

5) What additional remarks, pertinent to the study, would you like to contribute?

Frankly, I think the main fault with magazine science fiction is that the product is inferior. The quality of the writing is poor, but quite in keeping with the rates being paid. When you consider that today's rates on many science fiction publications are virtually the same as were being offered 20 years ago, how can you expect to encourage new writers into the field? You normally get what you pay for, and that's just about what science fiction magazines are getting.

The field has never had what I would consider an outstanding group of authors. Many of them were just plain hacks; others were guys turning out fiction to make a buck on the side. Still others were doing it as a hobby to get away from it all. But the fact remains the large majority of them were not—and are not today—good writers. Idea men, yes. Writers, no.

Of course, it's not a field where you expect to find the leading names of the literary world. Most of them would need months of research to turn out a real science fiction story, one that a hack blessed with a scientific background could probably grind out in a few days.

Perhaps it's the fact I'm getting older and more selective as to what I enjoy reading, but the general run of science fiction novel I read today is just plain rank. It's inferior to material I have read in the past. But, again, we're getting what the magazines are paying for.

I think it is a poor criterion for the science fiction field when an author such as Robert Heinlein can sell out-and-out juveniles to one of the leading so-called adult publications. And to top it, I hear veteran fans proclaiming these novels as the best thing they've read during the year. Gentlemen, these are stories about kids written for kids.

Heinlein is generally regarded as one of the finest writers produced in the science fiction field in the past 25 years. Still, rereading his early efforts I would hardly term him a first-rate author in comparison with his contemporaries in the general field of literature. If he was any more than a good, competent writer of science fiction and juveniles, would he have spent close to 25 years in this type of work?

This is not meant as an attack on Bob Heinlein. I've just used him as an example to point up the sad state magazine science fiction has reached.

Perhaps science fiction is going to go the way of most other pulp fiction. The mystery and detective fields look like they'll go on forever, but I see no similar enthusiasm for science fiction. Still, in the 1930s we had only three science fiction magazines and *Weird Tales*. Today we have more than that, but we're wondering if magazine science fiction is dead.

I hope that the illness is a temporary thing and that we may one day see not MORE science fiction magazines, but a few GOOD ones publishing GOOD material. I do not see this happening until the money is forthcoming to lure the men who can do the job into the field.

DERLETH, AUGUST

You ask what killed science fiction. I'm not sure that anything did. There will always be a core audience for science fiction, just as there will be for any division of fantasy. If you are at all familiar with things I have written and said about fantasy, you will remember that I went on record long ago as saying that for fantasy of any kind there always has been and always will be a relatively limited audience, and that any seeming boom in the field would fairly soon return to the normal core audience. What you have currently is NOT the death of science fiction, but a return to the core audience, and what you want to find out is what factors at this time contributed to the destruction of the boom.

As a publisher in the book field of 20 years' experience, there does not seem to me any mystery about that. In the first place, too much romantic-adventure fare thinly disguised as science fiction glutted the market, turning away potential new readers, tiring old buyers who found it difficult to distinguish at the counters once old familiar names began to fade out. In the second place, the appearance of paperbacks undercut the hardcover publishers already fighting a glutted market. The magazine field suffered for a variety of reasons, one of which is allied to the book field. Essentially the competition of the paperbacks struck hardest at the magazines. But other factors were also present. Too many magazines in the field for the integral size of the market, for one. Too much editorial meddling on the part of some editors—sometimes this meddling made considerably better stories out of submissions, but just as often it blunted different approaches and variants. Too much editorial riding of favorite horses—I don't refer to favorite contributors here, but to science fiction variations, themes, directions. What editors often lose sight of is the essential fact that a science fiction story of merit is NOT a good story because it has gimmicks, or because it has a startling theme, or because it is better written than most (though this helps), but simply because it is a good story to begin with. There has also been some harm brought to the field by inept, however slickly convincing, criticism. One highly touted science fiction critic is actually one of the most damaging in this regard, indifferent as an author, glittering but empty as a critic. The ideal, in my view, in the field of science fiction criticism, is P. Schuyler Miller in *Astounding Science Fiction*.

Returning to the "good story" theme above for a moment—the failure of editors to keep open minds, for instance, has harmed the field. I refer to the editorial attitude that space operas, for example, are dead, or that psychiatric themes are in, etc., failing to leave room for good stories no matter what their themes may be. Ghosts have altered, too, in the past 20 years—I'm just doing an article on that theme—but a good traditional ghost story still has an appreciative audience.

Now as to your questions specifically:

1) No, I don't feel that magazine science fiction is dead.

No single person or event is responsible for the present situation. In regard to what is responsible

2) In my opinion, see above. There is no such thing, or course, as a pinpointing of responsibility. Various factors contributed, and these factors were and are in general beyond the control of those readers interested in the field. As someone in the field for a long time, but always on the non-sf-fantasy end of it, it always seemed to me symptomatic and ridiculously childish that so many science fiction people were at odds with so many others, that people who liked one kind of science fiction decried others—i.e., the *Lensman* lovers had no use for the followers of *Null A*, and so on. This puerile attitude which was held and still is being held by many fans leaves no room for tolerance; there is a stupid insistence that science fiction must be "my kind" or none on the part of these people, who are often the vociferous fellows who write to the magazines at great length. This lunatic fringe is the noisiest, and may mislead editors.

3) Apart from insistence upon good stories rather than upon novel themes or old themes or gimmicks, I don't know that there is anything we can do to correct a situation which, in science fiction specifically, comes up against rapid technological advances at the same time that its boom is evaporating. The insistence on the part of some editors that science fiction is NOT fantasy, that it is NOT mere entertainment (which it most certainly is and always will be if it intends to keep on existing at all), that it IS prophetic fiction has of course boomeranged; science has in some divisions passed science fiction, and the result is that the "prophets" are being deserted. Once we lose sight of the fact that science fiction is an entertainment and NOTHING MORE,

Afterthoughts...

That's a beautiful job on *Who Killed Science Fiction?* I especially appreciate your comments closing the report...

– August Derleth, May 1960

science fiction is on the way to extinction. Anything else, call it prophecy or whatever you like, belongs in the article field, the nonfiction classification.

4) My comments on paperbacks as above. They are largely indistinguishable from science fiction magazines, save that they lack departments.

5) No additional remarks; I've put down quite enough already.

One other factor ought, in justice to science fiction publishers and editors, to be mentioned in passing. A magazine which say in 1950 had reached its maximum potential audience even against keen competition found it impossible to increase circulation or advertising costs sufficiently to offset rising production costs as those costs began to climb, and eventually had to fold. This is what happened to many of the magazines in the field in 1953-6. Arkham reached its nadir in 1955, for instance; we are doing just ten times the business in 1959 that we did in 1955.

DEVET, CHARLES V.

1) No, I do not feel that magazine science fiction is dead. However, it will remain limited.

2) Responsible for the condition: The large block of science fiction readers who only read it occasionally is getting enough science fiction type reading from actual happenings to satisfy their casual interest and they do not buy the magazines any more.

3) What can we do to correct it? Very little.

4) Should we look to the original paperback as a point of salvation? To a limited degree.

5) Additional remarks: The field is in a period of change. What the final result will be is difficult to exactly prognosticate. I believe a few of the best science fiction magazines will survive. Some of the general pulps and slicks will print a few more science fiction stories to capture that audience. Pocketbooks will enjoy a slightly greater audience.

DEVORE, HOWARD

Howard DeVore

1) It is my opinion that *magazine* science fiction is not dead, that we will go on, year after year, reading the same low form that is now being produced. I do believe the field will continue to narrow down—until we are supporting not more than six magazines. There will be momentary booms lasting from six months to a year, where some new magazines will appear, but will prob-

ably vanish at the next slump. Three, or perhaps four of the major contenders will remain constant. *Astounding* and *F&SF* will be among these. I doubt that *Galaxy* will occupy the No. 3 spot.

2) There is doubt in my mind as to what has caused the great slowdown, more than anything I would assume it to be vast utterances by loudmouthed, fatassed politicians, continually assuring the general population that we are well ahead of the Russians, and that the populace need not concern itself with space flight—the politicians will handle all of the little minor details, everything in fact, except the vast millions that will be needed. There is general public apathy concerning space flight. What was once though impossible has become accepted theory and is no longer worth worrying over.

A secondary reason, of course, would be that vast womb, television; the comic book that turns its own pages. This has lowered the amount of printed matter consumed (and I'm *not* interested in some set of figures designed to show that television stimulates the imagination and leads children and adults to do research on their own—the sale of "factual" biographies of Wyatt Earp will have little effect on science fiction sales).

3) Personally, I fear there is little that we can do to stimulate science fiction sales, or interest in the field. The average American citizen knows little or nothing of the technological processes involved, and is quite happy that way. He is much more interested in baseball averages, and a can of really *cold* beer! Science fiction is not for the masses, and I fear nothing will change this situation. The lovers of science fiction are so few that they simply cannot convince the multitudes around them, this has been demonstrated time after time over the years—I think we have all tried to interest friends in science fiction with little or no success. Oh, some particularly close friend may be persuaded to read an outstanding story and may even admit liking it, *BUT* will he voluntarily go out and buy a second piece from the newsstand? The only group that seems to be influenced by science fiction is the young college crowd. Ten years ago a fair portion of them were tempted to try this material, and a much smaller percentage have continued to enjoy it; however, it is my opinion that their college atmosphere served only to introduce them at that particular time. I think eventually they would have experimented with, and learned to enjoy science fiction on their own. While I do not feel that "Fans Are Slans" I do think that they have a much wider range of reading tastes and they are of the group that have learned to appreciate the *ideas* behind a book rather than the selection of dirty words telling how "this hot broad lays everyone in sight."

4) There is some possibility that the *original* paperback will provide a reasonable income for a very small select group of writers, and that this might enable them to expose the general public to science fiction, however, I'm afraid that most of the paperback readers would wind up as casual read-

ers. These are helpful, of course, but only *frequent* readers can be expected to support any sort of science fiction publishing.

It is very unlikely that any magazine can continue to exist unless assured of a firm sale of so many thousand copies. They must be purchased by people who buy one, two, or ten science fiction magazines and books per month. The buyer who switches from science fiction to westerns or *Playboy* will never contribute any measurable income to the field.

NOW, assuming that we could consider the *original* paperback a salvation, who is going to publish this "original" paperback? The stands are cluttered now with paperbacks from firms who bought the paperback rights ten years ago! Many of these books saw magazine, hardcover, and perhaps a *first* paperback edition in those long dead days. Firms which only a few years ago were proudly announcing that they had the best science fiction writers in the field writing for them, are now sneaking around buying up cheap reprint rights. Much of this trash did not deserve first publication, let alone the continual reprinting, frequently from the editor's own files. I consider it the lowest form of theft to issue a book, and then three years later reprint the same book, using the same plates (or standing type), and merely changing the background colors of the cover or dust jacket.

5) I have few opinions other than the above. I may have been a trifle brief, but there seems no question that science fiction is in a bad position and frankly, I see little or no hope for the immediate future. I have spent 23 years following the field, and while I may long for the dear dead days when science fiction was thrilling, I am well prepared to coast along until it shows a gradual revival!

I sometimes think that perhaps Sam Moskowitz was right, or at least partially so, in that the fans may have lost their sense of wonder. But then, so have the writers. They are being forced to turn out stereotyped material to fit an editor's policies, which change only in desperation. An editor making a decent living by purveying a particular type story feels little compulsion to seek out newer, different material. Consequently, the feeling grows, with writers treading in his footsteps—hacking out rewrites of the previous issue.

EDMONDSON, G.C.

1) I don't imagine magazine science fiction will ever die completely, but it seems to be going through one of its periodic slumps. There are only three real magazines and I stopped reading two of them years ago. Bob Mills is

doing a fine job on the third, but he's tired too. How long before he pulls the plug like Anthony Boucher?

2) The present situation is due largely to the fact that wages, prices, and everything else have gone up in the last 30 years and rates have gone down. We're actually working for about one-tenth the money we used to get. Sputnik contributed also to the decline, downgrading science fiction into hackneyed adventure.

3) The only real hope for science fiction is a brand new approach, something along the lines of what Josephine Tey's *Daughter of Time* did to the whodunit field. If I knew what this new approach was, I'd be writing it instead of this.

4) A good question. I'll answer it when my agent sends word about the first half of the clinker I'm currently writing.

5) Too damned much's been said already. There hasn't been a new idea in science fiction since Boucher introduced the theology cycle nearly ten years ago. There are only so many switcheroos on a given situation and, after two wars and a Sputnik, there's no use dusting off the old sense of wonder for anything less than the Second Coming.

It might help if writers were all kept incommunicado from the mass media and most of all, from each other. It's great to moan about stereotyping and lack of individuality, but when we're all exposed to the same stimuli. Entirely too many times, I've gotten an idea, mulled over it, slept on it, finally gotten around to blocking it out, and just as I'm about to write, along comes *F&SF* and Poul Anderson's beaten me by six months. With only one planet, one history, and two sexes, this sort of duplication is bound to occur.

I can't help feeling that television and recreation without reading has left us in the same position as the last dinosaur. There's a wonderful future of some kind ahead, but it isn't the one we old fogeys dream about. And wonderful as it is, I suspect there just isn't a place in it for us. John Barrymore's last years were pitiful; he went on parodying himself. How long can I write parodies of parodies?

Marcus Aurelius probably felt this way when he tried to make sense out of Christianity.

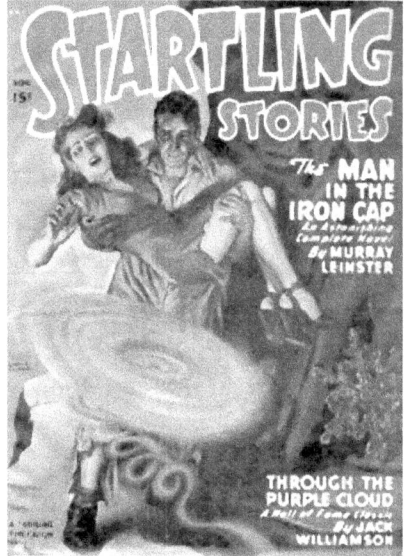

EMSHWILLER, EDWARD

[See the ritual scene depicted on the front cover…---E.K.]

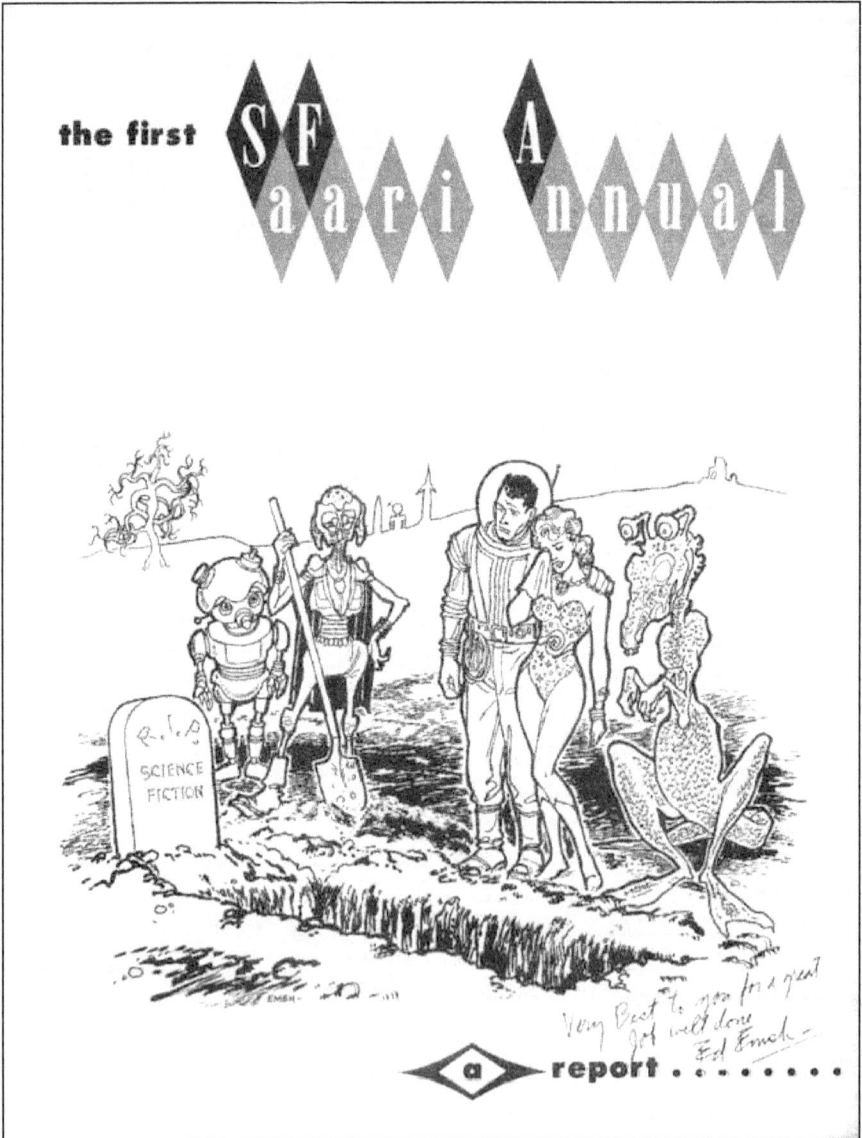

FARMER, PHILIP JOSÉ

1) I don't feel that magazine science fiction is dead. I do feel that it is only half alive and that it is going to stay so. But the present number of science fiction magazines will remain established or, at least, the top three will continue publishing steadily. And they will continue publishing about the same quality of stories as present. That is, an occasional original and stimulating story, quite a few well-written but nonoriginal stories, and a mass of the same old tripe, both well written and otherwise. I should break this down into the type the three so-called top magazines will publish. *Astounding*, soon to become *Analog Science Fact Fiction* (a laughable and ridiculous title by the way) will continue to publish the same kind of stories it has for the past three or four years. These will consist of an occasional excellent and non-Campbellian story which will delight with its originality. And a mass of stories based on Campbell's ideas, that is, his obsession with psi-phenomena and a future society based on rigorous class lines. Not that there is anything basically wrong with these ideas. The trouble is that Campbell insists on buying these stories to the exclusion of others, and while the majority of them are entertaining, the very reiteration of the theme becomes monotonous and will continue to be so. Writers who want to sell steadily to him listen to his ideas, which are fed to them through his editorials or personally, and they write his stories and feed them back to him and are rewarded with checks and so continue to give him the type of stories he wants. And so on in a vicious feedback. And speaking of feeding, I am fed up. Perhaps one could forgive Campbell for pushing the psi theme if one thought the theme valid and valuable. But all one has to do is remember Dianetics and his sincere pushing of it to become skeptical. Besides, if this psi does exist, what of it? There is no indication whatever that it can be controlled. Campbell's stories have characters in which psi is a well-controlled ability. But all evidence I have seen for it, including Campbell's own articles and editorials, indicates that it is wild to the wildest degree. As well expect to hitch a tiger to the plow and get a good day's furrowing as expect to produce any predictable and beneficial results from the manipulation of psi. But, as I said, the theme can make a good science fiction story. Not when one-half or two-thirds of every issue of *Astounding* is devoted to the theme, however.

Now, *Galaxy*. For some years now this magazine has offered a few, very few, great stories. And a mass of trite, skim-the-surface, pesudo-*New Yorker* stories which are a waste of time to read. For two years now I have purchased very few *Galaxy*s, and those I did were purchased because I wanted to read

Willy Ley's articles. I used to buy *Galaxy* even when it was noticeably on the decline through sheer loyalty to science fiction. I thought I should support science fiction. But now I don't even do that. It hurts me not to buy one; I feel like a traitor. But why buy a magazine I will throw down in disgust, half read? Is it because Gold can't get good stories? Is the type he has been printing the best he can secure? I don't think so. He shies away from good meaty stories with valid science fiction backgrounds. I know because of personal experience. Mine and several other writers. And the curious thing is that while Gold won't buy these strong and original stories for his own magazine, he is eager to purchase them for Galaxy-Beacon Press, the pocketbook outfit for which he is consulting editor. Gold has seen his magazine decline in quality and in circulation, yet he does not buy stories that might bring up his magazine, if not to its original level, at least to a higher level. And it is not because he can't get good stories. As a point, consider *F&SF*. They pay less than *Galaxy*, so *Galaxy* should get first chance at the stories that *F&SF* buys. Yet Gold bounces them and they go to Bob Mills, and *F&SF* wins the Hugos for being the best science fiction magazine of the year.

Now, *F&SF*. High-quality fantasy, as good now as when it started. And they publish more straight science fiction stories than when they started. They have the fewest taboos of any of the magazines and are willing to try almost—not quite—any new type of story. It's still a pleasure to read the magazine all the way through, something I don't do with *Galaxy* and *Astounding* despite my interest and love for science fiction. The magazine is not half dead as are the other two, in my opinion. Yet it still doesn't fully satisfy. Perhaps it doesn't because the other two are so unsatisfying. If the other two published the mass of good meaty stories they used to, then *F&SF* might be fully satisfying, as a good salad is with a steak. But *F&SF* now has to shoulder the burden the other two should be carrying. It has to be, not just a salad, but an antipasto. And too much antipasto is…too much. *F&SF*, instead of being a complementary magazine, now stands alone and doesn't quite cut the mustard, if an antipasto can be accused of such a crime. No fault of its own. It's not getting the proper support.

Summary: Science fiction isn't dead, just half dead.

2) Do I feel that any single person, action, incident, etc., is responsible? Part of this question is answered in No. one. But I feel that the main responsibility, the main cause, is that the world has changed. This is no longer 1929 or 1947. Science fiction has passed through its glorious birth, its growing-up pains, its fevers and fits, its malaise, its Renaissance, and is now entering, has entered, middle age. Man is on the point of landing on Mars and Venus. Another ten or fifteen years, and he will be there. The only thing left for science fiction writers will be to write of interstellar adventure and of the future of Earth, something they are doing now. You see very few stories about adventures taking place

in the solar system. As Fred Brown said in *What Mad Universe?* the science fiction writers have become adventure story writers. Not quite, but they're on the threshold of being so. And there is a general feeling that the scientists have now taken over the province of the science fiction writers. It's not quite true, for there is a tremendous room left for stories on sociological, psychological, and biological themes. But the number of writers who can deal effectively with these themes is relatively limited, and so long as most of the editors prefer to ride other hobby horses, these themes will not be properly developed.

Another cause: The price of science fiction magazines has been steadily climbing. Some magazines now charge 50 cents a copy. But this raise in price covers the cost of paying for paper and printing. The writers are not paid a penny more than they were ten years ago, and prospects are that they will not in the future. So, even if a writer loves science fiction dearly and would rather write science fiction than anything, he still turns to westerns or detectives or mainstream. He has to make a living. And with a quarter of the thought and originality and hard work it takes to write science fiction, he can write detectives or westerns and make twice as much money.

The above causes for the present situation, however, are only contributing factors. The main responsibility for the present situation in science fiction lies, as I first stated, in the changing of the world. The *Zeitgeist*, the *Weltaschauung*, have altered faces. The world is a little older, a little wearier, a little wiser, and a lot less optimistic. For the present, at least. And while I think we actually have more reason for optimism than we did 17 or ten or even five years ago, the world as a whole is not optimistic. It's seen the dreams, some of them, of science fiction come true. And the response is a big Like so we're here? Like so what? So more of the predictions and extrapolations of science fiction come true? Then what? We live in a world that *is* science fiction; science is progressing at a fantastically fast and geometric rate; it takes all a man's time just to read at a gallop of the new inventions; the world is changing fast, fast, fast; we live in the most revolutionary period in history. The last surviving veteran of the Civil War was born before the telegraph line was put into commercial operation and before the first steamship established a regular transatlantic route. The world population was 950 million; it is now 2,750,000,000 and may be double that by A.D. 2000. And the world has changed most noticeably since 1939, and with it has come the slow decline of that sense of wonder of which we talk so much, once knew so well, and now so rarely feel. Why read of things to make you wonder when you live in a world that continually wonders you?

The above is to be taken with a pinch of salt; there are still individuals who feel that wonder and there will be stories written that will arouse that wonder. But they will be few and far between, and most of the science fiction stories will be run of the mill. Unless we have another Renaissance in science fiction, and

I think we owe a vote of thanks and a gasp of admiration for the tremendous labor of love (and love of labor) to those responsible for putting out *Who Killed Science Fiction?* Too bad it didn't do much else but furnish interesting reading. If only a definite and logical answer could result... On the whole, I thought that Bester's and Bloch's contributions were the most significant. Though the poor editors caught so much abuse, the publishers must bear the blame for the low word rates. However, maybe they wouldn't make any profit then, so who can blame them? And Bester was right when he said that everything changes, including science fiction, and that writers must change with it or pass out or away. Strange, isn't it, that a field supposedly dedicated to the future, to mutation, has so many conservatives, die-hards, and fossils in it. Let's hope science fiction evolves instead of becoming an extinct or scarce species.

Another thing. After reading *Who Killed Science Fiction?* and then Bester's defense of Horace Gold in *PITFCS*-135, I shamefacedly came to the conclusion that too much kicking of Horace was done and not enough praise. Bester is right. I know from my own limited experience with Horace that he is a tremendously creative editor and generous to boot. And, after blowing my top in *Who Killed Science Fiction?*, and feeling better, I began to think that I had blamed Horace for too much. After all, *Astounding* had its Dark Ages and its Golden Age, too, and that *Galaxy* could enter another. Though pessimistic for a while after reading *Who Killed Science Fiction?*, I have regained my innate optimism. As Eric Frank Russell said, science fiction has met a lot of ups and downs.

– Philip José Farmer, *PITFCS*-137, October 1960

that is something no one can predict on the basis of today's situation.

3) What can we do to correct the present situation? Nothing. Either events beyond our conscious control better the situation or events will worsen it.

4) We can't look to the original paperbacks as a point of salvation. There are no lengthy letter columns in the paperbacks to create a sense of togetherness, to stimulate a controversial and at the same time a brotherly feeling. This sense and feeling will have to be carried on by the fanzines, which means that only a very small group will have them.

I don't see any revival of the magazine letter columns; for one thing, the price of paper and printing is against it. Alas for the good old days!

5) No additional remarks pertinent to the study except that I hope that I am wrong.

FREAS, FRANK KELLY

[Not only did Kelly Freas contribute the following answers to the symposium, but also the ingenious double title pages.* The lay-out design for the first and second title pages and the text copy for those pages were also created by him, to completely execute his visual presentation of "Who Killed Science Fiction?" There are, unfortunately, too few collectors and fans who will use commercial time in the pursuit of a devoted hobby. Thank you, Kelly! – E.K.]

I feel thoroughly unqualified to answer your questionnaire, but if I think on it awhile, I should be able to recommend someone…!

Well, hell—one more damned opinion…

1) No—merely moribund. There are still enough of us to keep it going a few more years.

2) In order of increasing importance:

(a) Sputniks

(b) Movies and television

(c) Professionalism

3)   (a) Pray

(b) See below

4) Only so far as we might learn from it.

5) Duck, man—

To elaborate…

1) Science fiction is dying of old age. Granted, we are currently enjoying a relatively productive (if mediocre) and respectable (i.e.-slightly fatigued) middle age—how can you stop getting older? In a very few years more, the loss of the elder generation is going to start being felt…then the present one will start dropping off. Oh, yes—there is a younger generation…ever notice how much smaller it is?

2) (a) It should be noted that the depressing effect of Sputnik I hit *all*, not merely science fiction, therefore cannot be given too much blame.

I admit that it's hard to overstate the stench of this horse, but after all, it *is* dead. Obviously *some kids* like it and that ought to indicate something.

Uh-huh. I suspect we have "improved" ourselves right off the market. "Pulp" always a dirty word with us…Nevertheless, there was enthusiasm, vi-tality, excitement, in a large part of the airiest literary junk.

---

*The reference here is to the 1960 edition of *Who Killed Science Fiction?*—E.K.

WHO KILLED

Science Fiction?

an affectionate autopsy ......

So everybody worked *real* hard…
So everybody got *real* good…
So we are producing literature, yet…
So who the hell wants it?

I recently had occasion to read a story by one of the gentlemen of the old school (pulp, that is) of science fiction. It was a positive blot on the face of literature. The plot was asinine, juvenile, illogical, and stupid. The characters were inept, inconsistent, unconvincing stereotypes. The writing was ghastly.

I haven't enjoyed a story so much in years.

If he had nothing else, he did have enthusiasm. He was excited about this ridiculous thing: he was obviously writing straight from his Rover Boy's heart, and enjoying every minute of it.

But we don't want to do anything like that, do we…?

Besides, the sort of publisher who would print such bilge is not the type with which we wish our name associated.

Quite right, too.

Whither, science fiction?

3) (a) You never can tell…

(b) The urge to improve is more or less universal, and when present, quite irresistible. So we learn, and we practice, and we get better and better—at making buggy whips, perhaps?

4) We can't very well revive the old pulps, but there is certainly something to be learned from them. As a reader, I say that the stories were better, on the average. You tell *me* why.

Incidentally, from a professional standpoint, I think most of the artwork was better too, 20 years ago. But that's another subject entirely.

Frankly, I think we have had it. Yes, it will probably be another 20 to 30 years before the last science fiction magazine finally stops selling enough copies to pay for the office space it takes up, and the fan publishers may keep things going a mite longer.

But the writing is on the wall; we are not bringing in the kids the way our elders snatched us up, bug-eyed .... *us?* and panting, with their crummy space operas and their rowdy-dow adventures. What's more, we can't. The whole emotional climate of the country has changed— *their* escape literature is nonfiction, something like "Ten Sticky Fingers—the autobiography of a fig-plucker."

But meanwhile, we *are* still here, all 243,000 of us, and I do like to read a good story now and then, even if it does make me think.

GERNSBACK, HUGO

Throughout the years I have made my position clear about the decline of *science* fiction. The science fiction now in existence is no longer "science." Usually the material consists of fairy tales.

[At this point Mr. Gernsback called my attention to his editorial, "STATUS OF SCIENCE FICTION, Snob Appeal or Mass Appeal?" in the December 1953 issue of *Science Fiction+*, in which he stated his views on the subject of this study as many as six years ago. In shame I confess to have forgotten this particular editorial, and since it is so very pertinent to the present study, I could not resist quoting the following brief excerpts. The entire editorial is recommended for further study.—E.K.]

"…The science fiction fan knows far more about science fiction authors, artists, editors, and everything that goes into the magazines than do the publishers themselves. And why shouldn't they? Few publishers ever have necessary time to read as much science fiction over as long a time as has the arduous science fiction fan.

"From all this it becomes clear why the science fiction fan sets the pace for science fiction today. He not only influences the author, but the editor and publisher as well. He—and only he—is the main body *critique* today. All this is quite as it should be—because it helps to drive the art to higher accomplishments.

"Unfortunately, also, the best and most assiduous critics in the world often unwittingly generate forces which in time may destroy the very edifice which they helped so laboriously to rear.

"*Modern science fiction today tends to gravitate more and more into the realm of the esoteric and sophisticated literature, to the exclusion of all other types.* It is as if music were to go entirely symphonic to the exclusion of all popular and other types. The great danger for science fiction is that its generative source—its supply of authors—

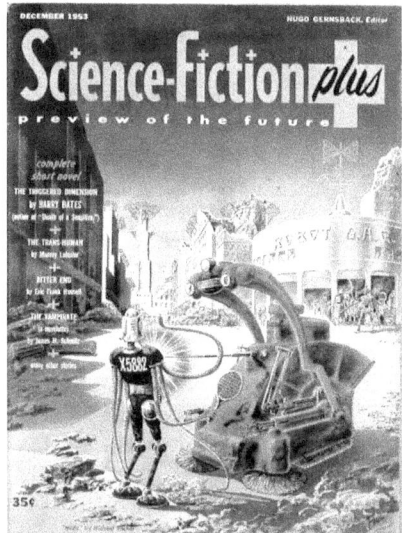

is so meager. Good science fiction authors are few, extremely few. Most of them have become esoteric—'high brow.' They and their confreres disdain the 'popular' story—they call it 'corny,' 'dated,' 'passé.'"

> **Afterthoughts...**
>
> Thank you very much for your interesting Annual *[Who Killed Science Fiction?}*. I must compliment you on it, as it is really well gotten up. I think it will be of great use to publishers and authors alike...
>
> – Hugo Gernsback, May 1960

And I give you below the answers to the specific questions you ask:

1) Science fiction is by no means dead. It is, however, being killed off by the lack of science in stories. Today, when the American public is looking forward to science in stories, it gets pap and kindergarten-variety material. Only about one in every 50 stories contains scientific facts as a basis for its action.

2) See No. 1.

3) What can we do to correct it? It can only be corrected by putting science back in stories, as we did in the old days of science fiction when practically every story I printed had good science in it. This is what the public today wants and demands.

4) (Original paperback question.) I have no opinion on this.

5) Additional remarks: Sometime next year you will see a very ambitious novel of mine which is chock full of science. It will probably run under the title *The Ultimate World*.

GOLD, HORACE L.

Magazine science fiction is very far from dead. There *is* an overconcentration on psi that *could* be dangerous if it excluded all the other themes science fiction should explore, but the solution is easy—lay off psi.

I have in a couple of editorials explored what you and "countless" people are now decrying, and there's no mystery, no killer, no sleuthing at all called for.

Magazine readerships—*all* magazine readerships—turn over; the accepted average, based on a great deal of research, is five years. Exceptions are taken into consideration in establishing the average. In science fiction, the exceptions seem more numerous than they really are because they very vocally turn against rather than away from the field they once loved. Has the beautiful bride become a hag? No, the five-year honeymoon has ended—and what you and "countless" others decry is a personal five-year Golden Age for those who've followed you.

Writers and artists also turn over in all fields. There are no statistics on this, except that it always feels worse than it is. Worse for the editor because he has to bring newcomers along all the time. Worse for the writers and artists because so many aimed at science fiction as a goal, hit it, enjoyed it—and now find the goal falling behind them.

I'll let those who relish analyses analyze the causes thereof, in Freudian or Jungian or any other such terms, but the terms aren't necessary. The truly immense majority of readers who turn over after five years do so quietly, matter-of-factly; they don't expect to be interested—or to be kept interested by "critical soul-searching"—in any one thing forever, and their places are taken by readers leaving one field or another for the very same reason. And it's just as simple, though more painful, for writers and artists—in *individual* instances. The same immense majority goes without fuss or feathers. The vocal ones are again in the same tiny but highly audible minority. Certainly I sympathize with them, and wish they could stay, and know that some will return from time to time—but a goal isn't a goal when it's reached, explored, exploited, for up ahead is another goal, visible to the majority, socked in to the minority, who hoot through the fog till they can see it, and leave, and have others take their places in much the manner that they'll be replacing others in other fields, who'll have left for the identical reason.

But I *do* have one recommendation to make. No writer should try to make his living out of science fiction. It's fine as a sideline, supplement, hobby, anything you wish, but *not* a main source of income. It never was and shouldn't be.

GRAHAM, ROGER PHILLIPS

Rog Phillips

You ask five interesting questions, Earl, but the answers to them, as far as the writers are concerned, are the same that they were ten years ago. Magazine science fiction is not dead. It has its ups and downs. The present situation so far as sales figures go is caused, as everyone knows, by the magazine distributors. It's being corrected slowly, but unfortunately some of the magazines that folded will never reappear.

3 & 4) Are answerable together. All any of us can do is what we've always had to do—deal with our individual relationship to the field as best we can, and not blow our top at raw deals we get.

This, of course, contributes nothing to your projected study. But the fact still remains that a really good story will find a quick sale from any editor in the field, because every editor knows he is publishing too much low-grade stuff he wouldn't buy if better stories were available.

The bad thing about looking to the paperbacks as a point of salvation is that spending two months on a story that doesn't sell is worse than spending two months on five short stories, one of which sells. It's up to the individual writer.

5) There are two types of magazines: (1) those who pay the writers from their advertising revenue, (2) those who pay their writers from their sales revenue. To illustrate what I mean about this, let's look at the picture in the San Francisco area. One science fiction prozine I know of sends 1,000 copies to be distributed among 2,500 outlets. Only 600 copies are sold. The distributor has to tear the front covers off the remaining 400, bundle them, and mail them to the publisher. For all this work, he and the outlets split a ripe $60 plum among themselves each month. If some teenage fan steals his copy of the magazine, the distributor has to subtract two bits from his $60 take.

At the same time, two boxcars of a certain weekly magazine from Philly arrive every week. The distributor could sell them off the boxcars to a scrap paper dealer and get enough to pay the publisher his cut, and still make money. Each of his outlets makes a couple of bucks a week from this magazine, and he makes as much from each outlet. The unsold copies are sold as scrap paper. The writers in this magazine are paid entirely from advertising revenue, as are the paper company and the printers.

Actually, it is surprising that any of the science fiction magazines continue publication. Possibly a questionnaire sent to Street & Smith, Ziff-Davis, and Mercury Publications, asking their motives for continuing publication, would reveal some very startling things. Or maybe it would not get a frank response but only a booster letter saying they do it for money.

GREENBERG, MARTIN

1) I don't feel that magazine science fiction is dead; however, I do believe the magazines are making their own graves by bad editorial judgment.

2) I believe the present situation is due to several factors. The movies, of course, do not help us by labeling horror movies as science fiction. The current attempts to reach the moon certainly hurt us since there is no speculation involved, story and picture are available in detail through all types of publications. I feel that science fiction, while its aspects are many, is primarily an escape medium. The great adventure stories of the past are certainly gone from the scene and this should not be. We could have the adventure story

back with the better writing demanded today, but the magazine editors are so concerned with their own pet foibles they will not look at the market as a whole but see only their own narrow viewpoint.

3) We can do very little: If we stop supporting the magazines, they'll fold. If we write to the editors, they'll send logical letters back to say why they do what they do and it will sound perfectly justifiable and the other magazine is wrong, etc....

4) The paperbacks have a disadvantage in that the average paperback is edited by a man or woman who has no science fiction background. Ballantine Books, and of course this is a personal opinion, has missed more good bets by lack of editorial judgment than any publisher. They obviously take what's given to them—and luckily half of these are decent stories. They could have been great stories, handled right.

5) It is certainly valid to use stories with a psychological twist, to explore psionics. However the basic facts are that science fiction is escape fiction, its appeal is in the sense of wonder of what will be tomorrow and what we will find out there. I truly believe the current slump is due to a lack of interest. Do you remember years ago, when a group of fans got together they'd discuss stories and characters? I spoke with some of the current fans at the Detroit World Science Fiction Convention and you know, I don't think they even read the stories. When questioned they were vague on so many points as to raise doubts as to their validity as fans.

Afterthoughts...

Who Killed Science Fiction? certainly was an adventure in reading...I was glad to see that I was not alone in my opinion there was one more point I had overlooked in my summary and that was the indiscriminate publishing practices by some of the major publishing houses and small ones are not to be overlooked. If you want support I will gladly back you in the use of the word science fiction. What does he want to call it fantasy for; it certainly must have a classification and science fiction certainly is proper. I've spent twelve years building this name up and I'd hate to change it now...

– Marty Greenberg,
May 1960

GRENNELL, DEAN A.

1) No, I don't feel that magazine science fiction is dead.

2) I do not especially feel that any single person, action, incident, etc., is responsible for the present situation.

3) As far as the current situation is concerned, I can't see a need for correction.

4) I'm in favor of original paperbacks.

5) I, personally, find that the current *Astounding* and *Fantasy and Science Fiction* supply me with satisfactory science fiction and all of it I have time to read.

GUNN, JAMES E.

On March 31, 1955, I wrote a letter to Tony Boucher, inspired by his comment in *F&SF* that we needed to take a closer look at science fiction, in which I summed up my feelings about this beloved field of ours. I don't think I can do better in answer to your questions than to quote from that letter, and the remainder comes from that source, excerpted and with some updating to make it comprehensible.

I've been studying science fiction as a literary medium for more than five years now (now ten), but it wasn't until a little over a year ago (1953-54) that I began to feel that science fiction had taken the wrong turn somewhere. I think the great debate on what science fiction is and what it should be is long overdue, and it may be because we've never thrashed out any general area of agreement that science fiction is in its present predicament.

We can never agree on more than a broad definition of science fiction, but perhaps we can agree on what constitutes the mainstream of science fiction and where we have wandered away from it. As a beginning, we must accept the thesis that the mainstream of science fiction is entertainment; and if science fiction is going to be popular, it must be popular entertainment. Whatever else science fiction is, it should be entertainment first and other things in addition, on other levels or other depths.

We have been misled—authors and editors—in a search for a spurious maturity. Any maturity is spurious which tries to deny its origins and its childhood, which tries to change itself into something else. Maturity isn't something to be sought and found. It is grown into, and you either have it or you don't.

Entertainment is a broad term which can cover a multitude of stories and story types. But it's significant that you used the word "excitement" in your review of Arthur Clarke's *Earthlight*. I used the word myself in a letter to Jack Williamson in February of 1954:

> *It seems to me that science fiction has lost something in the last few years; it has gained some things, too, but I wonder whether they quite make up for it. I wonder if what ails the magazine field currently isn't a paucity of excitement, if circulation wouldn't jump tremendously under the impetus of a new serial by van Vogt or Heinlein...Science fiction had something in the 1940s that it doesn't have any more: a vigor, a sweep, a dream, an excitement. Nowadays there is a great deal of maturity, subtlety, cleverness, good writing, but very little excitement...*

And we aren't the only ones who are worried or puzzled or alarmed. In the January *Astounding*, P. Schuyler Miller laments the passing from science fiction of that quality he calls "adventure." And there have been others and will be more.

We must face the fact we should have faced long ago: the popular reader doesn't want to be instructed, edified, improved, dazzled, impressed, lulled, or any other substitute for fiction. Fiction is people, and fiction is emotion, and popular fiction is people doing things in an exciting way and feeling excited about it. The popular reader wants to be entertained, and his definition of entertainment is suspense, action, surprise, excitement. He does not like the "literary" story. He does not like satire or essay or parody. He wants a story about a person with whom he can identify himself, who gets in a suspenseful situation and has to fight his way out of it. This is what science fiction used to be, and I don't think it's anything to be ashamed of. I think, instead, that it's unfortunate we didn't make the most of it.

To my mind, the golden age of science fiction was the late 1930s and the 1940s when Heinlein and van Vogt and Kuttner and Hubbard and a handful of others were writing the type of stories I've described, the kind that aren't seen any more. Is it just nostalgia? Are we, who grew up with the science fiction magazines, the ones who have grown old and jaded? Does science fiction still have as potent a spell for the novice and the young in spirit? I don't think so. I used to haunt the newsstands for the latest magazine; it was torment waiting. I don't think that's true for anyone today. For me it isn't, and I don't think it is for many others. Where has the excitement gone?

We have a great many able new writers, but where are the van Vogts, the Heinleins, the Kuttners, the Hubbards among them? Where are the storytellers? I don't see any. Many as writers are just as good or better in their ways, but are these the ways that are good for science fiction? I submit that they are not, and it has been proved that they are not.

Science fiction has been betrayed in many ways: by those who have sought to capitalize on its presumptive popularity and sought its least common denominator, by those who have underestimated the reading and viewing and listening public and the appeal and excitement of the drama of ideas, but also by those of us who should have known better. We have had our delusions of grandeur; we have committed the unpardonable sin of the storyteller—we have been dull. We have sought art for its own sake. Our primary function is to hold our audience and to add to it; we must never forget that.

I have been referring to magazines, because it is obvious that the book field is the tail and doesn't wag the dog (almost five years later, this is not so obvious). And so to the editors must fall a large share of the responsibility. If the editors won't buy the story of the storyteller, the storyteller must turn to something else; it is his nature that he must have an audience (it might be proved that he has turned to the paperback). The editors, in turn, are at the mercy of the readers, but this discipline is difficult to interpret, and too often the readers can't analyze what they like and want.

Why haven't there been any new Heinleins, any new van Vogts? Their talents are not unique. Their excitement about what they were doing, which poured through into their fiction, was not exclusive. The reason, I think, is because the budding Heinlein, the embryo van Vogt, has had his stories rejected by the leading magazines instead of encouragement, and he has turned to other modes of expression. It is illuminating that you said of *Earthlight*, "More books like this, and there'd probably be no need for the questions I posed above." But which of the major science fiction magazines would publish *Earthlight* today if it were submitted by an unknown author? The question is academic. But I'll tell you who published the short novel from which it was expanded: *Thrilling Wonder Stories* (August 1951).

Where did we go wrong? I think it was in trying to mutate science fiction into something else instead of improving on what we had. Satire, for instance. There have been satires written within the science fiction domain, and no one denies them a place within it. But satire is not the mainstream of science fiction; it is only essay disguised. Unlike the mainstream, it cannot, by its basic structure, carry its conviction within itself.

I suggest that it's time for the satirists, the aesthetes, the parodists, and the essayists to give science fiction back to the storytellers. Cleverness is not enough. Fine writing is not enough. The reader of popular fiction demands emotional satisfaction, and if he cannot find it in science fiction he will seek it somewhere else. If science fiction takes the path of the little magazine, seeking self-expression instead of artistry, experimentation instead of communication, then it must accept the fate of the little magazine: small circulation and limited readership.

The function of the artist is to communicate; unless he does this he has failed as an artist. In order to communicate he uses the best means he can find. In science fiction, as in any popular fiction or in any popular medium anywhere, any time (the Elizabethan stage, for instance), the best means are the storyteller's means. A return to storytelling does not necessarily mean a sacrifice of quality (take Shakespeare, take Cervantes, take Tolstoy and Dostoevski, take Dickens, take Melville, take Hemingway). Within it there is all the room in this world and many others for good writing and meaningful characterization. As authors and editors we must start asking ourselves the right questions: "Is this the most entertaining (not the cleverest) way this can be written?" or "Is this the most exciting (not the most inevitable) development?"

People read fiction for emotional satisfaction; they read *science* fiction for something extra. Perhaps it is because science fiction is (can be) more exciting. Perhaps it is for meaning. Perhaps it is because our society, like science fiction itself, is oriented toward the future. But the emotional satisfaction comes first, and if it isn't there all the other things won't help.

I would like to go into other things like the trap of the incidental story (if people want to read about meaningless incidents, why read science fiction?). Archibald MacLeish wrote once that a poem must not mean but be. A science fiction story is just the other way around.

KEMP, NANCY

Nancy Kemp

1) Yes, I believe that magazine science fiction is dead.

2) No, I do not feel that any *single* thing is responsible for the present situation. There are a combination of contributory factors: low rates; poor stories; inadequate distribution; inept editorships.

3) Wider distribution, if it could be achieved, would be a major corrective measure. Depending, of course, on the possibility of producing better stories and a more equitable word rate for the authors of those stories. Call it a cycle, vicious or otherwise, wherein each correction is dependent upon another. But the best, and only, starting point is that of better distribution.

4) Yes, we should look to the original paperback as a point of salvation.

KNIGHT, DAMON

1) No, I don't think magazine science fiction is dead. As you know, science fiction in magazines goes through periodic booms and slumps, and this one is right on schedule. 1960 should be a big year, if the pattern holds as it always has.

2) No, I don't think we should be looking for a villain or scapegoat. Like anything else that's regulated by supply and demand, science fiction goes through a cycle of over- and under-supply. It would be true as far as it goes to say that the people who jump on the bandwagon during a boom are responsible for the slump that follows, but short of putting science fiction under the control of some sort of czar who would limit the number of magazines, there's nothing we can do about it.

3) See above.

4) Well, the paperbacks are doing better, as you know, partly because paperbacks have already been through their disastrous slump, which shook out a lot of marginal producers; partly because paperbacks stay on sale longer, etc., etc. But I don't think they are taking the place of magazines, or are likely to.

LEIBER, FRITZ

Fritz Leiber

1) I do not think that magazine science fiction is dead, but I imagine it will continue curtailed, the equivalent of some half-dozen monthlies, at a guess. (Death in some 20 years is likely.)

2) Numerous factors are responsible for this curtailment:

a. Television and other forms of mass-media entertainment are cutting deeply into the *reading*-for-escape habit. Considerable fantasy and science fiction of varying quality is available on television, in the movies, etc.

b. The paperback book with its one-shot advantages of no limited sale time is gradually killing off magazine fiction.

c. There is now (in public libraries especially) a store of good hardcover (and paperback) science fiction adequate to satisfy the appetites of many of the young people who get the science fiction bug.

d. Progress and speculation in space flight, atomics, robotics, and similar fields are no longer under a general editorial taboo. We can read this stuff in the mass media; we no longer have to get this information from science fiction stories.

3) We can continue to publish amateur magazines, which will likely increasingly become a haven for the "difficult," imagination-stretching science fiction story.

4) The original science fiction paperback is certainly a point of salvation. *Star SF, Avon Fantasy Reader*, and others have set excellent precedents for the one-shot type story-assembly.

5) I think it's tempting, but dangerous, to analogize from the death of fantasy magazines (a sigh for *Weird Tales*!) to the death of science fiction magazines. For one thing, the latter have to a considerable degree replaced and engulfed the former. Finally, with man entering space, it seems clear to me that the space adventure story, at the very least, will continue.

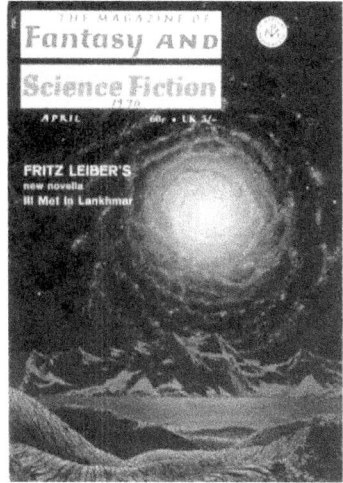

LEY, WILLY

1) No, I don't think that magazine science fiction is dead, it just isn't feeling very well right now. The interesting trouble, at the moment, is that it has become impossible to explain science fiction to an outsider. In the past one could say "stories based on the assumption that a new invention is being made or has been made." The public now will look you straight in the eye and insist that nothing beyond atomic energy and space travel can be imagined.

2) Not a single event, incident or person. But I do believe that the trend to harp on crank items has done a great deal of harm. Of course Ray Palmer must get first blame with his [Richard] Shaver business. Hans Santesson— insists on saying that flying saucers might be real and now even prints occultistic junk. And John Campbell, after running off the rail with Dianetics, is now wild about psi. I know his answer: space ships are nearly here, atomic energy is here, science fiction has to look forward. But dealing with psi is still a mistake; occultists and mystics may love it, but most people reject it violently. The reason is obviously psychological, though I can't say why. Most people just do not wish to hear about powers (if they exist, which I personally doubt) that are not physics and/or nucleonics.

3) Go after the editors and ask them not to print any nonfiction that is not factual, especially nothing occult or flying saucerish.

4) No. Or maybe for novels. But it would be no fun to wait until one man/woman has written enough short stories to fill a book. Besides, if one does wait, they don't read well in succession. The variety a magazine can offer is infinitely superior.

5) I probably have made enough enemies by now as it is.

LOWNDES, ROBERT A.W.

1) Not dead, but possibly dying in the sense that all popular magazine fiction may be dying. By "popular magazine fiction" I refer to the type of magazine that was once known as the "pulps" and remains with us in digest-size publications. The sports and western titles have gone. The detective titles are mostly gone, and of these we have mostly ultra-cheap, sensational, sadistic crime fiction which has nothing to do with the classic detective story. The remainder consists of publications that are split between reprints of the better (purportedly) stories published in the last decades and new material mostly by authors who made their name in the "good old days."

2) There are two elements necessary to a continuing audience for any type of fiction: (1) The steady reader. (2) The new reader. No publication can endure very many years on the basis of "steady readers"; there is a considerable turnover going on all the time, and even in that category of the enthusiasts, any given individual is likely to lose interest for a time, or, for a time be forced to discontinue regular support. I myself have gone through periods when I was "fed up" with science fiction. I've always come back, and usually tried to collect and catch up on the issues of the better magazines that I missed, but that doesn't replace the sales that were lost during my apostasy. Multiply that by "n" and you can see why "constant reader" just doesn't form a strong enough backbone.

The "new reader" may be a transient who picks up one issue only, or who, having been satisfied once will try again months later when he's in the mood for more, and a certain percentage of these transients will subscribe or become regular customers. But what has supported the magazines for years has been the flesh of transients upon the bone of the regulars.

What has happened? For the most part, the volume of transients has fallen to a very low figure—not enough to support adequately even the few remaining titles in the science fiction field. The disappearance of competition—or some competition—can, at times, help the remnant, providing that the reason for the death of a competitor signifies no more than distaste for that particular brand of science fiction. Unfortunately, this is not universally the case. While some may buy *Abstract Science Fiction* once *Abstruse Science Fiction* no longer appears on the stands, most likely others will not be interested in the *Abstract* brand—and others will have been repelled from science fiction completely because of dissatisfaction with what they found in the now-defunct magazine.

Without defining "good" and "bad" in this frame, it is still a truism that good competition helps a magazine, while bad competition injures it. A good competitor will leave a reader in a friendly frame of mind toward the field—and maybe next month he'll buy your magazine, too; and maybe he'll add it to his list or switch to you. Bad competition drives him away; he won't look at any science fiction magazine again, even a good one like yours. (This isn't 100% but describes what has happened in many instances. Bad movies and TV science fiction have also hurt good science fiction magazines in the same way.)

There is further a special situation in the field of distribution. When American News went out of the magazine distribution business, a gap appeared that hasn't been filled. Most of the science fiction titles had to find new vehicles of distribution—and found themselves up against individual, independent wholesalers who were not interested in handling these magazines and refused to take them or to do much of anything with them when they did. (This hit the detective titles in the same way.) Result: In many of the big cities, various science fiction titles cannot be found at any newsstand. We have received a steady flow of letters from readers of all our publications who have not been able to find our magazines. They asked their dealers; the dealers contacted the wholesaler—to be told that "we don't handle these books." Finis. *Some* have subscribed, but only a small percentage do that—after all, there is a difference between laying out 35¢, 40¢, or 50¢ once a month, or once every other month, and laying out the cost of a year's subscription all at once. And a large percentage of readership lay amongst people for whom subscribing was difficult. The real enthusiasts, of course, get their subscriptions in; but the larger number isn't that determined. In this frame, it makes no difference how "good" a good magazine was; if it doesn't get to the newsstand, then it doesn't matter what is inside those covers that no one sees.

General interest in science fiction waxes and wanes. There was a "fad" for awhile, and that could recur, theoretically. But my feeling remains that there is an audience for a certain number of good titles (at all levels of science fiction), titles which can make a profit (though not a fortune) if the books can get on the newsstands. Television has hurt magazine sales in general and I would say to the extent that there is no longer *big* money to be made in popular magazines as there was back in the days of the great pulp empires.

3) Who is—or are—"we?" I don't think that "we" are in a position to do anything about it—except to support sure that we buy our copies each issue,

subscribing if necessary, and show a tolerant understanding of the difficulties the magazines are laboring under when "we" write to editors. (By "tolerant understanding" I do not mean pulling punches about what "we" may not like, or think bad—positively not that—but in the tone of the criticism and complaints.) And by letting editors know "we" are still with them even though less than radiantly satisfied.

4) What do you mean? Should we (ah, this vague "we" again!) forget about the magazines and just buy pocketbooks? You don't expect me to say "yes" to that, do you? But seriously, I think that "salvation" in the sense of a continuing supply of science fiction—and a possibility for good science fiction—is more likely to come through the pocketbooks than the magazines. I'll continue to hope for the magazines as long as there are any left, and suggest that "we" continue to support them up to the end—hoping that we don't see the end. The situation doesn't look promising but, as I indicated above, I do not think that "we" can do anything significant about it. But what's it going to cost us to try? Nothing shattering—and if, concurrently with "our" support, the magazine field picks up, we can always enjoy the somewhat irrational but satisfying feeling that our efforts helped.

5) No additional remarks at present. See forthcoming editorials in *Future* and *Science Fiction Stories*.

McLAUGHLIN, DEAN

Magazine science fiction is not dead—yet. There remain a number of science fiction magazines, and most of these are published on a monthly schedule. I could even name two magazines which, if there be any justice in this world, should continue to be published up until the crack of doom or the next ice age.

Provided, that is, they can maintain the standards they have maintained up until now.

I don't know if they can do this.

I must admit, the prospects look bleak. Even the best magazines seem to be publishing a large proportion of drab, uninteresting, and unstimulating stuff. The question might well be asked whether there is enough genuinely good science fiction being written to supply the existing magazines, and all the evidence—including some fairly direct testimony—seems to indicate that the answer is a disgusted NO. As a consequence, the lower-budget magazines are able to publish only the cats and dogs which the better-paying magazines have declined as not fit company for their masthead, plus—perhaps—a thin trickle of superior material which has failed to sell higher up the ladder for reasons of editorial prejudice.

But this is a chicken-and-egg situation. There was a time, not long ago, when the quality of the average science fiction story was considerably higher than it is today. Without digging into the back files and amassing a horrendous volume of statistics, I think it is possible to maintain that no more science fiction is being published in magazines today than—say—ten or fifteen years ago. (There may have been fewer magazines in those days—I'm not sure—but, with maybe a couple of exceptions, they were all bigger.) Therefore, the suggestion that as much *good* science fiction is being published as there was in the "good old days" doesn't seem to hold water.

Something must have happened, therefore, to cut down the quality of the stories being written. Editors do not willingly publish bad stories, and do so only when they can't get enough good ones. Nor do writers deliberately write bad stories. At least, I hope they don't.

But one phenomenon is very obvious. It has been characterized by the number of top-ranking writers in the field who—with a gigantic yowl of GERONIMO!—have vanished in search of greener pastures.

I ask you now, why?

The ugly fact is, science fiction writing is not, on the average, a very remunerative business. To the best of my knowledge, only one man has been able to make a comfortable living writing science fiction. For all the others, their science fiction writing must be supplemented by writing in other fields, or by other income. And when the "other writing" is more rewarding financially, the writer is either a fool, a bad businessman, or (honor to them, if any such there be) someone who just plain wants to write science fiction more than anything else. So the full-time writers, with only a few exceptions, devote most of their efforts toward other markets—particularly, at present, the

true-trash-for-men magazines and those other men's magazines—*Playboy* and its imitators—which appear to be dedicated to the proposition, and also to the principle, that sex is good clean fun.

(Before I'm accused of a holier than thou attitude, I might add that I have recently made a sale to *Rogue*. However, I do not plan to follow up with a full-scale entry into this good-paying field—I don't usually write their breed of copy; the writer writes the stories he can think of—not the ones he can't. The ones I think of happen to be science fiction.)

It is possible that the full-time writer is exposed to another influence—his agent. An agent, by definition, is a businessman, and he is only incidentally interested in artistic satisfaction. And the agent is not without influence over his writers. I have no doubt that at least some agents have persuaded their authors into more lucrative fields—which has helped both writer and agent financially, but many times has left science fiction the poorer.

Conclusion: only the part-time writer is financially able to devote all his writing to science fiction. Unfortunately, there are too few good part-time writers. Most of them, if they were any good, would be turning it out full time. Unable to do this, either for lack of talent or lack of productivity, they *can* continue to write science fiction. But even to these, the call of greener pastures is not unheard—and off they go.

This raises the question, what makes the pastures greener? Several facts emerge. First of all, the men's magazines, almost without exception, pay more than the best-paying science fiction magazine. And even confession magazines consider 3 cents per word rock bottom. Most science fiction magazines can't pay that kind of money for the simple reason that they don't have that kind of money; they don't sell enough copies to justify any greater payment than they have been making.

Second, the past couple of years has seen several very fine science fiction magazines cease publication. We all regret this, but we cannot argue with the cold fact that they were losing money, and none of the publishers had enough money that they didn't care what happened to it. As a consequence, science fiction writers have had fewer places in which their work could be published, and the competition for the remaining available space began to look fearsome. Being a cautious lot (remember, you can't eat rejection slips—you've had enough to swallow as it is), the writers have declined to compete—have sought out markets where the competition wasn't so tight.

This brings us to the final point. For the present, at least, the men's magazines are plentiful—there is a large market for copy—and they at least give the appearance of being financially successful. And for the writer who must make his bread and butter from his writing, it is very discouraging to devote time and effort to a story only to discover that the market it was written for no longer exists.

The question of why science fiction magazines have poor sales goes deeper—into such matters as the entertainment tastes of the American public, which I won't attempt to discuss. The fact exists that science fiction magazines do not sell very well, and very probably several of those now publishing are publishing at a deficit. We might as well face it.

However, two things are wroth mentioning. First, the recent developments toward space flight may well be providing the imaginative stimulation which people once sought in science fiction. If this is a cause of recent setbacks in science fiction, it is probably only temporary. Once the novelty has worn off, the mind must find other wonders to be stimulated by. Already, satellites are commonplace, and moon shots will become equally prosaic before long.

Second, it is worth pointing out that most science fiction magazines are given very poor distribution. They do not reach the retail stands where they could be sold. Whether this is a consequence of poor showings in the past—certainly one factor—or whether it simply reflects the fierce competition which exists for display space on the newsstands—this is something I can't answer.

I do believe, though, that since the collapse of American News Co. a few years ago (and, granted, its existence was—at best—a very mixed blessing) most science fiction magazines have had for their distributors (their national distributors, that is—not to be confused with the local magazine wholesalers) second-string, weak-kneed outfits which—since they lack top-ranking magazines in their lists—are unable to exert much persuasion on the local wholesalers through which they must work. *Astounding* is the one notable exception to this statement—and *Astounding* is the one science fiction magazine that can be found almost anywhere where magazines are for sale.

It may be that, as the number of magazines being published dwindles, the quality of the stories being published may improve. This may have already happened, but I see few signs. Certainly, we can expect the more marginal writers to fall by the wayside, or go elsewhere. But also some of the remaining real talents will be persuaded to seek publication in fields where the opportunity of making a sale is not so restricted. Therefore, while I have hopes, I remain pessimistic.

I do not mean to say, by all this, that magazine science fiction is dead. It must be borne in mind that, proportionately, more science fiction magazines have survived into the present day than have mystery magazines, western magazines, sports-story magazines, or magazines devoted to love stories (unless you count confession magazines). I *do* believe that magazine science fiction is presently in a very weakened condition, and seems to be getting even weaker. But we still have that occasional work of real worth, entertainment value, and originality—and still, in some magazines, at least, a fairly high level of general competence—and a thing should be judged in terms of its successes, not its failures.

I don't know if anything can be done to improve the present situation. Certainly, no obvious salvation is in sight. If the writers could be put under some kind of obligation to write nothing but masterpieces, and if editors could be persuaded to publish only masterpieces, we might get somewhere. But this is not possible. The writers—those still writing—are doing the best they know how, even though this is often not good enough. Editors would greatly enjoy publishing nothing but masterpieces; unfortunately, they have to publish stories selected from the manuscripts offered them.

And the only way to woo back those who have deserted would be to present them with a healthy, well-established market for their stories.

All we need, in other words, is a philanthropist with a million bucks who doesn't care what happens to it.

Nor do I believe that the expanding paperback market offers a completely satisfactory substitute. Certainly, in most categories, the pocketbook has replaced the magazine as a source of entertainment literature. This may well happen also with science fiction—but I don't like it. It is my belief that the pocketbook does not quite replace the magazine.

Most of the science fiction magazines concentrate on novelettes and short stories. *Astounding* and *Galaxy* do publish serials, and *Amazing* does run things which are called novels—usually rather short novels. But, while there have been many fine and memorable novels in science fiction, the novelette is the natural form of the science fiction story as we know it today.

I say the novelette rather than the short story because most of the time it is impractical to compress a fully realized science fiction setting, idea content, and plot into a short story's restricted length. On the other hand, the novel tends to depend too much on plot construction rather than idea content—which may make a very good story, but which tends to overshadow science fiction's special qualities.

Unlike the magazine, the pocketbook emphasizes the novel and almost ignores the shorter forms. The only exceptions are the *Star Science Fiction* collections of original short stories (which are almost like issues of a magazine in basic nature, if not in format or publication schedule) and the collections of short stories reprinted from the magazines.

We can ignore the reprint collections in this discussion, since they depend on the magazines for their material. The collections of original short stories and novelettes are another matter, and it may well be that, some day, they will replace the magazine. But I doubt it.

Anthologies like the *Star* series certainly have advantages over the magazines. Not only do they receive, in general, much better distribution, but they are not pulled off sale after a month or two to make room for the next issue.

Several issues of a series can be displayed side by side, and there is nothing odd about it. In practice, it doesn't usually work out quite so ideally; the average pocketbook has an effective on-sale period running only a few weeks. Or less. Nevertheless, there is not the same compulsion to remove pocketbooks from sale (unless they are just plain not selling) as for dated magazines.

But neither does the pocketbook series build up the same identification as an entity that a magazine does. The *Star* series is, of course, a try in that direction, but with wide-spaced and indefinitely scheduled publication dates, plus the pocketbook format, each issue in the series tends to be thought of as an individual collection of short stories, not as part of a series.

Also, science fiction pocketbooks, while presumably profitable to their publishers, are considerably less profitable than other types of pocketbooks. Most pocketbook publishers report science fiction books as having the smallest average sale of any of the generalized types of fiction. Even so notable a series as Judith Merril's annual anthologies, published by Dell Books, is given what can only be described as token distribution, which is a good indication of what Dell's sales department thinks of its potential. (I do not make this statement carelessly; the local wholesaler in my area—in spite of his protests!—receives a far smaller allotment of the Merril anthology than of even the dreariest Dell western.)

Finally, most science fiction pocketbooks are selected for publication by editors who do not have an understanding of science fiction's basic nature, virtues, and advantages. To them, it is simply another form of entertainment fiction. This is fine if all you want is space opera. This is fine so long as much of the work being published in pocketbooks is derived from magazine sources. And this is fine so long as the stories are written by writers familiar with and sympathetic to the traditions and qualities of science fiction.

But the traditions and qualities were developed in the magazines and have been maintained by the magazines. Cut off from this source, an inevitable process of drift would begin. Perhaps there would be some profit in this—an unchanging literature, or one with a too-rigid tradition, is well along to becoming a dead literature. But it would be adrift without guidance. There would be a tendency for science fiction in pocketbooks to become more "commercial" and less thoughtful than the science fiction we know. (Consider the recent evolution of the "mystery" novel.) I vividly (and with disgust) recall the slickly conceived and executed stories of Kendell Foster Crossen during the early fifties; they are an example of what I mean. They looked like science fiction, and even had some of the taste. But they were certainly not what I think of when I think of science fiction.

For the same reason, while it is true that—at last—general magazines are publishing some science fiction, I doubt that this field offers any real hope. Restricted by that fearful, bone-headed image of the average reader, the general magazine is compelled to publish only the most rudimentary sort of science fiction, and very old-hat stuff it is, most of the time.

Perhaps I am too pessimistic. I hope I am. But I do not foresee any great improvement in conditions in the science fiction magazine field. Nor do I see any practical way by which conditions can be improved. I do not like this, but dislike of a fact bears no relation to whether or not it is true. We might as well face it—with hope, with stubbornness, but not with confidence.

MESKYS, EDMUND R.

Edmund R Meskys

1) Maybe not dead, but it will continue to decline in 1960. During the last six months I have heard rumors of the impending folding of virtually every magazine in the field. The *one* magazine about which I heard no such rumor is, strangely enough, *Amazing Stories*. The credibility of these rumors ranged from unlikely to probable, and I would be surprised if more than seven of the present nine magazines are still being published a year from now, or less than five. After a few fold over the next few years, things might stabilize and five or so continue to exist for quite a time. I guess that if some publisher decided to take a risk and put out a new magazine because he has nothing better to do (the way the first *Famous Monsters* was produced) others might jump on the bandwagon to start another boomlet like, but smaller than, that of 1957 started by *Infinity*.

2) Several things; progress, distribution, the boom of 1953 and 1957, and movies in descending order of importance.

I have basically the same thoughts on the effects of scientific and engineering progress on science fiction as was expressed by L. Sprague de Camp at the 1959 Philadelphia conference. I remember reading a remainder copy of Nicolson's *Voyages to the Moon* just about the time the United States first announced project Vanguard and wondering how long it would take for science fiction to die. As you undoubtedly remember, *Voyages* tells of the speculative aeronautical and astronautical fiction published before the first balloon flight, and ends with the note that after a period of great popularity this form of literature died as people realized the nature and difficulties of air travel. By analogy, this should spell the doom of space opera, and the realistic yarns will probably merge with war books (viz. Frank Harvey's borderline *Air Force!*).

Distribution and display is what killed *Satellite*, and will probably finish off *Science Fiction Stories, Future*, and *Fantastic Universe*. I don't know how it is outside of New York City, but these three are virtually impossible to find here. And despite the article "The Undistributed Middle" in *Inside* a few years back,

I put the blame on the distributor and not the newsie. My dealer knows I buy everything except *F&SF*, and tries to get it for me. At times, he has requested a magazine from the distributor five or six times before he got a copy of it, and then just one. Of the magazines they do send him, they usually send only one copy. If something happens and they send two or even three, the extras *are* sold before the next issue comes out, but they persist in only sending one copy.

The booms, especially that of 1952, produced so much gorsh dern awful crud that it must have driven a number of people from the field. If someone had picked up the second issue of *Spaceway* or any issue of *Cosmos*, out of curiosity, I doubt that anything could convince him to ever try science fiction again. These are the only real crudzines I remember, but there must have been others (many of which I never read).

Least of all, the movies and "comics" must have scared a number of potential people out of trying the stuff (viz. "Worst Foot Forward" in *Inside*).

3) Buy *all* of the magazines, which will be a little, but not much help. Of course, if that is done, then poor stories must be vigorously stepped on with letters. I stopped buying *F&SF* because the annish had four terrible stories which made me quite angry. Had I followed my own advice, I would have written a blistering letter instead of just dropping the magazine. I have also dropped *Galaxy Novels* for similar reasons.

4) It will augment the meager supplies found in magazine form, but I expect a large part will be borderline like *Air Force!, Bombs In Orbit, Red Alert*, etc., or disguised as *The Rest Shall Die, Live and Let Die, Atlas Shrugged* (although the last two are reprints), etc.

5) A sizeable amount of science fiction will be appearing, apparently, for the next few years in disguised form (as the books cited in item #4). P. Schuyler Miller talks at length of this trend in the January, 1960 *Astounding* under the title "Integration." Good science fiction, not labeled as such, has recently appeared in *The Saturday Evening Post* and *Good Housekeeping*, among other places, and on TV (*Murder and the Android*). Anyhow, if science fiction *is* integrated with mainstream, this will probably cause another decline in, if not extinction of, the field of pure science fiction magazines. Also, it could spell the end of science fiction fandom (although an active amateur publishing fandom would probably remain, having no connections with science fiction).

At the last ESFA meeting several people brought up the idea that Campbell is trying to escape the death of the field by developing a new market. Explicitly, he hopes to sell his magazine primarily by the subscription with very limited newsstand distribution. Also, he hopes that his audience will consist mainly of scientists. That is, his magazine would become a fictional *Scientific American,* having the same audience and method of distribution.

I don't think he's aiming at the scientists, what with all of the cracks he's recently been making about them, but he might be aiming at the engineers and lab

THE LONGEST VOYAGE, By Poul Anderson

Premature Funeral

Last year Earl Kemp, the Chicago fan who is one of he proprietors of Advent: Publishers, put out a harmless appearing little questionnaire headed "Who Killed Science Fiction?" In it he asked five questions:

1. Do you feel that magazine science fiction is dead?

2. Do you feel that any single person, incident, et cetera is responsible for the present situation? If not, what is responsible?

3. What can we do to correct it?

4. Should we look to the original paperback as a point, of salvation?

5. What additional remarks would you like to contribute?

technicians. If this is what he is aiming for, and he succeeds, then *Astounding* might still be around after the regular market has vanished and all the others are gone. Another thing said then was that he is giving the magazine such a personality and flavor that, should something happen to him, it is doubtful that Street and Smith will be able to find a replacement to carry on.

MILLER, P. SCHUYLER

ON THE DEATH BY SLOW POISON OF SCIENCE FICTION

1) *Is magazine science fiction dead?*

I think this has now become merely an aspect of the question: "Are fiction magazines dead?" The question may be even broader: "Are American general-interest magazines dead?" (I think that scientific and special-interest magazines: trade, hobbies, fashion, some "upper-bracket" literary, will continue.)

I am afraid all magazines are dying, for reasons I will guess at under No. two. A year or so ago, when I spot-checked the whole city of Pittsburgh in search of a missing issue of *F&SF*, I found one large drug store in one of the major sectors of the city which had not had a new issue of *The Saturday Evening Post* for two weeks—and didn't care. And we're worrying about *Satellite*!

2) *Whodunit?*

I suspect that the passing of science fiction is one element in a Toynbeean "time of troubles," and as such is the result of an involved complex of cultural forces. (This is an involved way of saying "I don't know, but I hate distributors.")

a. *Ourselves.* We, as a people, don't read as we used to. For the present generation, television is probably the reason, but that doesn't excuse the generation just before television, who weren't reading either.

I'll qualify this to say that we don't read as a chosen form of entertainment. We do read for information, and this may account for the success of the "high-priced" paperbacks on a vast variety of nonfictional topics. The writers' magazines say there's a better market for articles than for fiction. Even the girly magazines are read primarily by freeloaders: I can always tell when a new lot is in, because I can't get near the magazine stand in Kaufmann's Department Store book section.

Because reading is no longer important to us, we can take it or let it go. I suspect that Ed Wood and I are the only people in Pittsburgh who try to get hold of all the science fiction and fantasy magazines, and Ed is the one who really tries, because I haven't seen Ray Palmer's *Flying Saucers* for more than two years, and couldn't care less. I hunt for them out of habit, and as a completist, but I don't read them all, or even try to. Others read one or two magazines consistently, and don't care whether the ones they

The questionnaire went to 108 writers, editors, artists, and fans, and drew 70 replies; ranging from a classically short one from our own John W. Campbell— "Dead? We're going better than ever before!"—to several pages of intense social criticism. Earl published the meat of these replies in a 107-page book that went only to the contributors and the members of the Spectator Amateur Press Society last April, and is enlarging on it in a symposium at the Pittcon, a month ahead as this is written. You can't buy "Who Killed?" from anyone but the 125 people who originally got it, so I've hesitated to comment on it here. However, there are too many meaty ideas involved to let it go any further, and I doubt that waiting two more months, until after the Pittcon debate, will add anything.

What you read here will be superficial: it has to be. A complete report would involve quoting just about everything anybody said, then analyzing the replies and editorializing on them— something Earl resisted himself. What I pick and choose out of the mass of commentary will also be colored by my own ideas.

Let's begin with the question itself; "Who killed (magazine) science fiction?" Since the symposium appeared, there has been a widespread hooraw in fandom over John Campbell's "ostrich" reply, which was equally terse on the other four questions. This is a little odd, and makes me wonder how many of the hissers have read "Who Killed?" because most of the contributors said exactly the same thing, if at greater length:

"Magazine science fiction isn't dead"—though it is apparently, in Willy Ley's words "just not feeling very well right now." This illness is what is really under discussion.

One issue can be established by counting: the *quantity* of magazine science fiction has fallen off since the all-time peak of 1953, when there were 45 titles on the stands in the United States and England. As of August 1, 1960 we have six American magazines, three British ones, and one or possibly two weird-horror reprint titles which may or may not survive, but should be counted since the other total included *Weird Tales* and various fantasies. This is a fairly objective fact, whose reasons can be explored.

There is also a feeling abroad that the *quality* of today's science fiction has deteriorated since the "Good old days" of the mid-1940s. This is a purely subjective evalua-

don't buy are published or not. I suppose this is partly the effect of the one-time glut of magazines, when the people who had tried to read everything finally gave up because of the quantity and lack of quality.

b. *The Outlets.* With mighty few exceptions, stores now carry magazines—at least in cities—as a service to their customers. There is not enough profit in them to make the deal good business. In high-rent districts (downtown; fashionable, or university neighborhoods), the space devoted to magazine display is losing money for the drug store or newsstand that handles them, because the same space could be used for records or cosmetics or patent medicines, on which the profit is good.

Since the outlets sell magazines as a service to regular customers, what happens when the customers no longer care whether issues appear regularly? The store owner doesn't give a damn either, and lets the distributor bring what he will, when he feels like it.

In some places the nuisance factor is throwing magazines out completely. Adolescents and tired businessmen free-loading sex magazines and leaving them thumb-smudged and drool-marked...kids bugging through the comics...girls with the movie and rock-and-roll magazines...keep "serious" readers from getting near the rack, or even into the store.

But the key fact is that in most places, stores no longer want to sell magazines—science fiction or any other kind.

c. *The Distributor.* Here is my personal villain, against whom I was preaching as far back as the Cleveland World Science Fiction Convention. Ed Wood's experiences on a nationwide scale, including such big cities as Chicago, and my own this past weekend in New York, convince me that I am right.

Distributors can solve the whole thing if they want to. They can take the responsibility and initiative that the store owner and the reader no longer take, or force them to take. But they aren't, and they won't. They don't give a damn either, and through some economic perversion that I can't fathom, they seem to feel that they can make more money not selling magazines than trying to sell them. Science fiction magazines, anyway.

AXIOM I: If you want to sell magazines, you display them where the greatest numbers of people will see them—in the downtown business district, in well-to-do residential districts, in "highbrow" university sections. They don't in Pittsburgh: apparently to find magazines, you have to go out into the suburbs.

AXIOM II: If you want to sell magazines, you display them regularly and consistently, month after month, so that faithful readers can count on picking them up. T'ain't so here. Big downtown outlets that *do* care what they get are given two or three copies of a new issue, or none at all, and a corner drug store that has never sold more than two or three copies is given 15 or 20— which are promptly sent back. I

tion which has no "real" basis, since personal tastes as to what is "good" science fiction vary widely and sometimes irrationally.

The question of quality is also, I would say, a rejection by a primarily intellectual circle—an inner circle of the science fiction world who are concerned with what is happening to it as a philosophical and literary problem. And with this in mind, I'd like to direct your attention to an article by Leo Rosten, author of *The Education of H*Y*R*A*N K*A*P*L*A*N**, its sequel, and many more weighty books and articles. Mr. Rosten has lectured on political science at Yale, is a faculty associate of Columbia, and was a senior staff member of the Rand Corporation, and will shortly be lecturing at the University of California at Berkeley. He is, you might say, an intellectual. He is also a. realist.

Leo Rosten's article, "The Intellectual and Mass Media: Can They Ever Get Along Together?" appeared first in the Spring 1960 issue of *Daedalus,* the journal of the American Academy of Arts and Sciences; it was reprinted in *Printers' Ink* for July 1st. There is nothing about science fiction in it, but there are several statements that I think help explain the answers in "Who Killed?"

First as to quantity: "Relatively few people in any society... have reasonably good taste or care deeply about ideas... Intellectuals seem unable to reconcile themselves to the fact that their hunger for more news, better plays, more serious debate, deeper involvement in ideas is not a hunger characteristic of many. They cannot believe that the subjects dear to their hearts bore or repel or overtax the capacities of their fellow citizens."

The contributors to "Who Killed?" came to grips with two pragmatic points that the intellectual wing of fandom, as Mr. Rosten points out for all magazines—and television, and the movies—does not accept that magazine science fiction is primarily a medium for *entertainment* of its readers, although with many other values unique to itself; and that it is a *minor* branch of fiction, appealing to a minority of readers.

Rog Phillips enlarges on this point in the symposium, pointing out that the mass-circulation magazines such as the *Saturday Evening Post, Cosmopolitan, McCall's*, live off their advertising, whereas any minor magazine *like Analog*, or *Galaxy*, or *Amazing* must live off its sales, Now, magazine advertising—*in magazines that have not gone out of business entirely*—is booming, in spite of television. But public taste in magazines is changing: all-fiction magazines are going out; "men's"

tried to get the November *Fantastic Universe*, which has not been put on sale in Pittsburgh, in New York last weekend, and couldn't find it in any of the large newsstands. Larry Shaw recommended the stands near the New York Public Library, but they are no longer open on Sunday and they close early on Saturday nights. In Pittsburgh, copies of an issue of *F&SF* have been returned for credit (the logo-types, that is) the day they were received, with no attempt to distribute them at all. I believe the same thing happened to the last three issues of *Super-Science*.

Publishers can keep beating on distributors when this state of affairs is called to their attention. I pass the word on when I can. But I've given up with Ray Palmer's stuff, and I failed on *Super-Science* because nobody knew whether it was still being published. Most science fiction readers don't care about other magazines as long as they get their one favorite, so who tells the publisher? Nobody.

d. *Mathematics*. No science fiction magazine prints enough copies so that each issue can be placed on sale in every community in these United States, let alone every drug store and newsstand.

Let's round off the population at 170 million and the print order of *Astounding* at 85,000 copies a month. This means *one magazine for every 2,000 people*. The Pittsburgh area has about a million people, and was sent 500 copies of the *F&SF* issue that Triangle News never distributed, so my approximation is fairly close. Since mighty few distributors—even the old noble, community spirited kind who don't exist—can afford to lug one copy to every hamlet of 2,000 people, they send 'em out a few here and a few there, and skip other outlets entirely. Fifteen years ago, when things were good, an Albany distributor told me that when he got only a few copies of any magazine, he dumped them all in one place, in Albany, and never took any to other outlets there or in surrounding towns in his territory. The bookkeeping was easier that way...

3) *How do we fix it?*

I dunno, or I'd have been peddling my program long ago.

It still seems to me that the distributor is the key—if there is a key. If the safe door isn't welded shut.

As long as he can make as much money by not selling magazines, or by selling only a few magazines and leaving the rest on the railroad siding (no trucking costs; no time spent opening cartons and counting copies; no bookkeeping; no pickups to make; neighborhood deliveries once or twice a week), he is going to do so.

I suspect that if it were not for the fact that he has to distribute the big national weeklies—principally *Life* and *Time* (I discovered that the *Post* no longer matters, you recall)—the distributor would take out other magazines all together, one day a month. One truck and one driver could cover the territory in rotation. Sludgeville gets *Astounding* on the first Monday, and Benson Cen-

and scandal magazines are coming in to replace them as non-TV entertainment. So are hobby magazines of many kinds.

The next point comes from Robert Lowndes, editor of the probably deceased *Future* and *Science Fiction,* and I believe of the Avalon books. It is amplified and underlined in various degrees by Horace Gold of *Galaxy* and John Carnell of the British magazines.

Any magazine has two kinds of readers: the steady readers, and the new readers—and there are never enough steady readers to support the magazine. One common comment is that the most critical science fiction fans no longer read the magazines they criticize. Horace Gold says the turnover of new readers takes place in about five years; Sidney Coleman makes it two years. A friend of mine, Francis Beck, some years ago did some record keeping on active membership in hobby organizations, and carne out with four years.

Whether *Analog* or any other science fiction magazine keeps its dribble of regular readers doesn't really matter in keeping it solvent: it must have a continual influx of new readers to match the inevitable loss. And here the arguments as to quantity and quality do both come to focus, and comments in "Who Killed?" take on meaning.

As to quantity: the reading public is swinging away from

reading fiction for entertainment, to television, to the paperback books, to participant sports such as bowling or spectator sports like baseball and football. Cities like Pittsburgh build a multimillion-dollar arena because it can be kept filled with sports events, but they starve the public library. Science fiction isn't the only sufferer: other pulp magazines went first—and how long is it since the balcony of your downtown movie was open?

Distribution is bad, and getting worse. Ted Carnell reports that this is a worldwide problem, though seemingly worse here than in Britain or Europe. You can't pick up new readers for science fiction if they can't pick up science fiction magazines on the newsstands—and get them there consistently, every issue.

Several contributors argue that bad science fiction, especially in the monster movies, TV, and during the "boom" days of the magazines, is giving the whole field a bad name. Old ladies made a department-store rental library, which I use, get rid of its adult science fiction because "that stuff isn't fit for children!"—for whom, of course, it was never intended. Andre Norton reports a reaction against the flood of poor juvenile science fiction reaching libraries, Would that it were all as good as hers, Robert Heinlein's and some others!

ter doesn't get it until the last Friday. (Quite a few years ago, I once found the August issue of *Blue Book* in a country drug store before the July issue had gone on sale in Albany and Schenectady.)

A couple of years ago, when I was doing an article on the *Time-Life* printing lab for my company magazine, they refused to let me use pictures showing my company's equipment in their lab, though they had plenty of it. The reason: "New York says we're in the business of selling advertising—not publishing." They had turned Alcoa down the week before, for the same reason.

If the big national consumer advertisers decide to pull out of the magazines, there will be no magazines. When that happens, there will be no distribution, no outlets, no magazine stands. *All* magazines will be like the present literary quarterlies and specialty magazines, sold as a service in bookstores which have to get them direct from the publisher.

And will there be any science fiction magazines then?

If magazines as such don't collapse, then there must be some way of blackmailing distributors into selling the magazines they contract to distribute. I don't know what it is, but until two years ago, Ray Palmer and Bill Crawford could get stacks of their poorest stuff on every corner rack, when you had to hunt all over town for *Astounding* and *Galaxy* and *F&SF*. How did they do it? Why can I now find stacks of *If*, but no *Galaxy*? *Future* everywhere, but no *Original SF*? The

October *Fantastic Universe* rather well circulated—on the day the November issue went on sale in New York?

4) *Is the paperback the answer?*
I am coming around to the idea that it may replace both magazines and hardcover books in the United States. For some strange reason, people will pick up a paperback who wouldn't be seen with a magazine—or a "real" book. With a few exceptions, the winners in my *Astounding* popularity poll, a few years ago, were all books that had come out in paperback editions—because the fans who sent in lists hadn't read any other kind. Right now, I suspect that only a serial or a paperback stands a chance of winning a Hugo. A hardcover original just won't be read by enough people in the year it's published; the fans wait for the paperback edition, or for the remainders.

Since science fiction is at present well represented in the paperback field, I think this may be—as you put it—the "point of salvation." What were once serials can appear as paperback novels—and as better novels, since there is no need for the artificial installment structure. Original anthologies like Ballantine's *Star* series may replace short stories.

5) *We're being integrated.*
There is one other factor in the picture—or so I said in the column I sent to Campbell last month—which affects hardbound books, and may affect paperbacks, though it doesn't now seem as important as it once did in magazines.

Another quote from Mr. Rosten's article belongs here: "Intellectuals tend to judge the highbrow by its peaks and non-highbrow by its average. If we look at the peaks in both cases, how much do the mass media suffer by comparison?"

F.M. Busby, who will probably chair the 1961 World Science Fiction Convention in Seattle, seconds this with the opinion that a new reader, going over the output of the "great" days of 1946 and that of 1959 would consider more of the 1959 stories really good, Theodore Sturgeon once attacked it from the other side with what has become known as Sturgeon's Law: "Ninety per cent of *everything* is crud." The remaining ten per cent is what we call "good" and ten per cent of that—one story in a hundred—is "really good."

"Doc" Lowndes makes an important point along these lines: "Good competition helps a magazine, while bad competition *injures* it. A good competitor will leave a reader in a friendly frame of mind toward the field...bad competition drives him away; he won't look at any science fiction magazine again." This is where the unutterably bad movies hurt the good magazines, too. The *general level* of science fiction must be good to a *general* reader.

John Campbell, for all his satisfaction with the state of the art as represented in this magazine, would be the last to say that he gets enough good stories. "Who Killed?" goes into reasons for this. Basically, the reason is economical: the best writers can make much more in other fields—so they do. *ASF* is the best paying market in the field, so it gets the best but it would delight in getting still better.

Here Isaac Asimov contributes the paradoxical point that the top science fiction editors have been too good for their own good. They set standards of writing quality much higher than the standards of the other pulps and most "slick" magazines, and they spotted their best writers and held them to those standards until they were too good for science fiction. John Campbell stands out here, but all the good editors have done it.

There are some pretty bitter attacks on "literary" science fiction in "Who Killed?" Poul Anderson, Marion Zimmer Bradley—who has about the best-balanced response in the whole symposium—Dr. E. E. Smith, James E. Gunn, Frank Kelley Freas are a few who have at the point. I belabored it myself in 1955 at the Cleveland convention, under a literarily obscure tide. The point is simply that so long as we judge "good" science fiction by the presence of private jokes, verbal games, *avant garde* style, personal conceits, and incomprehensible stereotypes,

Science fiction deliberately segregated itself in 1926, with the first issue of *Amazing*. Hugo Gernsback began to preach a new religion, and in 1926 he built himself a church to preach in. We happily piled into a literary ghetto around the church. We were chosen; we were different; we were elite; we didn't want to be the same as other people. And we didn't want them mucking around with our science fiction, when they didn't know what it was all about.

So science fiction left the general field of popular fiction, where it had flourished in the Munsey era, and became a movement. It became ingrown. It developed its own code of ethics...its own stereotypes (spacewarps; BEMs; time travel; gimmicks)...its own language...its own inner hierarchy (the sectors of fandom)...gospels (fanzines)...heresies (Shaver; Dianetics; psi)...pilgrimages (conventions). Stories were full of private jokes, and allusions that only the elite could follow.

We deliberately froze out new readers: neo-fans, who just wanted something different in a good story. We did mighty little missionary work or proselytizing. *We didn't want outsiders.*

Now—as it must to any minority—comes discrimination from the people we kept outside. They have misconceptions about us, and about science fiction. They won't buy our baskets and wood carving, that we set outside the ghetto gate for tourists. They pay better wages to their own kind, and they may not hire us at all. From being a smug, contented, self-segregated minority, we've become an oppressed minority. Our talented young people get out…try to pass as ordinary writers and artists. Some of them come home on vacation visits, but they feel uncomfortable in the old environment. They're becoming outsiders themselves. They can't understand what the beatniks of the new generation are talking about.

So much for analogy. It seems to me that science fiction is again becoming integrated into the main stream of fiction. More and more writers *from outside*, with no special background in science fiction, are selling novels on science fiction themes—some good, some quite crude and clumsy by our standards. Science fiction elements are getting back into mystery plots; experienced novelists are having fun with fantasy. So, if the magazines do die, it may not matter. Science fiction may be back where it used to be in the days of Burroughs and Merritt and John Taine and many another: a minor part of fiction, that good writers aren't ashamed to write, and major publishers aren't ashamed to sell. (Mez Bradley said a while back, in *Yandro*, that this is the future of good science fiction movies: they'll just be good movies, with no label attached.)

And for my money, if science fiction can restore to popular fiction some of the elements of storytelling and imagination and idea—juggling that have been missing for a long time, it may save reading as a part of American culture.

then good science fiction offers nothing to a new reader, and because of its special content offers nothing to an intellectual from some other field.

To put it differently: if we select our standards of excellence to suit the "little" literary magazines, then we should be satisfied to have science fiction magazines with. the negligible, often subsidized circulation of a "little" magazine.

I think it was Damon Knight who coined the phrase, "a high level of mediocrity." Looking at "Who Killed?" I find a pretty general agreement that editors would be selling more magazines—if anyone can sell more magazines—by concentrating on this rising mediocrity. This means fewer "far out" themes and ideas except in stories by the most competent writers. It means more adventure, more color, more story-telling by gifted story-tellers. It means more Murray Leinster perhaps, and Poul Anderson, and Leigh Brackett, and Edmond Hamilton, and E.E. Smith, and Eric Frank Russell—whose very pertinent comments I've completely passed over here. It may mean looking for and finding another Edgar Rice Burroughs with that extra edge of quality that we've come to expect.

Above this high level of

mediocrity, which starts attracting youngsters and oldsters who are fed up with television and paperback sex-and-sadism, the best writers will contribute those peaks that Leo Rosten described. There won't be any more of them than there ever were, but they'll stand out more. A plateau is a hellish place to hike: you can't see where you are or where you're going, or where you want to go, especially if it's all cluttered up with beautiful shrubs and trees—of literary style and self-parody, for example—that distract your attention and start you wandering in circles, Add a few peaks, though, and you can see where you're going; you have a goal—and beyond the first peak another one. They are guides to the tenderfoot and landmarks to the experienced traveler. From them, or part-way up them, the dull plateau suddenly seems to have structure and sense.

And, lest I seem to have allowed the editors to go scott-free in a symposium in which they are actually under constant fire, with and without reason, let's make one last point: it is their job to build those peaks if they can't find one ready made, by training new writers if the old ones are no longer available, and to keep enough of the brush cleared off the high plateau so that the tourists can see the stars.

– P. Schuyler Miller,
Analog Science Fact & Fiction, December 1960

Text courtesy John Boston Collection. Cover scan courtesy Jacques Hamon Collection
http://www.noosfere.com/showcase/

MILLS, ROBERT P.

1) No, I do not feel that magazine science fiction is dead. In terms of *F&SF*, at least, I believe that there is a solid—though not enormous—body of readers who are steadily interested in imaginative, reasonably literate short fiction. I believe that there are many more readers who would enjoy that sort of fiction if they knew about it—and who will sooner or later find out about it. I wish the number were larger; I suspect it is not, for two major, and a number of minor, reasons: The major reasons:

(a) "Science fiction" connotes cheap pulp to almost everybody I know who does not read it. Unfortunately, there is some reason for this reputation—an unfortunate percentage of the writing in the field is undeniably bad.

(b) There is not enough fresh, good writing in the field. A fair amount of competent reworking of old themes, a much too large amount of incompetent reworking of old themes and working out of ridiculous themes, and virtually no stimulating new concepts worked out with inspiration or high skill.

However, despite the regrettably small percentage, some good stories are being written, and I suspect that their numbers will increase.

It is true of all forms of literature that rich periods are followed by slack periods, and slack periods by rich periods. It is unreasonable to expect talent to flow in a steady stream as water does from a faucet.

4) Original paperbacks are good for the field, I think, because they offer a source of income within the field to writers who do not wish to go outside the field, but at the same time must earn more money than they presently can from science fiction magazines.

5) These remarks take off in general from *F&SF*'s editorial approach to the field, because that is the approach with which I am most familiar. I should think, however, that the problems and prospects of most other magazines in the field are essentially very much the same.

NORTON, ANDRÉ

[signature: André Norton]

Since my own sales, orders from publishers, etc., have increased very much during the past two years, I am not a very good judge of the "death" of science fiction. However, I do write for a specialized group in which there is not too much competition, so I cannot take my own experiences as a measuring stick. I do feel that my field—that of teenage science fiction—was badly hit by very poor editorial selection of books which happened in a rush about four or five years ago. Librarians who admittedly knew little of the field bought heavily of this poor stuff and now fight shy of the whole genre, not being able to tell one type of book from another.

I cannot judge about the magazines. Myself, I read *Astounding* with a lot of pleasure, *Galaxy* with not so much enjoyment, and *The Magazine of Fantasy and Science Fiction* third. I dropped my subscription to two others due to the poor quality of the stories—the "lunatic fringe" articles about flying saucers, etc.

The original paperback is good—I know from my own fan mail that many of my books first fall, as originals or paperback reprints, into the hands of readers who will not, or do not buy the more expensive trade editions. To my mind, the wider spread the circle of readers the better, and the level of paperbacks is higher than the corresponding issues in historical adventure or mystery. A lot of good writing can be found in the paperbacks.

It is my opinion that the group of the faithful will always be limited. In the first place, I am told over and over again by librarians and teachers that the younger readers of science fiction are all in the upper IQ group and that they are impatient with sloppy writing. Those readers call for more stuff, but it must fit their standards and not be a cheap superman or monsters-from-Mars type. Since these younger readers are of superior ability, it must also be true that when they collect or read adult material, they are still of the better-educated, imaginative, wide-read crowd, and you must produce quality for them. The number of readers may long be limited to the same group, and since they are well grounded in the basic story plots, etc., the authors will have to produce better than potboilers to hold them.

Sorry that I cannot offer you better than this. But I only know how my own small field is affected.

O'MEARA, JAMES H.

James H. O'Meara

1) I feel that magazine science fiction is dying. It will be a slow, lingering death—but death will come eventually. Very soon the only place where you will be able to get competent science fiction of any sort will be in the men's magazines. The rates they pay will be the only place that writers can go in order to earn a living.

2) I feel that Campbell influenced the field to a great extent. He influences it because most of the writers slant their stories for him since he pays the best rates within the field. If they do not sell to *Astounding*, they are placed with lower-paying magazines.

3) I don't know of anything that can be done to correct the decline in the magazine field. There is a tremendous demand for science fiction, but for some reason it does not carry into the magazine field. Even better distribution of the magazines would not help. The demand for science fiction magazines is just not there.

4) I think the original paperback is in a much better position in the field. It is not that they get better distribution. I think it is because readers, for some reason, would rather buy a paperback than a magazine.

5) When I was in high school, science fiction had always been the most popular fiction form in the school library. It is a Catholic high school for boys and has about 1,200 students. It is a new school and I was in the second class to be graduated from it. The library was opened in my junior year and gave me an opportunity to see the development of it from the beginning. When the library opened, it had 19 books under the science fiction classification. The demand for science fiction, even from the first day the library was opened, was so great that two years later there were 57 titles in the science fiction classification.

The demand for science fiction was so great that it was the most popular type of fiction during the two years that I used the library.

When I returned for a visit to my school after almost four years, I stopped in at the library and checked to see if there had been any change in the reading habits of the students. The card catalogue which I checked had 87 titles under the science fiction heading. I asked the librarian about the popularity of science fiction and she told me that it is the most popular type of fiction in the library and that at least a third of the students read it. Admittedly, most of the books in the library are juveniles, but there are at least 20 good adult science fiction books and the Heinlein juveniles are so popular that there are three copies of each and they are almost worn out from heavy use.

The thing that is so hard to understand is this: If science fiction is so popular, why don't the magazines sell? It can't be only money, because when I was in school the students who were interested in science fiction always had paperbacks but they never had magazines. Even magazines designed for the younger readers were never seen. The students interested in science fiction seemed to get what they wanted from the library and paperbacks.

There is a great potential market for science fiction here but these younger readers just don't seem to be interested in magazines, and after they graduate they seem to be less interested in science fiction. If there was some way to keep these younger readers interested in science fiction after they graduate and go out into jobs or the army, it would help the whole field, by providing replacements for the older readers whose periodic rotation take them away. The interest of these younger readers seems to die after they get out of high school, and their connection with the field, if any, is that they occasionally pick up a paperback.

I feel that there will always be a demand for hardcover books for the libraries and that the paperbacks will continue to do well, but the magazines will slowly die out. The demand for juvenile science fiction, especially, will continue to be great and the paperbacks can count on a large readership from those people who are still mildly interested in science fiction.

PALMER, RAYMOND A.

1) Yes, I feel that magazine science fiction is dead.

2) No, I do not feel that any single person, action, incident, etc., is responsible. Actual events today are more amazing. Also a reaction to "fiction" is very violent in *all* fields, but particularly science fiction.

4) Looking to original paperbacks, and books, for fans is the only answer—and there *will* be a market.

5) *Why* doesn't *Fandom*—(next convention) take up the subject of forming a book club of their own, publish and buy their own selection of science fiction book manuscripts, and use the profits to finance future conventions? Two thousand members who agree to buy four books a year at $3.50 can thus salvage all *good* science fiction written today! Count on me as a life member!

PALMER, RODNEY

[See item under Starrett, Vincent.-E.K.]

[In response to the mention by Vincent Starrett in the *Chicago Tribune Magazine of Books*, I received three replies. One was a pamphlet; the most repulsive, stupid, asinine tract that I have ever witnessed. Another was simply a kind soul who mailed me the clipping from their paper without comment, and this was appreciated. The third, a serious reply to a serious query, is the following by Rodney Palmer. As far as I have been able to determine, Mr. Palmer, a Chicagoan, has no professional connection with the field of science fiction, and has never made contact with Chicago fandom. As a complete outside-the-field view, Mr. Palmer's reply certainly deserves our undivided attention. It must be remembered that Mr. Palmer is not writing in direct response to the questionnaire, and is not covering the specific five points.—E.K.]

This is a subject upon which I've done quite a bit of thinking and wondering myself. I don't believe science fiction is dead, but it's been knocked around quite a bit. We still have Robert Sheckley, Poul Anderson, Fred Pohl— though I take the liberty of presuming that Sheckley is in a class by himself. The field that it might be said Ray Bradbury abandoned, he took up with a vengeance, because somebody, somewhere, likes science fiction and won't let the field starve for good reading.

Here's my position: My father read science fiction—the big flat *Amazing*s, and occasional *Astounding*, maybe *Weird Tales*. Mostly I associate my interest with the pulp-adventure science fiction era—the very good early *Amazing*s under Ray Palmer, *Startling, Thrilling Wonder, Captain Future*.

I could never dig *Astounding* in the Street & Smith era, and I can't dig it today.

I think science fiction ought to possess sentiment. Somebody once said that sentiment was the soul of art, but don't quote me. I'm not sure. I do know that most of the stories I liked impressed me with the grandeur of the subject—one felt depths of distance, space, majestic worlds.

I think that, disastrously, science fiction started to take itself too seriously. No humor. When was the last time you read a really funny science fiction story? "Pete Manx?" Some of the humorous time-travel paradoxes, the robot stories? Sure, some science fiction was zany. But it was just three or four thousand words of comedy relief at the back of the book. I vote for some pseudo-science once in a while. Why not, if a good story emerges?

Sentiment: Sentimental about the future, as we sometimes are of the past. "Lost Planet" by Barry Storm, in *Thrilling Wonder*, embodies the idea I'm trying to get at. Sentiment, not mush.

And so what if the manly virtues are exaggerated a bit in a science fiction story? Exaggeration—pulp action style—can isolate a point and put it over.

I would say sentiment, action, comedy relief in its place, a scientific gimmick with emphasis on weird results rather than technical causes. The slant ought to be exaggerated-masculine-virtuous with disdain for the boudoir; adventure, roughhouse, the call to far worlds.

A prop of early science fiction was the older man—usually a scientist—who was usually a friend of the hero, and who often fought right beside him, rayguns blasting and all.

PRICE, GEORGE W.

George W Price

1) No, it is not dead, yet, though it has certainly declined. There are still nine magazines, which is the same as when I started reading science fiction in 1947. But the magazines now seem to lack the health and enthusiasm which they had then. It is not yet possible to say whether the magazines will continue to decline down to ultimate death, or whether they can stabilize on a lower level.

2) I do not blame any single person for this decline. I believe that the largest single cause—though by no means the only cause—is the attempt to make science fiction into "literature." It is hard to set a date, but about 1948 there began to arise delusions of "maturity" and "social significance."

Authors and editors had been content to write and publish material frankly aimed at various levels of intellect and scientific interest, ranging from the highly cerebral stories of *Astounding* to the wild adventure of *Planet*. No one, least of all the editors of *Planet*, claimed that it was great literature; it was just fun to read. Of course, I do not claim that everything published in those days was good; much of it was crud, in obedience to Sturgeon's Law ("Ninety percent of *everything* is crud"). But science fiction compared well with other fields of writing.

Then standard book publishers discovered science fiction. It was at once noticed that the stories selected for anthologization were very predominately from *Astounding*. The obvious, if erroneous, conclusion was drawn that—only *ASF*-type stories are "good." That, I think, was the first turning point. A trend began toward copying *ASF*. *Galaxy* was started as a shamelessly exact replica of *Astounding*.

Within about two years, *Galaxy* introduced, or at least made explicit, the second tendency which has contributed to our downfall. This was the emphasis on "literacy," in the very snobbish sense. Here came the concentration on slick writing and "character development" at the expense of the science-fictional qualities.

Apparently we have forgotten what science fiction is; we have allowed, and even encouraged, a blurring of the distinction between science fiction and mainstream. We have fallen under the delusion that "good" writing must devote itself to "character development," to which the scientific and futuristic elements must defer. It is perfectly true that in mainstream fiction the world of society and technology serves merely as a backdrop against which the study of human character proceeds. In this sense, the best mainstream fiction is timeless. In science fiction, on the other hand, it is the future world of society and technology that is the primary subject, and the development of individual character is—or at least should be—distinctly secondary. In contradistinction to mainstream, in science fiction the development of character has point only insofar as it demonstrates the nature of the future society and its technology, by showing how these affect and shape various personalities. To be sure, there can be no sharp dividing line between science fiction in the sense I have outlined, and mainstream. Stories dealing with sociology or psychology, for instance, can hardly avoid character analysis, nor should it be avoided, so long as it arises naturally from the speculative ideas which are the science-fictional bases of the stories. But let us bear in mind that science fiction is not just "mainstream laid in the future."

Above, I attributed the decline of science fiction partially to 1) copying *Astounding*, and 2) the delusion of "maturity." Now, it is not that the *ASF*-type story is bad (personally, it's my favorite), or that maturity is wrong per se. But these elements have been pushed to the exclusion of all others, such as the afore-mentioned adventure stories of the *Planet* variety, until the latter have virtually disappeared. This has been hailed as the "coming of age" of science fiction.

The difficulty is that there are really very few good *ASF*-type stories or truly mature stories being written. The result has been a tremendous out-pouring of bad imitations.

There are enough good, thoughtful stories being produced to supply per-haps three monthly magazines. *Astounding* (or should we now say *Analog*?) and *Fantasy and Science Fiction* make two, and there is no third, the remain-ing good, thoughtful stories being distributed more or less evenly through the other seven magazines. Those seven, consequently, assay very high in crud. Most of them, most of the time, read as if they subsisted on Campbell's and Mills' rejects. (*Galaxy* is now a special case. *Sui generis*; it is not only full of pseudomaturity and overslick writing, it also tries to be *cute*.)

I hesitate to make statements as to what other people think, but I strongly suspect that by choosing this path of pseudomaturity, we have cut off a large number of prospective readers. The new reader, no matter what magazine he samples, will find pretty much the same kind of story; and by the sheer statistics of it, the stories will probably be bad. If the *ASF-F&SF* type stories do not appeal to him—assuming that he sticks long enough to read the *good* examples—then he is repelled from science fiction.

If we had a few magazines publishing good adventure stories, they would, I suggest, first bring in many readers who are not attracted by the more thoughtful stories. Second, they would be an introduction to the field for those, especially youngsters, who as they mature will find an appetite for more cerebral material.

It is to the discredit of fandom that it actively denigrated and derided the unthoughtful adventure fiction, without bothering to draw the necessary distinction between good and bad adventure stories. To qualify as good, an adventure story should be entertaining in its plot, readable in its writing, and reasonably accurate in such science as it may mention. It is pointless to denounce stories for not having deep character study, brilliant speculation, or cosmic significance, if they were not intended to be more than passing entertainment for relaxed moments.

For examples of what I consider top-notch adventure science fiction, I nominate the series of "Galactic Barbarian" stories that Poul Anderson did for *Planet* from about 1948 to 1952. Anderson's tales particularly appealed to me because they proved that it is possible to have action without stupidity, sex without pornography or psychosis, and conflict without sadism. Well, there is only one Poul Anderson, and perhaps it would be too much to expect that other authors could write adventure up to his standard. But surely there must be any number who could write passably good adventure stories, where now they write poor *ASF-F&SF* type stories, and probably heave a sigh of relief for being able to make the change.

To sum up my view of what has caused the decline of science fiction: There has been a disastrous drive to puff science fiction up to the status of great literature, with the result that we have suffered a deluge of pseudomature garbage, while the less complex adventure stories which should be the ballasting bulk of science fiction have been grossly neglected and even scorned.

3) My recommendations for corrective measures are obvious from the preceding comments. The editors—and the critics, including organized fandom—should realize that there will never be much good thoughtful science fiction written, and the magazines should therefore be filled out with good adventure stories rather than with pretentious half-literate balderdash. As readers and critics, we should be careful to keep our criticism appropriate to the type of story. That is, it is not legitimate to lambaste a simple adventure story for being a simple adventure story; it should be criticized in terms of whether it is a *good* or *bad* adventure story.

4) The paperbacks have certain commercial advantages over the magazines, notably better distribution and a prolonged on-sale time. Therefore, it seems quite probable that novels will appear more and more as original paperbacks. Even now, *Astounding* is the only magazine that runs serials regularly. I see no reason why there should not be peaceful coexistence between the paperbacks and the magazines, with the former carrying the novels and the latter handling everything of less than novel length. If the magazines finally go under, I believe that it will be due to their own shortcomings, as already discussed, rather than paperback competition. I doubt if the disappearance of the magazines would lead to a corresponding increase in paperbacks carrying short stories. Rather, the market for shorter works will simply contract, and possibly vanish. Should this prove to be the case, the paperbacks could be called at best only a partial salvation. I think we can be reasonably sure that science fiction novels will continue to appear indefinitely, but the outlook for short stories is very uncertain. I am reminded that, prior to the advent of the science fiction magazines, nearly all imaginative fiction was in novel length, for original book publication.

5) There have been a few recent signs of increasing health in the field, in terms of story value, if not economically. First, I think that *Amazing* has shown a commendable improvement since adopting the policy of a novel in each issue. Almost all of these novels have been at least passable, and a few have been quite good. Second, the publication of Heinlein's *Starship Soldier* marks a healthy step into controversy. However, it is far too early to claim that we are due for a renaissance, or even a revival.

REYNOLDS, MACK

1) No, I do not feel that magazine science fiction is dead. Sick, but not dead.

2) Certainly no person, or even combination of persons is responsible for the present situation. I think our main difficulty has been a lack of ability to keep up with developing times. I know I'm being far from original in pointing out that it became necessary to seek new themes when our former ones moved out of our magazines onto the front pages. If we are to regain as our readers those persons with imagination, we must deal with other than the old saws that we have been writing and rewriting for so long.

3) The question then, of course, becomes what themes? I am of the opinion that this decade is going to be one of the most decisive ones that man has ever seen. And I believe that people of imagination will be increasingly caught up in the social changes the decade will see. I think then that at least one of our new themes should be the social sciences which, along with sex and humor, have been all but undealt with in science fiction. I know, the cry goes up, "But the science fiction reader is not interested in social sciences!" And it makes me laugh. Probably the biggest science fiction bestseller ever to hit America was Ralph Bellamy's *Looking Backward*. At least one of Jack London's bestsellers, *The Iron Heel* was science fiction. George Orwell's *1984* and Aldous Huxley's *Brave New World* are more recent examples. James Hilton's *Lost Horizon** is also a recent modern example. These were all *top* bestsellers. And they all dealt with socioeconomic questions.

Frankly, and I'm speaking now as a reader, I'm getting sick and tired of reading stories based 10,000 years in the future where all the sciences have progressed fabulously except for one. In *The Weapon Shops* stories what is the form of government? Feudalism. In the *Foundation* stories, what kind of socioeconomic system prevails? Feudalism. Hell, far from evolving new societies, they don't even have capitalism; they've gone backward.

I don't believe I am alone, as a science fiction reader, in being fascinated with what is going on in the world and what will de-

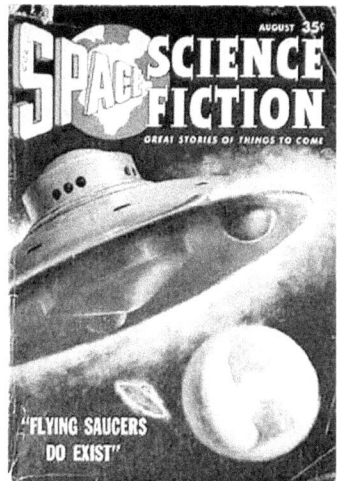

---

*Insignificant fact for the day: James Hilton's *Lost Horizon* appeared in paperback as book number 1, the first title ever published by Pocket Books, Inc.—E.K.

velop in the next comparatively few years. I'd like to see some stories based on the current battle for men's minds. I'd like to see some stories based on anarchism, technocracy, socialism, industrial feudalism, syndicalism, and communism (both the pseudo and real varieties). On an adult basis, of course, we've had enough of the good guys and bad guys crud.

4) No opinion, but I'm anxious to read those of others.

5) None.

RUSSELL, ERIC FRANK,

1) No, I do not think that magazine science fiction is dead. The demand fluctuates, always has done and will continue to do so. It has its ups and downs. Every time there's an up the excitable call it a "boom" and every time there's a down the gloomy-minded view it as a "collapse." I'm now old enough and ugly enough to have become philosophical about such things and to accept it as inevitable that changes must occur as time rolls on and that, on the whole, adverse changes are counterbalanced by beneficial ones.

2) No. I don't see anything genuinely abnormal about the present situation. Tough problems exist—but tough problems always have existed. Thirty years ago the big problem was that of building an economically satisfactory readership for stuff then generally regarded as "ridiculous." Today, the big problem is that of how to retain at one and the same time readers 30 years apart in taste and outlook. It isn't easy and it won't get any easier.

3) What can we do to correct it? Nothing that is not being done already. Given that they are in their right minds, publishers, authors, and editors do the best they can, because it pays them to do so. But the readership has the final say; if anyone's best isn't good enough for them, they cease to buy it. To that there is no answer for the obvious reason that nobody can do more than his best. So the inefficient magazine folds up and the efficient one keeps going. By "efficient" I mean the magazine that succeeds in pleasing the largest proportion of its readers most of the time.

4) Should we look to the original paperback as a point of salvation? I think the influence of paperbacks is, if anything, beneficial insofar as they tend to introduce a bigger readership to science fiction. But since such paperbacks are bought mostly by readers who are already science fiction addicts, the percentage of gain isn't large. On the whole, I don't think paper-

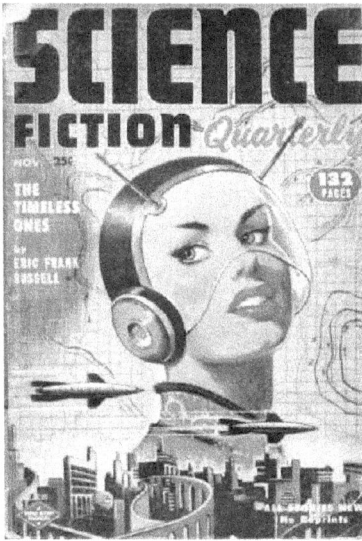

backs have much influence on science fiction magazine sales and what influence they do have is to the good. Further, I consider them complementary to magazines but not a substitute for them. In any single issue a magazine has something a paperback lacks, namely, variety. Readers who want variety—which plenty do—buy magazines, either instead of or in addition to the paperbacks.

5) In the long, long ago the science fiction magazines catered for a readership 95% of whom were in the fifteen- to 25-year-old age group. Today, the range stretches from twelve to 55 years—with a tiny minority of old-timers actually in their sixties. The youngsters enjoy and regard as "new" various ideas, themes, and plots that the oldsters consider to be old hat, worn to death years ago. They also regard as "silly" and "farfetched" themes that oldsters consider "refreshing" and "thought-provoking"—psionic plots, for example. Further to complicate matters, it is natural for young people to want action (as in space operas) and equally natural for oldsters to be more interested in thoughtful themes based on human problems. Worse still, it's natural for young readers to be intensely vocal about their likes and dislikes while older ones say little and content themselves with buying or ceasing to buy. The unfortunate editor who seeks reactions from his readership is therefore likely to get a distorted view from a vocal minority and, if he falls into the trap of trying to cater for it, will do so at the risk of losing the readers who don't bother to speak up.

We're getting rapidly to the point where it is going to become well nigh impossible to cater to any one magazine for tastes so widely divergent. A magazine with a deliberate "middle-aged" policy should come off best but even that won't succeed wholly. Seems to me that as time goes on the position will sort itself out and we'll end up with some magazines aimed at and only at the young readership while others are slanted at and only at the older ones. Each of these two types may have a minor overlap with the other, gained from elderly readers still young in mind and from young readers old beyond their years, but, on the whole, they'll be quite different kinds of magazines aimed at quite different kinds of mentalities.

In other words, the entire science fiction field is splitting in two and the $64 question is whether either portion is large enough by itself to maintain a magazine by its own strength alone. There comes a point—say, for argument's sake, a circulation figure of 40,000 per month—below which it

Afterthoughts....

Got to hand it to you—you certainly made a real topnotch job of *Who Killed Science Fiction?* Most interesting thing I've read for a long, long time. I've spent a week seeking a word adequate to describe it and the best I can get is the French expression: *Formidable!* It's nice to learn what other writers are thinking and why they're thinking it—especially for one like me who is so far from the main bunch and hasn't been in on a gab-fest for years. True, having listened to the lot of them I'm no wiser about the basic problem than I was at the beginning, but the listening has been fun...A feature that struck me in particular was the way in which many contributors reached in precisely the manner that one would expect from their pro-writings. Derleth was obviously Derleth, Asimov unmistakably Asimov, deCamp typically deCamp and P.S. Miller recognizably P.S. Miller. This individuality was emphasized by Gen. Kemp, so to speak, assembling them on parade. It proves, I think, that a man's writings are in fact "little pieces of himself."...The general opinion, or the majority opinion in the symposium seems to be agreed on four points: (1) There's a bad smell coming from somewhere, (2) Everyone thinks the guy with the most innocent face did it, (3) It's been there for years and (4) It's likely to remain. Not very enlightening. But what the hell, a good book can be enjoyable and therefore justifiable while adding little to the reader's wisdom.... By the time you get this you may still be prostrate with exhaustion. If so, it may help to be told by one reader that the effort was worthwhile. I congratulate you on it—and thanks a million!

– Eric Frank Russell, May 1960

just isn't a business proposition to publish a magazine. I've no opinion about whether a magazine is likely to get by in such circumstances; it's something that remains to be seen.

As for authors, assuming that each and every one of them is doing his genuine best to provide entertainment the best way he knows how, I cannot see how they can do any more. The writer not doing his best will pay for it eventually by killing his own market stone dead. On every writer's lap there sits an unwelcome ghost named Nemesis.

RUSSELL, RAY

Let me preface my remarks by saying that even though I have written some science fiction and have, as an editor, published some, I have not written or edited enough of it to consider myself anywhere near an authority. I am, however, a fan.

You ask, first of all, if I think magazine science fiction is dead. I do believe that a fiction in the specialized science fiction magazines, which heretofore has been excellent, has been on the decline. These magazines, which were paying not bad money in the boom years, are paying very little money now; hence, writers are either sending their stories to the slicks, writing hurriedly and badly and in volume in order to keep alive at the low rates, or they are abandoning science fiction altogether and are going to mystery, detective, and so on. I base this knowledge on personal observation and on talks I have had with writers.

I have always felt that the big circulation slick magazines should publish much more science fiction than they do. At one time, magazines like *Collier's* would publish an occasional science fiction story. *Collier's* is now dead, and with the single exception of *Playboy*, I can not offhand think of any slick magazine that is receptive to this genre. Even some of the *Playboy* imitators, though they imitate *Playboy* in many ways, do not publish science fiction. A man who was an editor on one such magazine told me that it was a policy of the magazine to reject science fiction because "it might alienate the older readers" (!). But *Playboy*, if I may toot our own horn a bit, has always been receptive to science fiction and always will be. I don't know if you saw a recent issue of Ted Cogswell's *Publications of the Institute of Twenty-First Century Studies* in which I made some comment about *Playboy*'s attitude toward science fiction. Here is a copy of the pertinent quote:

As a matter of fact, purely by accident, the last two stories to cop our Bonus were in the science-fantasy field: Richard Matheson's "The Distributor" and George Langelaan's "The Fly." In other words, each author received a total of $3,000 for a single story. And we pay *no lower* than $500, which is our going rate for short-shorts.

True, we can never hope to publish as much science fiction as a specialized science fiction magazine, but we do use a great deal of it: we've published plenty of Beaumont, Sheckley, Matheson, Slesar, et al., and hardly a year goes by without at least one of our science fiction or fantasy pieces ending up in an anthology. We publish a science fiction or fantasy story in almost *every* issue. The hardbound anthology, *The Permanent Playboy* (Crown, 1959), contains ten stories in this genre.

I really don't know what to say about the original paperback. I would hate to see science fiction restricted to the novel form, since, in my opinion, the best science fiction has always taken the form of the short story, with only occasionally excellent novels.

One more thought, and then I'll be through: whether or not the low rates among the specialized magazines are causing a decline in the quality of science fiction, or whether it is a decline in public interest in this genre that has forced the publishers to pay less, is a chicken-or-the-egg question and I do not feel qualified to even attempt an answer. I do think we are going through a slump of general public disinterest in science fiction, but we have all lived through such slumps before, and I am quite confident that we will come out of it, *if* science fiction writers will look to their laurels rather than rest on their laurels. By this I mean: let them not go on writing slightly new twists on the old gimmicks. Let them, rather, dare to break fresh ground in their story ideas and in their writing styles. If blame must be placed some- where, perhaps science fiction writers should not be so eager to place that blame on the reading public or on editors. Perhaps the writers themselves are to blame for allowing themselves to get into a rut. Anyway, it is something for them to think about.

SELDES, TIMOTHY

Walter Bradbury has left Doubleday and I have taken over our science fiction list which I handled with him. I am not so experienced in the field as he is, but for what it is worth, here are my answers to your questions:

1) No, I do not feel that magazine science fiction is dead.

2) I think that there was a revival of interest in science fiction after the war, and then again after Sputnik, had the literary and dramatic level of sci- ence fiction been up to it.

3) I think science fiction could have capitalized on this interest, but with very few exceptions it wasn't right for books purely as a moneymaking device.

4) Yes, we should look to the original paperback as a point of salvation, but for any book with any value at all there is no reason not to have a hard- bound edition since it will then sell in paperback, and by having the hard- bound edition, one leaves open the chances for book club and movie sales.

SHAW, LARRY T.

Larry T. Shaw

I don't think there's too much point in going into great detail about what's wrong with magazine science fiction, since there are so many obvious things wrong, but we may get somewhere by tackling the question of what can be done about it.

1) I don't think magazine science fiction is quite dead—but it is, as you said yourself, in a deplorable state. The magazines that are still alive now may all continue, though at least two of them are very shaky. However, the bulk of what they are publishing is science fiction only by the most generous definition, and what I'd really like is to see a few magazines containing stuff that satisfied me better. And, of course, most of the current crop ignore fandom almost entirely, which is bad for fandom.

To skip to question number four, I don't think the paperbacks are a point of salvation. I expect a lot of comparatively good science fiction will be published in them in the future. But I like magazines. It's as simple as that, as far as I'm concerned. A magazine is a personality, a regular part of the reader's life, and something to look forward to. For me, it fulfills a need that a book doesn't, no matter how good the book is. And, again, the books won't do much to steer people into fandom, where the magazines can, at least potentially.

2) No, I don't feel that any single person, incident, etc., is responsible for the current state of affairs. Many things are responsible. But I refuse to agree with those who feel that the *age* of science fiction is dead because of historical trends, the state of the world, etc. The distribution situation is responsible, to a great extent. The fact that other types of pulps died first is important; when a science fiction magazine could be published as part of a chain of fiction magazines, each one making a small profit, it had much more chance of surviving. Now science fiction magazines are published either by very small publishers, who *must* make money on every issue of everything they put out, or by very big outfits who aren't interested in the small profits that a science fiction magazine can bring in because they have bigger fish to fry.

I think that point is crucial and worth stressing. A science fiction magazine will never make a *big* profit. Unless the publisher is satisfied with a comparatively modest return, he won't continue to publish one. Judging by the publishers I've known, and keeping this fact in mind, we're lucky to have as many science fiction magazines as there are.

I've also come around to the view, after long and painful examination of the facts and my own conscience, that many people who appear to love science fiction—not excluding myself—have contributed to its sickness by

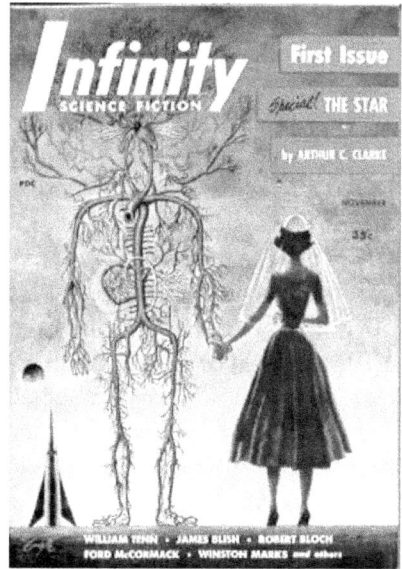

trying to make it too literate and too respectable. We've criticized the living daylights out of it in the hope of making it appeal, not to the general public, but to the *Saturday Review* type of critic. We did all we could to kick out the adventure, the plain good storytelling, and the guts. I do *not* say that all science fiction should be blood and thunder. I do say—it seems obvious as hell to me now—that when the swashbuckle went out of science fiction, it lost most of its appeal. If we have to put up with the swashbuckle (assuming we don't like it, although that certainly isn't true in many cases) for the sake of the ideas embedded therein, what's wrong with that? While science fiction obviously appeals to a limited audience, it still needs many of the qualities of good mass-appeal fiction in order to survive. We threw an awful lot of those qualities away, not because we had to but because we chose to.

And, of course, most of the good writers went somewhere else. That's natural; most writers develop new interests as they grow older, and they want to make more money as they grow more experienced. We need—and have needed for a long time—new writers. They're not easy to find; I can testify to the ridiculously low quality of today's average (or even today's best) slushpile.

And the magazines, let's face it, grew smaller and smaller. Perhaps 35 cents doesn't represent much more of an outlay to today's reader than 20 cents did to the reader of 20 years ago, but what does he get for it? Then, the magazines being fatter, he stood a good chance of finding at least one story he could enjoy in each. Today, each magazine contains a pitiful handful of stories, most of them very much alike in tone. The odds have shifted. Nowadays, you don't *gamble* your 35 cents; you donate it to charity or to a sentimental memory.

3) So, to correct the situation, we need a publisher who is willing to invest a fair chunk of dough in the hopes of a very small return. If the return is only going to be financial, in fact, we probably won't find him. If he will invest because operating a good science fiction magazine is in itself rewarding to him, we may.

We need good writers. The outsiders who think of writing science fiction as a way to make a living won't do. You can't make a living writing science fiction. At least, you can't make a living that will satisfy you for very long. You have to make your living elsewhere, and write science fiction largely for the love of it. That in turn means an editor can't just put a notice in *Writer's Digest* and sit back to wait for great manuscripts. He has to work, and work full-time, at finding good writers and good stories.

Do I think the writers and stories could be found, under favorable circumstances? Yes, I do. I'd love to try.

We need, if possible, something to offer the readers to make up for the sheer quantity we have lost. That's a tough nut to crack, but I think it could be done. A magazine can make up in personality for a lack of bulk. It's hard to make many publishers believe this, however.

Unfortunately, none of this is any good unless we can solve the distribution problem. It may not be completely true to say that any magazine will sell if all the copies printed are displayed prominently, but it's not far from the truth, either. As we all know, today's newsdealer doesn't even open a lot of the bundles he gets. Thousands and thousands of copies, representing the total potential profit in some cases, just go down the drain. The only solution I can see to that is to offer the newsdealer some tangible reward for displaying your magazine, and the only tangible reward that I think would work is money. The only way to do that is for the publisher to take a smaller profit on each copy sold. Of course, he has to find a good, established distributor who is willing to take on his product to begin with.

In short, it might be done…but only with a strictly non-greedy publisher who loved science fiction. I haven't been looking actively for such a publisher, but I'm in the middle of the publishing world and I keep my eyes open. At the moment, I see no traces of such a paragon. But I haven't given up hope yet.

To sum up: there is no reason for science fiction, per se, to die. The problems involved in keeping one or more good science fiction magazine alive and healthy are purely practical ones. Practical problems can be solved—but, brother, these are not easy ones; and finding the solutions will have to start with finding a fairly sizeable quantity of money.

SILVERBERG, ROBERT

In brief response to your questions:

1) Yes, I think magazine science fiction *is* dead—even though the corpse is still moving. There are nine magazines right now, of which only one (*Astounding*) offers any sort of attractive rate to its writers, and of which only three (*Astounding* and the Ziff-Davis mags) pay its writers promptly. A field which cannot afford to pay on acceptance, or to pay much more than a cent a word, is a pretty feeble one from the writer's viewpoint—and more and more writers are deserting the science fiction mags as a result, preferring to earn their livings in fields where the pay is higher and faster and where the market is not quite so thin. Furthermore, of the nine magazines, only *Astounding* and *F&SF* seem reasonably secure; folding rumors surround each of the other seven constantly, and within a

Afterthoughts...

Who Killed Science Fiction? is certainly a monumental job, and I want to express appreciation for it; it's a handsome volume, compiled with obvious care (imagine—an index!) and will certainly stand as a definitive statement of what people were thinking about sf in 1959. I have but one major and one minor regret about the whole undertaking—the major regret being that it should have been necessary at all to conduct a symposium on such a topic, the minor one being that some of your remarks in back appeared to lower the generally lofty and serious tone of the rest of the book, as well as taking unfair advantage of the contributors. Your comments might well have been better placed in a supplementary volume that would contain everyone else's comments as well. And it really was tasteless to reply to Sid Coleman's thoughtful article that way; local fannish pranks and jabs can be fun, but they shouldn't be immortalized in works of serious intent. None of us were fooling around up front; why drag the whole thing down to the level of an apazine in the back?…Otherwise, though, a swell job, beautifully produced. I don't find myself with any specific comments on the individual contributions, though I do feel a number of folks are off beam in

month's time all seven could easily be blown away. A field with only two magazines in it is not a living field. And the prospects of new titles entering are slim—there hasn't been a new title since 1957.

2) What is responsible? Neither Russia's space tactics nor the editorial crochets of individual editors nor the high cost of living. The trouble, simply, is distribution. The collapse of the ANC signaled the collapse of science fiction. Only *ASF* gets adequate distribution today, and they aren't totally pleased. The public can't buy magazines it can't find. The editor of today's weakest-selling science fiction magazine told me that in those areas where his magazine *is* sold, it does extremely well. But if your magazine only reaches half the outlets of the country, it has to come pretty close to selling out in order to break even.

3) What can we do to correct it? Not a damned thing, except form our own distributing company. Distribution now is a monopoly of arrogant petty potentates who can't be bothered putting such low-return items as fiction magazines on the stands. Science fiction in magazine form will survive only if we distribute them ourselves—and that's one company I wouldn't care to invest much in.

4) Yes, I think the original paperback is the chief chance of survival for science fiction. The paperback houses have good distribution, in the main, and their books can remain on sale indefinitely. Ace has shown that there is a month-in, month-out mar-

ket for science fiction paperbacks, and most of the other companies have committed themselves to at least three or four books a year. Of course, this might mean the end of the science fiction short story—but the short western and the short detective story are similarly at the edge of extinction.

5) Additional remarks? Not many from here; it's an unpleasant situation, both for the fans and for the people who, like me, once earned most or all of their living from writing science fiction. After a nasty period of conversion, I'm now busily at work in other fields, and will be writing science fiction–only when and if I have some free time and an irresistible idea. (I'll continue to write science fiction novels, though.) I think science fiction has reached the peak of its curve of popularity, and, strangely by the distributors, will drop back to become once again the arcane thing it was in 1948—except for the crud so-called science fiction in the movies and on television, which will remain to haunt us. From a fan's point of view, the best thing to do seems to be to retire to the study and spend the rest of their days with back issues; the science fiction magazines of the future, bouncing along with their penny-a-word rates, will only attract amateur writers, and the prospect of future classics is thin. But there's always *Adventures in Time and Space* to return to, and the large-size *Astounding*s, and the early *Galaxy*s—rearward march, full speed behind!

places. The fellow who dropped *F&SF* because, quote, it had four terrible stories in the annish, deserves some sort of fugghead award, though. My God, when a magazine publishes one *good* story an issue these days it deserves loud applause! And F&SF certainly manages to achieve that…The field is certainly a lot deader than it was when you sent your questionnaire out. Six magazines now, and only four editors. The loss of *Future,* SFS, and *Fantastic Universe* will have a crippling effect rarely considered; these three magazines, low-paying though they were, served as salvage markets for excellent but unconventional stories that lay outside the rather narrow requirements of the Big Three. A fiction field must have such salvage markets. The way we're heading, we'll soon be down just to our Big Three, each of which has very definite ideas about what it wants to print. Even if they paid 10c a word, they wouldn't attract many writers. In the past, I could aim a story at the top ranks and, even if I missed, could be sure of getting at least a penny a word for my time. Without the salvage markets I can't take the risk of rejection, not while I can have a 100% sales record in other fields. A 6,000-word story submitted to Campbell might take a week to write, and might get bounced, but at least I could be sure of getting

$60 for it *someplace*. Not much for a week's work, but at least it covered expenses. Today, if I sat down to do a story for JW, I'd be faced with the situation of getting either $180 for it or nothing at all. This all-or-nothing deal is hardly attractive, and so, even though Campbell's rates are as high as they ever were, the lack of salvage markets is costing him writers. A situation like this feeds on itself. Writers either leave sf completely, as so many have done, or, if they remain, concentrate on writing sure-shot bell-ringers. They concentrate very hard indeed on writing a story that will satisfy Campbell, Gold, or Mills—usually by writing one just like stories Campbell, Gold, or Mills have already published. This produces a lot of safe little stories, and allows the writers to keep clothed and fed, but is hardly going to result in classics. When *Infinity* and *Future* and *Fantastic Universe* were around, a writer could stick his neck out, experiment, and (if he had any ability) could be fairly sure of some return for his trouble… When there's no incentive to experiment, a fiction field dies fast. Even the most talented newcomer needs a sympathetic low-paying market to help him along. In today's all-or-nothing situation, sf in the short form is just about doomed. Since novel-writing has always been an all-or-nothing proposition, nothing much has changed there, and several active salvage markets do exist for the offbeat novel, for the experiment that fails to please Doubleday or Simon & Schuster, or Ballantine or Avon…Let's all be grateful that we've been such diligent collectors in the past. As I said in my article, we can always go back to the juicy years of not too long ago. Mater of fact, there's a yarn in a '49 *TWS* I've been meaning to get down from the shelf for a while; now's as good a time as any.…

– Robert Silverberg, May 1960

SMITH, E.E., Ph.D.

I'm glad you're making a study of the science fiction field as it is, and I hope it does some good. I'm very glad to contribute as, over the last couple of years, I have done a lot of thinking on the subject. My answers to your questions are:

1) No, magazine science fiction is not dead. With *Astounding, Amazing,* and *Fantastic*—and also *F&SF*, whatever it is-monthly and going strong; and with at least five others in an apparently fairly strong bimonthly position, the term "dead" scarcely applies. It is, however, sick; with a sickness that can very well prove fatal.

2) No, I do not feel that any single person, action, or event is responsible for the condition. In my opinion, the principal offenders are the various eager-beaver publishers who dashed into a field about which they knew nothing and cared less. As I see it, there are four major errors involved:

a. Overcrowding of the field. So many publishers rushed in to tap the supposed bonanza that there were far too many alleged "SF" magazines published; more than the field could possibly support and vastly more than could be filled with even acceptable material.

b. Failure of main-line support. In an attempt to lure main-line readers into the science fiction field, editors used many main-line authors (who knew nothing whatever of either science or science fiction) and a great deal of main-line material very thinly and very incompetently disguised as science fiction. Small, safe, insipid tales told in a small, safe, insipid way; bastard-type material that did not attract main-line readers and that disgusted real science fiction readers.

c. Wrong approach to solution of problem. In an attempt to placate "literary" reviewers and other main-line Pooh-bahs, many magazines concentrated on what they called "writing"—in which slick and precious writing and trick endings were all that were necessary. The fact that there were no ideas involved and that nothing of interest happened had nothing to do with the case. Thus, as might have been expected, main-line readers did not come in and real science fiction readers quit in droves.

d. Failure to face facts. At least, it seems to me to be a fact that the general public never has been, is not now, and probably never will be really interested in the branch of literature we know as science fiction. There is a hard core of perhaps ten or fifteen thousand (I'm guessing now) science fiction addicts (such as I) who will buy and try to read any and all magazines put out under the label. There are perhaps ninety thousand (another guess) other, more selective science fiction readers who will buy any and all GOOD SCIENCE FICTION magazines. However, most of this group want STORY VALUE, not slick and precious writing. Thus, it is my considered opinion that a science fiction magazine, so edited as to contain stories having real story value, could sell something over 100,000 copies per month; but I do not believe that *any* science fiction magazine, however edited, could sell much more than that.

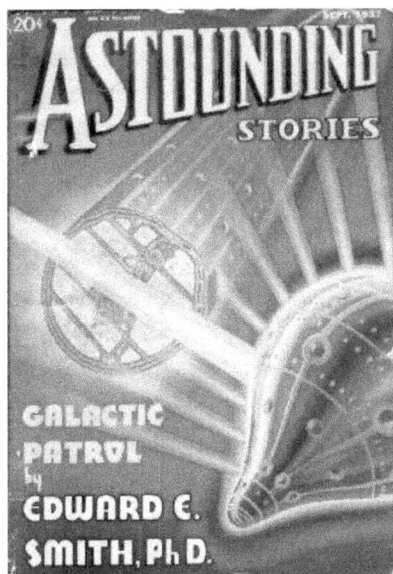

Please note that by "science fiction magazine" I mean one that would publish *real* science fiction; and by "story value" I do NOT mean the famous "Sense of Wonder." I mean that the story must be interesting enough to hold the reader's attention—to compel reader identification—and to make the reader feel, after he has read it, that he has read something worthwhile; something worth re-reading. And such stories, in today's science fiction magazines, are DAMNED scarce.

3) I do not know of anything we as fans or magazine buyers can do about the situation, except to keep on doing what many thousands of readers have already done—stop buying the magazines we do not like. Unfortunately, I personally am still buying them all; but I don't know how much longer even I will keep on buying crap that I simply can not read. I do not believe that letters-to-the-editor will help: there aren't enough of us who will write such letters and they are ignored. I think we will have to let economic forces do the work—when enough of the present magazines have folded to cut the survivors down to a number that the field can support, perhaps we can influence the surviving editors to publish *good* science fiction.

4) No. In my opinion, paperbacks supplement magazines, but do not and never can replace them, for many reasons; four of which are as follows:

a. Every science fiction magazine tries out new authors; some of whom eventually make good. Paperbacks do not; they can't. They *must* have large sales; hence the unknown stands just about the chance of the proverbial celluloid cat in hell. In other words, magazines *develop* writers, paperbacks do not. Thus, if the science fiction magazines disappear, science fiction as a field will disappear very shortly thereafter.

b. Each magazine develops a personality and commands at least some reader loyalty; pocketbooks do not. Thus, I would keep on buying *Astounding*, even though for three months running half of its stories were stinkers, because I would know that it was in a temporary slump. But if I bought one paperback of *Original Science Fiction Stories* (which I did), and found it *full* of stinkers (which I did), I would never buy another (which I haven't up to now). The paperback *novel*, of course, by a Heinlein or a Leinster, is a different breed of cat entirely.

c. Availability. We know when and where to look for our favorite science fiction magazines and they are recognizable on sight. If, however, I had to wade through the helter-skelter conglomerate of paperbacks on the average newsstand—even if I knew what I was looking for—I would stop buying science fiction entirely except for works of authors I know and like.

d. Identification. Unless someone develops a vastly better system of advertising or announcing paperbacks than any I know of at present, the average reader will not know even what to look for.

5) Additional remarks. First, I question very seriously your use of the

word "salvation" in item No. four. It carries (at least it seems to me to carry) the implication that the science fiction field should, by some innate right, number in the millions instead of in the thousands. Why? I do not consider such thinking realistic. The field has always, actually, been small; I see nothing to justify belief in any tremendous increase in the number of persons having the type of mind to which *real* science fiction so uniquely appeals.

Second, it seems to me that the editors of the science fiction magazines, facing the fact that there are a dozen magazines in a field that can support properly only three or four, have made such desperate attempts to enlist outside support that they have deliberately diluted the product; and in so doing have not only failed to attract any significant number of mainline readers, but also have alienated a great many readers such as I myself am.

Third, in my opinion, fandom itself is far from blameless. For many years there has been a movement to divorce fandom from science fiction; to make fan activities ends in themselves, with little or no relationship to the "professional" science fiction magazines. This movement has been growing and is still growing. Its influence can be seen best, perhaps, in the fact that *The Magazine of Fantasy and Science Fiction* has, for two years straight, been chosen by the "FANS" as the best professional "science fiction" magazine. For, as a matter of fact, *F&SF* is not a science fiction magazine at all. (It isn't even good fantasy.) For that reason, and that reason alone, it has succeeded in reaching a considerable number of main-line readers. It has received more approval from the literati, the cognoscenti and the upper-case critics than any real science fiction magazine ever did or ever will. It has "succeeded"— but it has done so by NOT PUBLISHING SCIENCE FICTION. Instead, it emphasizes the so-called "literary" values, including mawkishness, imbecility, frustration, stupidity, and futility—and to me, three-quarters of the stories it runs are simply unreadable. Unreadable because (again in my opinion) slick, precious, affected, and strained writing never have taken and never will take the place of imagination, of well-worked-out ideas, and of honest-to-God STORY VALUE.

Fourth, if fandom does divorce itself from science fiction, I give it not over three years of independent life.

As you've noticed, Earl, I haven't pulled my punches. You asked for my opinions—in detail—you've got 'em!

STARRETT, VINCENT

[There was no direct reply to the questionnaire, but the following appeared in the Chicago *Tribune Magazine of Books*. There were three responses to this item in Mr. Starrett's column, "Books Alive." See the item carried separately under the heading PALMER, RODNEY.—E.K.]

EARL KEMP...is circulating a questionnaire seeking an answer to the question, "Who killed science fiction?" If you have thoughts on the subject, address him, not me. I didn't know it was dead.

STOPA, JON

We killed science fiction. You know: America, from sea to shining sea. We've quit dreaming, and science fiction is dreams.

You can see it in science fiction itself. Take a "sociological" story: Have you ever read one about how things SHOULD be? Nope, they're all about how to get things back to the way they are NOW. Nobody seems to be able to think of a single improvement. Just get rid of a few things, i.e. slums, etc., seems to be the best anyone comes up with.

Or take the psi story. I've got nothing against psi: There might be something to it. BUT NOT THAT MUCH TO IT. There has been this kind of psi story, and that kind of psi story, until it's become stark raving clear that most of it is just a neurotic sigh for escape. Psi can be used legitimately (see Ted Sturgeon's *More Than Human*) to help explore an idea.

This mess that we're in is general—we came out of World War II with hopes of turning back the clock, and when we couldn't, we tried to, at least, hold the advancing hand.

There was a time when we had a dream—so we strode across a dusty continent...and almost tripped into the Pacific. We've been trying to catch our balance ever since, grabbing onto the "West" with its boots and saddles and oaters—grabbing onto "South" and its grubby teenagers who need a bath (and a haircut so that their hair would be at least as short as their sisters'.) and its Civil War buffs and its black hate—grabbing onto the "beatnik" with his dingy mind, shallow shadows, and delight with "Idea": As long as they are little and unimportant and, most of all, dead and unrevivable.

But this is not the place for a political tract—so enough....

TAKACS, STEPHEN

There is no science fiction field any longer. If I had stuck to selling science fiction during the past four years, I would have starved to death long ago! Since the first Russian Sputnik went up two years ago last October, it seems that every high school and college student in the US has quit reading science fiction: disillusioned and disgusted with American science! I know, during the past two years, I did not have any visits from any teenagers—and they used to form the backbone of the science fiction field. Not even during the summer vacation periods of 1958 and 1959 did any youngsters come in—I never see a young person anymore!

1) I certainly feel that magazine science fiction is dead—magazine rates to writers are so low that the best writers don't want to contribute any more. I speak to the writers personally here at my store, and they all admit they have quit. It pays more to write for the men's magazines—or direct to pocketbook publishers who pay a lot more than the magazines.

2) What is responsible? I am enclosing my speech that I gave at the Cleveland convention; this will explain! Two factors are responsible, 1) the tremendous advances made by Russia—our (US) repeated failures to catch up to them, plus 2) Arrangements by which readers can purchase books for very small amounts in passable hard-covers. These (30,000 to 40,000—figures are mine, E.K.) readers have, since 1953 been people who do not ordinarily buy hard bound books, confining themselves to buying the magazines as they came out. When the chance came to buy these bound editions, they turned away in droves from the "fan" publishers like Shasta, Fantasy Press, Prime Press, and Gnome Press. Bookshops during the past five years have "learned the ropes" and refuse to stock any hard bound science fiction. I know, I can't sell any myself—If I had not gone back to dealing in out-of-print books, I would have had to go out of business a long time ago. And when I say out-of-print books I don't mean *science fiction*—the demand is all for Lost Race novels, and for the weird-supernatural type, fantasy, etc., Burroughs, Talbot Mundy, H. Rider Haggard, everything *but* science fiction!

3) What can we do to correct it? I am afraid it is too late to correct the situation. The dozens of horror (science fiction) films released by Hollywood during the past few years, have so turned the public (intelligent public) from science fiction that the publishers are moving heaven and earth to take off the words "science fiction" from their titles of their magazines. I recently heard that *Astounding*, after 30 years, is changing the title to *Analog Science Fact Fiction* (!!!) to try to disguise the magazine in the hopes of getting more technicians to buy the magazine and to make it more respectable to the general public.

4) I certainly feel that we should look to the original paperbacks as a point of salvation—the entire future of the science fiction field rests in the

hands of the paperback publishers, and the more original novels they put out, the better for the field.

[As 'additional remarks,' Stephen attached the complete text of his Cleveland Convention speech, "Alas, What Boom?" with the stipulation that the most pertinent observations, those that had the greatest shock effect value at the time, be deleted from the manuscript. I do not have courage enough to override Stephen's wishes and print the entire text. It has been published though, in its entirety, I believe in *Science Fiction Times*, and is to be considered recommended reading for this study. – E.K.]

TUCKER, BOB

No one killed science fiction. It isn't dead.

When I first became acquainted with the literature (and it is, however questionable the quality), there were but three magazines being published on a somewhat-regular schedule with, of course, a "quarterly" or an "annual" thrown in now and then for the hell of it, and for a fast buck. These latter books were produced cheaply and remained on display a long time, so that if they sold at all they represented a nice profit for the publisher.

Because I've never known less than three magazines, I've always considered the field alive and kicking lustily as long as three (the same three) continued to exist. Thirty titles a year (or more) seemed a glut, an unhealthy glut which encouraged cannibalism, and I failed to mourn the passing of the superfluous magazines. I wouldn't consider magazine science fiction dead unless their number dropped to zero.

But at the same time, I realize it is a matter of relativity. To those readers who entered the field when ten, or 20, or 30 titles were being published, a drastic reduction of the (to them) normal number seemed to signal the death of all. Not so—but of course it is difficult to convince those who are used to more populous times (*not* prosperous, but populous).

I believe first, that the excess number of magazines (and their deplorably low level of fiction) helped to destroy themselves and each other; and second, that the number of hardcover and softcover books also contributed to the general destruction. The quality level of the fiction in these two kinds of books may or may not be higher than the levels in magazines, but it is a different level in some ways, and until this difference palls, the books will continue in number. (A decade ago when the hardcover publishers discovered magazine science fiction, they flooded the bookstores and libraries with reprintings of cheap novels and serials, and quickly killed the new market they were developing. Of late, the low quality short story collections seemed destined for the same end.)

What can we do to correct it? ("It" meaning the dearth of magazines.) Nothing. Don't try to correct it or you will again have 30 titles on the newsstands with no more decent stories to read than before. Buy and read the two, or three, or four magazines you have a genuine liking for, and let the jungle claim the unworthy. Not everyone will buy the same ones, but in the end the buying majority will save *some*, and the field will return to what I grew up to consider a normal state of affairs.

The same rule should be applied to the hardcovers and the paperbacks: buy those you honestly believe to be worth buying and let the devil take the rest.

VONNEGUT, KURT, JR.

Nobody killed science fiction. Science fiction is not dead. More money will be spent on stories with science in them during the next year than in any year in history will be spent by magazines, television, radio, book publishers, movies, and even Broadway.

So what is the beef?

The pulp writers can't make a living any more? Tant pis. They made intelligent readers want to throw up.

Anybody who announces that he is a science fiction writer is announcing that he is in damn bad company financially and artistically.

You are trying to conduct a post-mortem without a corpse. I would love to provide you with one. I would love to see the expression *science fiction* butchered this very minute in order that stories with science in them not be identified, in the minds of intelligent readers, with pulpers, beginners, and hacks.

Afterthoughts....

Thanks for the handsome present...My own contribution to *Who Killed Science Fiction?* was irresponsible, and I'm sorry for it. What it expressed more than anything else was my own isolation. I don't know anybody else in the field, not even fans, and so I tend to think of the field as something far far away and belonging to strangers. That is self-pitying thinking without merit...There seems to be fair agreement as to what the best pieces of work in the field have been. It might be interesting to make a list of those best pieces, a hundred of them, say—and, after each title, to name the thing most attacked, the thing most praised, and, in the barest possible terms, the intended moral. You might discover in that way the spiritual basis of the almost crazy affection many intelligent people have for the artificial catergory of writing known as science fiction...All the shoptalk by ink-stained wretches leads nowhere. Underneath all that shoptalk something very important spiritually may be going on. I hope so....

– Kurt Vonnegut, Jr., May 1960

WEST, WALLACE

1) No, I do not feel that magazine science fiction is dead, but only resting. And some very good and thoughtful stuff is being published in *Astounding, F&SF*, and the Columbia magazines. *Vide*: "The Sky People."

2) What is responsible? The current uncertain political and economic situation in the United States. All types of fiction are in the doldrums. Authors get little encouragement.

3) To correct the situation: End the cold war and get on with the business of living.

4) We should not look to the original paperback alone as a point of salvation. Magazines, hardcovers, fanzines, etc., should all help.

5) Seems to me the world is in a transition period now, from which we go over the edge or on to what H.G. Wells called "a storm of living." History shows authors don't work well in such a period.

WILLIAMSON, JACK

There are a good many reasons for the present unsatisfactory state of magazine science fiction. It has been hurt in a triple squeeze between television, the comics, and the paperbacks. As escape fiction, it is to some extent the victim of the events and inventions that it has most often prophesied— the Russians, for example, are busy removing the moon from the domain of the free imagination. People generally are reading less fiction; the interest in any literary form seems to be more or less cyclic. And all these damaging effects tend to snowball; as the market shrinks, many of the best writers turn to some other way of making a living, and the market shrinks again.

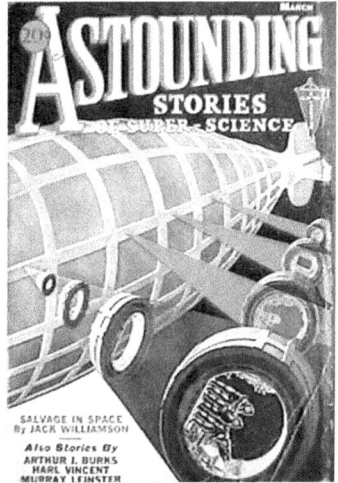

Yet I don't think the outlook is hopeless. There is still good science fiction in a few magazines, as well as a paperback market for science fiction novels. Magazine science fiction might be revived, I think, by a new editor with the enthusiasm that a few editors in the field have had, and the writers that such an editor might discover and develop. Thirty years ago, when I first discovered science fiction and began trying to write it, it was tremendously important to me as a new way of looking at this changing world and saying what I thought and felt about it. This study itself is evidence that some people still take science fiction seriously, yet I suspect that the essential trouble with magazine science fiction is simply that too few people, readers or editors, or publishers or writers, are serious enough about it. Once we have a trend in the other direction, with more serious readers interested in something that justifies their interest....

WOLLHEIM, DONALD A.

' I have finally gotten around to your letter asking opinions on "Who Killed Science Fiction?" So, to answer your questions:

1) I don't think magazine science fiction is dead. Of course not. It is just going through one of its regular setbacks, which happen continually because the field is not and never was quite as big as publishers suppose. It can't support two dozen magazines and when an imaginary book causes the band wagon to get overloaded, it's got to break down. The breaking down must and does damage all magazines alike.

Magazine science fiction is a vital necessity to the field. It serves as the breeding ground of new writers, the womb of new science fiction ideas and themes. It's the proper entry port for fandom and those enthusiasts who form the living guts of science fiction readerhood. It is the easiest market for the embryonic writer to break into—and that's damned important.

2) But why did the magazine field break down? Primarily as I said before because the field is not that general in interest to support too many magazines at once. Every now and then news begins to seep through the magazine publishing field to the effect that such and such a theme is selling like crazy. When that happens, there are always a dozen marginal operators who will hasten to leap on the rising rocket. If *True* magazine sells, suddenly there are several dozen men's magazines—and the others must and do get cruder and cruder as they try to shortcut the means to success by boiling out all but the most elementary factors in that success. If *Mad* moves, bingo, a dozen imitators (which die fast, as you can find out) in a field which never could support more than one such satire. If *Playboy* starts, again the mad rush to get rich quick—a hundred magazines becoming more and more salacious and cheaper.

Hence the recent boom in science fiction, which broke down. *Saturn*, which I edited because requested to do so by just such a marginal producer, had fairly good short stories in it, even though they were the selections from everyone's rejections. But I know they had at least some taste and passable quality. However, look at the overall appearance of the magazine—the cheapest printer in the trade, the shoddiest proofreading, the sloppiest art work. Likewise the rest of the fly-by-night science fiction titles of that boom... Some were better printed than *Saturn*, but they were still inferior to *Galaxy*, *Astounding*, and *F&SF*. So every time a fan, or a reader, who didn't happen to be a millionaire, bought one of these johnny-come-lately products, he just possibly didn't buy one of the better magazines that month. Hence the circulation of all was hurt. Since the field wasn't that big, it was simply spreading its limited readership thinner, to everyone's hurt.

Now this isn't a crime—it happens to be the way any business is conducted today. It happens continually in all fields of publishing, and of manufacturing also. Sometimes the field has really expanded, but often it's an illusion. It will happen again, too, in science fiction. I don't known when, but it surely will. And the same results....

(And I won't hesitate to edit a magazine similar to *Saturn* when next it happens, even though the end product may be the same. It's money in my pocket—and if I don't do it, someone with even less fan taste will surely do it... You may be interested to know that even with this alleged bust, I am advised by *Saturn*'s publisher that the five science fiction issues *did not lose* money! Each and every one of them cleared a profit...but a small one. However, the detective *Saturn*s cleared a bigger profit for a while.)

Now, besides the above, is there a single element we can say ruined our gal? I have a feeling there may be...and I'd say that the idiotic "psi" stuff initiated by Campbell (whom I regard otherwise as the best man in this science fiction magazine business) was a big factor in undermining the basic foundations of good science fiction. "Psi" is just the occult under pseudo-scientific terminology. You couldn't even peddle the occult to *Weird Tales* readers... Mr. Campbell is a wizard at understanding real science, but unfortunately he is so woefully, boneheadedly ignorant about anything outside of the physical sciences that he falls into the first trap any hokum artist hands him in psychology, sociology, or theology. (Remember Dianetics?)

Because I know that when plowing through the slush rejected by the biggies for *Saturn* I ran into an awful lot of psi material. Hence, when someone desperate for material on a low budget is scraping the barrel, he must take some of this simply because it may be readable and better written than other stuff, even if he disagrees with it. Hence the low quality of his new magazine gets even lower by real science fiction reader tastes.

3) What can be done? Nothing, I suppose. We can't shoot Campbell—he's too darn good and we shall have to put up with his foibles and hope the rest of the field doesn't follow him. And when somebody goes nosing around

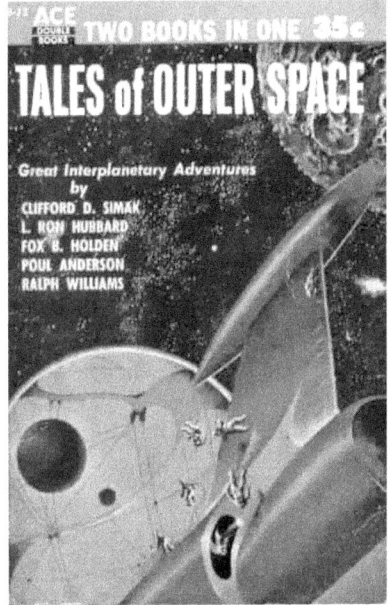

the New York publishers that "Oh boy, oh boy, *Galaxy* just tripled its circulation…" the boom will be on again.

4) No, we should not look to the original paperback as a point of salvation. The original paperback is a fine source of novel-length fiction, but I don't think it properly replaces magazine science fiction. Besides it tends to be too big a financial risk to allow a publisher (or his editor) to experiment too widely—and science fiction needs some medium for experimentation.

Besides, if science fiction is reduced to nothing but paperback novel publishing, it will mean the end of fandom. Because readers of paperbacks do not write letters—not to the editors and certainly not to each other.

Ace Books does about two or more science fiction novels a month, and must reach as many people regularly as the best and biggest magazines, yet our mail commenting on the science fiction we publish is nil. No comments, no mail.

How can you hold up fandom on that? How can an editor know the difference between a good original science fiction novel and a poor one if nobody writes to comment—and it may take a year to get any kind of a circulation report—and since each book is different, the policy line of the company is a lot less clearly defined than that of a periodical.

5) I guess I've said as much as I ought to.

WOOD, EDWARD

At a time when space travel seems but a matter of no more than a few years, the fact that magazine science fiction is so close to death is indeed incongruous. While a large portion of the blame will be rightly placed on the incredible distribution mess that has blighted America for years, to say it is the whole blame is a mistake. Consider *Playboy* or better yet, *Mad*; magazines that have hit a responsive cord in the American people and are not only successful but have dragged along with them imitators who also seem to be making money.

The verdict if and when rendered will be: SUICIDE!

Have the magazines offered science fiction that was really science fiction? Or have they offered incomprehensible double-talk devoid of imagination, idealism, scientific outlook, or even simple understanding? A sterile emphasis on literary context, sex, occultism, monsters, misplaced humor, baby talk, etc., have all been fads at one time or another in the broad spectrum of science fiction fantasy magazines. Since the ultimate reward of absurdity is ostracism, what is now upon us seems not harsh but rather overdue.

An inept expansion of magazine titles plus a mistaken commercialism coupled with a gigantic misunderstanding of what science fiction could do have all combined to accomplish what depression, a world war, and pulp shortages could not do. The number of the readers, publishers, editors, and writers who have assisted in this destruction is legion.

The science fiction magazine field is now in a trap from which escape is difficult. If a magazine were today to start publishing the greatest stories ever printed in the field, with high-caliber artwork and a top-grade format, it could not reach more than a small part of its potential audience. ONE CAN-NOT BUY MAGAZINES THAT CANNOT BE FOUND!

What is to be done?

Someone is sure to suggest subscription to the remaining magazines. While this sounds attractive, it contains some self-defeat in it. Suppose a few thousand dedicated fans subscribed and no longer bought the magazines on the stands. The few stands that do display a few magazines (believe me, they are mighty few!) might decide to drop them entirely. How would it be possible to gain new readers when they couldn't even find the magazines to sample them?

One can buy one copy of every issue of every magazine that shows up to indicate to the dealers and distributors that there are a few bucks to be made in the field.

Of course there is always the recourse of the apathetic, resignation to the situation. The end result of this is painfully obvious.

Personally, I shall read all the magazines I can obtain. I shall not subscribe. Nor will I beg anyone to read science fiction. I can try to explain to an interested person what science fiction is and what it is *not*. It is not possible to force something like science fiction on people who do not care for it. The loss is theirs…

If, as seems most likely, the science fiction magazines do disappear, the paperbacks and books should continue…for awhile.

Adding up the three decades plus of science fiction magazines one can truly say that it has been a wonderful time (this in spite of the many defects) for us who have read the magazines and it is indeed a pity that more people would not join us.

Afterword 1960
Like Morning Call

There is in the Vieux Carre of New Orleans a quaint restaurant named "Morning Call." Here there can be purchased coffee with chicory only, and some obscure pastry twists from a deep-fry vat that are referred to as "doughnuts." One goes to Morning Call in the morning, naturally, after a night on the town, after Carnival is dwindling to an end, as the early rays of sunshine bounce off the Mississippi and glitter across the Quarters.

Here one relives the experiences of the night, the delight of Al Hirt's trumpet at Dan's Pier 600, the pleasant song-fests at Pat O'Brien's and, last but by no means least, the moment of truth that comes for you and the dark-haired beauty in the little apartment over Rampart Street.

And one gags on the syrupy chicory-coffee and sprinkles confectioner's sugar from a shaker onto the grease-soaked doughnuts.

It was quite an heroic feat, going through the preceding 95 pages [in the 1960 edition of *Who Killed Science Fiction?*] of highly opinionated remarks without allowing my editorial blue pencil to intrude occasional remarks of my own. Only the most necessary comments were interjected; those adding to the continuity or explaining some perhaps obscure reference.

Some statements made in these contributions pleased me so much, or grated on my prerogative to such an extent, that I have to reply.

This then is like Morning Call. A moment of truth for *Who Killed Science Fiction?*

In the first bright flashes of a snow-covered morning, I find myself with the following words for:

ANDERSON, POUL: Your point No. five. I could not agree with you more completely about the question "who killed science fiction?" as being an outlet for suppressed aggressiveness. I found a large percent of the comments contributed falling into this category. Including your own remark that it is such an outlet. I could not disagree with you more completely about the need for such a study. Where in the hell would we be today if we left writing (i.e., science fiction and/or detection) to literary historians? I love science fiction, the people that manufacture this product and the purchasers. This includes you, John W. God, Jr., and Joe McFann from Podunk. What has happened within the field in the past *was* my business—what is currently happening *is* my business—what will ultimately happen *is* my business and I'll damn well attend to it!

BARRETT, DR. C.L.: Your point No. two. Ted Carnell came out of ga-fia [*Get Away From It All*—E.K.] for this study. Same point, and children. Honestly, Doc, I don't consider three to be such an unhandy number, except of course when buying school supplies, and shoes that somehow manage to last a whole week. I think it would be wonderful to have a dozen, would that I could afford so many... Need I mention that George and Mary Young are doing their little bit? How about Don and Margaret Ford? Do Dean and Jean Grennell hold the record in fandom?

BOUCHER, ANTHONY: Your remark, "This quality of boredom..." Once I hated Arthur Koestler for a very similar remark. Little did I know then that it prefaced a very prophetic article. Pray he doesn't revisit the field to sample the current crop. What devastation he could render this time, and justly so...

BRADLEY, MARION ZIMMER: Beautifully done, cuts to the core with perception and integrity. Thank you.

BUDRYS, A.J.: *Galaxy* cannot metamorphose into *The Saturday Evening Post*. As I see it from here, *Galaxy* could never be "under the dryer" reading because it radiates (or did radiate in the past) one, and only one theme in monotone: "One Small Room." A depressed view that "people are no damned good"; I hope this will never receive the mass treatment.

CAMPBELL, JOHN W., JR.: Your point No. one. I believe the 38 out of 70 "but" replies to this query are indications that the magazine field *is* indeed dying. Now you prove that you're "going better than ever"; I keep as close a watch as possible on circulation figures, which are to me and I presume Condé Nast, the best indication of how any book is "going." The "wool" will not stretch this far, assuming you're pulling it over your own eyes first. Your point No. two, if you haven't found it by now, it's quite possibly too late. Your point No. three, "it's fantasy fiction...that's in trouble"; this of course includes psi...to which I must repeat a joke I've heard many times, but don't know the source, "John Campbell is editing a new anthology, he's going to call it 'Psianthology.'" Joke No. two, source unknown, from *Yandro*, "*Analog*, the greatest idea since the Edsel!" I wish I had thought of that.

CLIFTON, MARK: "John Campbell put his finger on it..." Without a doubt Campbell is the greatest editor the field has ever known. No one within the field currently has so much power, literally controlling what material goes into what magazine, regardless of publisher or editor. Who else can dredge a superb story out of a mire of gibberish? If this percentage of "superb stories" slips any lower though, I fear I will not be alone in charging him with mismanagement of the power he wields. Psi is NOT the answer, and perhaps Campbell should skip some of the Wednesday sessions of passing out "Campbell ideas" to mirror hacks and let some of this psionic excrement settle under a little quick lime.

COLEMAN, SIDNEY: Brilliant and sparkling, as usual. Who wrote it for you this time?

DAVIDSON, AVRAM: No, Avram, the freshness has not departed from you. Your point No. five, look at your fanzines...never even mention science fiction. Is this the fault of the editor of the fanzine, or the fault of those capable of writing intelligently about science fiction? The two are not necessarily the same. I will call to your attention Norman Metcalf's *New Frontiers*, as being outside the type you mean, and what is this you are holding in your hand at the moment, if not a fanzine? Surely you will agree that science fiction is spoken here! True, all that glitters is not criticism by knight, neither is all that stinks to be referred to as "fanzine." I will assist on your inquiry into fantasy; when will you start?

DEVORE, HOWARD: Your point No. four. I cannot agree with you on reprints. No publisher is stupid enough to reprint a book when there is no demand for same. When a title is out of print, and in demand, I have nothing but praise for the publisher who will take the chance and risk his thousands. Example, Clifford D. Simak's *City*. There are others, badly in need of reprinting, e.g., Jack Vance's *Dying Earth*. And in another category entirely, there are those badly in need of bound editions for libraries, e.g., Alfred Bester's *Tiger, Tiger!*, Algis Budrys's *Who*, James Blish's *A Case of Conscience*. What is dishonest, though, is the practice of publishers who change titles from the original publication without mentioning the original, e.g., Ace Books; publishers who reprint British material copyrighted under the last convention rulings without credit or acknowledgment, e.g., Ace, Ballantine, and Hans Santesson's version of *New Worlds*. Such actions are inexcusable.

FREAS, FRANK KELLY: Remarkably true and entertaining. Thank you for contributing.

GOLD, HORACE: Thank God you aren't wearing blinders. At least you acknowledge that the situation does exist however your contributory reasons, true as they are, are very minor compared to the actual reasons. That you acknowledge them is at least a step in the right direction, the music of the masses must be drowning out the sound of distant drums.

GREENBERG, MARTIN: You are quite right in questioning the validity of some of the fans at the Detroit World Science Fiction Convention. Convention fans fall into many categories, the innocent bystanders, the "I-just-came-withs," the hucksters, the lookingforadrinks, the obnoxious, the painfully juvenile, the pain-in-the-ass variety, and others. Indeed, I remember the discussions about science fiction; a few of them that I have had have included you in the discussion group. We have a real crazy fan club here in Chicago, for eleven years now we've had regular, formal meetings almost every other week where we sit around and… you guessed it… talk about science fiction. We have a rather unfortunate reputation of being quiet, no feuding, no fussing, too damned little fanzineing, but by God I'll bet we discuss more science fiction per capita than any other group.

KNIGHT, DAMON: So, what's new?

LEIBER, FRITZ: Your point No. five, "a sigh for *Weird Tales*"; have you seen a new entry onto the scene called *Shock*? It bears looking into, if for no other reason than nostalgia.

LEY, WILLY: Your point No. three. A very loud seconding motion.

LOWNDES, ROBERT A.W.: I wish I could finance you, Doc. Either that or Mr. S. should keep his damned hands off. You have more integrity than any editor in the field, and not the slightest chance to exercise it. Pound for pound, and a quarter-cent not withstanding, you consistently deliver the impossible. This is maudlin, and probably serves no purpose, but, man, would I like to see what you could do with three cents a word plus bonus, payable on acceptance.

McLAUGHLIN, DEAN: Dean, sex *is* good clean fun. In life, literature, and the pursuit of a healthy romp in the hay. I do not think you should condemn *Playboy* for this dedication, after all, Hugh Hefner, Ray Russell, et al. know which side of the mattress the sheet is on. Nevertheless, your contribution was one of the really high points of the study. Thank you, Dean.

MILLER, P. SCHUYLER: Detailed and delightful reading; a very worthy contribution to the study. I had hoped for a large number of double-value contributions like yours, of great value content-wise, with a secondary, entertainment value. Miz Bradley, Budrys, McLaughlin, Price, Smith, Wollheim, and several others join you in giving this study a portion of entertainment. Thank you, Sky, for your work toward the success of this effort, and our very best wishes for the success of the Pittcon.

MILLS, ROBERT P.: Your point No. five, "the problems…of…most other magazines in the field…" Did you perhaps notice that at least one editor says he has no problems? Absurd! Man, we all got problems in this field. You [as editor of] *F&SF* are in an ideal position because you claim a measure of loyalty unique in the field—a firm, though small, unyielding group whose loyalties are not split three ways, among you, *Scientific American*, and now *Popular Mechanics*. With unfailing support from the publisher, you could outlast them all!

NORTON, ANDRÉ: Do not be sorry that this was all you could contribute. Your contribution was of special significance because of the branch of science fiction that you represent, the extremely popular juvenile field. Thank you very much for adding your views.

O'MEARA, JAMES H.: Your remarks about the younger, casual readers added support to Sidney Coleman's remarks. There is truly a Heinlein/Norton monopoly on quality fiction within the juvenile field, with continued integrity, the two of them could singlehandedly (or would that be double-handedly? quadruplehandedly?) supply all the excellent material this field could assimilate.

PALMER, RAYMOND A.: Your point No. five. Ideally I suppose, this "club" could work out. But there is NO ideal situation. There are no authors and/or agents who would go along on this deal. There are no fans willing to assume the momentous task of administering this "club". The profits would be dubious, to say the least. There are not 2,000 fans/members who would agree to buying anything four times a year for $3.50 a throw; even you, though you say it now, would probably poop out if your bluff were called. There are very few fans who would enter the administration of this "club" once they looked into the multiple income tax structures, could visualize the piles of crap mail they would receive. I know, because Advent: fits your description in all but one point, that of financing future conventions. Because there is nothing left with which to finance anything. Once you pay out $1.80 for the manufacture of a book that Doubleday could reproduce for less than ten cents a copy—once you pay the agents, the express bills, the jacket printing bills, the mountainous postal expenses, the packaging costs, etc.—then you get your periodic letter from Alphonse Q. Fugghead or one of his cousins describing his perfectly marvelous, delightful, science fiction type novel about this here guy who sprouts wings and flies off to Venus to fight the whatchamacallits that we really should publish because we're sure to make a million dollars off it and we can have it for only $5,000 advance on royalties, of course there is one catch, the manuscript is a little jumbled up. It appears that Alphonse wrote it at the age of fifteen, last year, using a No. 3 pencil, none too sharp, and writing on Kraft wrapping paper, all 675 pages of it. We can hardly wait to file Alphonse's letter…in the round file.…

PRICE, GEORGE: One of the better contributions; thank you, George.

REYNOLDS, MACK: One tends to forget that you are rather isolated over there [Turkey in 1960, Mexico in 1980.-E.K.], what with your iniquitous dens, hashish, and all, so that point No. four really has little meaning. I would like to recommend some to you, though: Budrys's *Who* and Vonnegut's *The Sirens of Titan*.

RUSSELL, ERIC FRANK: Your point No. five is very well taken. When one gets to be my age they stop and take a second thought before referring to someone else as an "elder sage," but you display a wisdom here of the field, and a devotion that does not come easy, nor without a great deal of work. You are one of my favorite authors, if that is any consideration, and *Sinister Barrier* is my number one recommendation for non-science fiction readers as a point of entry into the field.

RUSSELL, RAY: "Perhaps the writers themselves are to blame for allowing themselves to get into a rut." Fortunately $3,000 will pay one hell of a towing bill.…

SELDES, TIMOTHY: In filling Walter Bradbury's shoes, you have quite a task before you. Initially, you face a prejudiced audience. It is prejudiced because you are in a position to bring the finest quality science fiction to the greatest number of people, resulting in the greatest amount of income for the field and/or the author. But this is seldom the case. Instead, the Doubleday science fiction line just manages to crawl out of the box marked "mediocre." The major factor in your disfavor is that a sale to Doubleday means simultaneous, or at best a one-month delay, release through the Doubleday Science Fiction Book Club. This relieves the author of expecting any trade sale. The individual book purchaser knows that he has to wait only one month to get the book at one-third price. Admittedly the impact of the individual purchaser is infinitesimal, but the author, and especially the author's agent, will not recognize this fact. *The* sale is to institutions, and only to institutions. The book club revenue comes second. It is my thought that the club has been a major cause toward the almost complete disappearance of science fiction from the lines of all publishers, and an almost complete absence of science fiction titles (those that are published) from book stores. Why should they stock an item that won't be bought from them? The few special requests will be ordered for drop-shipment; let the others wait for either a remainder copy, a book club edition, or a paperback reprint. This has more bearing on your point No. four. You are wrong in that any book with any value at all in hardbound editions will sell to paperbacks. You say this as final, yet there are many books, highly successful in hardbound editions, that for some reason or other cannot be placed with any paperback publisher. "...Having the hardbound edition one leaves open the chances for book club and movie sales." The book club facet has already been mentioned here. For the life of me, I cannot understand your reference to movie sales. Many authors and/or agents are deserting the hardbound field for that very reason; that the publisher takes a cut of the club sale, of the movie sale, of the other dramatic sales, of the variety of potential resales. Titles that cry out for a place on your library shelf are available only in a crumbly, pulp-paper edition that's pulling loose from the cement on the spine. I can only repeat that Doubleday has the organization, the equipment, the facilities, the financial structure, and the personnel to produce the largest amount of quality science fiction this field has ever known. The selection of just what material to produce now rests with you; somehow I do not envy you this job, but I do sincerely wish you all the best...

SHAW, LARRY: Your point No. three. If you find this rich man, willing to finance a science fiction magazine, let me know. I'll be first in line....

SMITH, E.E., PH.D.: Well, Doc, I felt that someone should call a spade a spade; something is rotten in science fiction, but I didn't find it with this study. Perhaps, like Budrys, I was expecting someone to come up with the perfectly logical but as yet unrecognized solution. Your point No. five, subject three; I am, naturally, aware of the movement to which you refer, to divorce fandom from science fiction. I cannot say that it pleases me very much. Sure, the correspondence would continue for a while, and the fanzines as well, probably, but it would be an undeserved continuation. On the same subject, I must agree with the majority regarding *F&SF*; I see the continued awarding of the Hugo trophy to this title as a loud, deliberate booing of John Campbell; a protest against psi. *Galaxy*, of course, does not enter into the competition at all. *F&SF* is the most pleasing prozine published today, and will probably continue receiving the Hugos as long as *Analog* persists in pushing blatant quackery. Subject No. four, three years is perhaps too long a time; I would be inclined to cut this by half.

STARRETT, VINCENT: Thank you very much for the plug in "Books Alive," but if you receive consistently the percentage of quack mail that I got from this one little insertion, you have my deepest sympathy.

STOPA, JON: The army has got you waving too many flags, pal. Hurry back [from *Stars and Stripes*, Tokyo, Japan—E.K.] and pick up where you left off with those promising stories.

STURGEON, THEODORE: Extremely sorry you are not included here. Of all the people whose opinions were asked, only yours and one other I consider a definite loss to the study. A man who can stand in defiance of time and slan/fans should be included here. Only one thing would make me happier than having you contribute to this study: to discover very shortly now a new, original novel by you. In my worthless opinion, the science fiction field has produced two literary geniuses, you, and standing slightly outside the field itself, the other: Ray Bradbury, whom I steadfastly refuse to include within the category of science fiction itself--fantasy, yes; science fiction, NO.

VONNEGUT, KURT, JR.: *Bullshit!* I've spent the last twelve years doing my damnedest to bolster the label "science fiction" and you would love to butcher this label. I would be sorely tempted to refer you to the traditional cliché, "if you don't like the apples, get out of the tree" but then this would be extremely inappropriate, from the personal view. Because, kind-sir-who-annoys-me-muchly, I like your apples, by name *Player Piano* and *The Sirens of Titan*, and *I* do not want out of the tree!

WILLIAMSON, JACK: Yes, Jack, some of us do still take the field seriously, as seriously, apparently, as others (i.e., Vonnegut) detest it. I am deadly serious about it, and once your trend does start, I'm sure we only have to wait about.....

WOLLHEIM, DONALD A.: I admire your frank honesty with regards to *Saturn*, but despite this, feel that it did damage the field. And you, sir, are a cad for recognizing this fact and yet standing ready to do further damage to the field with a *Saturn*-copy, should the occasion arise. I felt your contribution to be one of the better ones made for the study. Thank you.

WOOD, EDWARD: I had the same feelings you do regarding subscriptions to the magazines, with added taboos. Like, for instance, receiving the subscription copy a week after the issue has already gone on sale, and naturally you have already purchased one, thinking yours was somehow lost in the mail. Then there are the copies that arrive completely and irreparably mutilated by the mishandling of the post office department, so that you wind up buying about two out of every three copies from the newsstand anyway, in order to maintain a somewhat uniform collection as far as physical condition is concerned.

There you have it, my replies to some of you that would never have been written had I not included them here. Forgive me for taking this public place for carrying on my petty, personal gripes and praise.

The end of the physical work required to produce this whole study is now rapidly coming into view. It has been a tremendous amount of work, far more difficult than I had ever dreamed when I began. I think, though, that it will all be worthwhile, sometime…in the future….

But for now, I'm just damned tired….

yours

EARL KEMP

I AM A SERIOUS PERSON

I THINK SERIOUSLY
I ACT SERIOUSLY

SOMETHING HAS GOT TO CHANGE

Appendix A
Science Fiction Magazines
1926 – 1960

compiled by Edward Wood

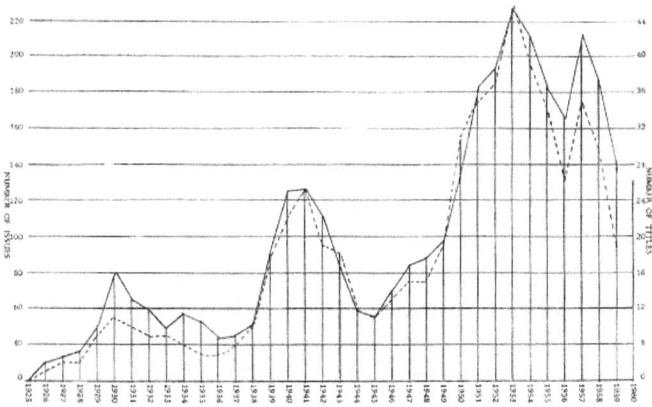

WE DON'T ALWAYS
SAY WHAT WE MEAN

Who Killed Science Fiction?
1980

"

"B

"Bi

"Bil

"Bill

"Billy

"Billy.

"Billy. Billy! You're time-tripping again."

Earl. Earl! You're Billy Pilgriming again. *Schlachthoffunf* and West Barnstable; Dresden and Valerie's tits—Goddamn, Kurt, you made it so *good*—God Bless You, Mr. I never knew what it was I was doing so much of until you explained it to me.

Now I enjoy it tremendously, this seemingly endless flitting about through space and time with no apparent reason, but with reason everywhere. Yet another symptom of the creeping senility that's been my avocation for far too many years. A facet, perhaps, of altogether too much time spent actually pursuing texture and sensation and experience, trying to assimilate an impossible amount into one hopelessly inadequate container.

The slightest stimulus now has the power to grab my mind off the thought of the moment—even in mid-thought—and divert it into some improbable other. People begin to overlap and *deja vu* all over the place. Dearly beloved people.

My children frequently find cause to complain that I confuse them each with another, thereby depriving them of their proper individuality, but they are so cyclic to me, the things they do that are similar. They reoccur again and again until, in my mind, I see each child replaying their previous sibling. Not consistently, of course, but when it happens my memory sees their predecessor and I speak—in haste—their name. The wrong name.

The right name at another time. My name, too, when it is.

Convolutions on top of convolutions—full throttle forward, moving backward down Interstate-national Mobius Laser-beam Route 66. "Get your kicks. It winds from Chicago to L.A." (Johnny Mercer).

Twenty whole fucking (Much better, Harlan, and you?) years. No, it *can't* be. There are many times when I'm not yet 20 myself, much less the things of me/my creations, my children, my books, my (alleged) artistic-attempts, my _____. Oh, I know they are, all of them, but I'm not until I am. In all honesty, though, I *have* grown a bit recently. For a good number of years I was positive I was 17 years old. However, during the last three years I've had a number of birthdays, spiraling past me on vaporous clouds of incomprehensibility, fueled by blood-and-gut energy…seven years in three. I'm 24 now. My children think it inconsiderate of me, being younger than they.

Did H. Allen Smith really get lost in the horse latitudes this way? I began to write a Foreword to this book, not a Foreword that would *be* the book, with nothing else following.

Reflections at 50

It was good enough for Edmund Wilson at 60, though he did it infinitely better, but—*Aha!*—can he take leftover accumulated yarns and weave them into a tapestry showing the songs of my soul?

Who was I then? 1960? Certainly a person me/now would not approve of, except for the abundance of energy that seemed, somehow, to get diverted onto a sidetrack where orange sunshine created a purple haze for me and Jimi, until he went *Star-Spangled-Banner*ing off alone, plucking the strings and making sounds for Janis to drink her Southern Comfort by while Morrison opened his fly, Miami-manipulating his "crawl-in' kingsnake" (*L.A. Woman*).

Short-tempered bastard then (still completely without patience today, only a bit more laid back), hell-bent on accomplishing *every*thing I could dream of on short schedules if not instantaneously. Actually setting timetables for myself and, miraculously, watching some produce materialize.

I know for a fact I wanted a Hugo.

(I could close my eyes and let that thought—smelling very much like burning Michoacan—rush me right past an Emmy or an Oscar to a Pulitzer. A Nobel. I suppose reason had to prevail somewhere even 20 years ago. I *can* remember convincing myself I should try for something a bit more practical. I could always move the earth the following year, unless something/one better came along.)

I definitely wanted a Hugo.

I was editing *SaFari* at the time for SAPS (The Spectator Amateur Press Society). Somehow the idea of doing an Annual to round out the year came to mind and, the more I thought about producing it, the more grandiose the issue became. I thought about making it a collector's item by severely restricting the edition itself (all previous issues of *SaFari* had been generally available to anyone who asked). Then I thought about enforcing its potential value by using contributions from as many BNFs (big name fans; is it really necessary to explain these vernacular words?) and professional writers as I could possibly assemble in the time allotted. Then 108 questionnaires were mailed out and 71 responses received, to make up the bulk of the symposium.

Right from the beginning I decided that no copies would be for sale, to further enhance the value of the book. It was published on April 15, 1960, in an actual-count edition of 125 copies and they were distributed in this fashion: The Spectator Amateur Press Society, 40; the contributors, 71; The Library of Congress, two; and friends of the immediate family, science fiction or otherwise, twelve. The original symposium, in gratitude for his work on behalf of Advent:, was dedicated to Damon Francis Knight ("for dfk from a creeping Jesus").

Jim O'Meara, my science fiction partner, and I loading up the car very early Saturday morning with cartons of blank paper and the pre-typed Multilith masters for *Who Killed Science Fiction?* Driving (Illinois to Ohio) to Lynn Hick-man's house in one quick stretch with only an occasional beer to ease toll-road congestion and help compress the time. A pity neither of us was into weed. Then. If it had been 1980 then, and we could have afforded it, a little coke could have definitely made *every*thing go better—*La chispa de la vida...* such a pity they had to dilute the formula. Wonder what an original Coca-Cola tasted like? How much white crystal did it take to make caramel-colored lemonade, souped up with caffeine (bad) and sugar (worse), a worldwide symbol?

The three of us, Lynn, Jim, and me, slaving over a whirling, clicking Multilith monster for hours, running off and backing-up the 107 numbered pages of *Who Killed Science Fiction?* Carolyn bringing us beers and making us stop long enough to eat dinner. Funny, after 20 years I still remember the broiled halibut steaks she made for us, with lemon slices...dinner was *that* good. I can't even remember what I had to eat last night.

Carolyn putting the kids to bed and Lynn putting me and Jim back to the duplicator...working late into the beery night before crashing. Finishing the printing later the next day before long-haul driving back to Chicago, the car loaded with printed sheets, the ink still drying.

Later, spreading the 55 stacks of printed sheets out around my kitchen, collating and stapling them, midwifing the birth pains of *Who Killed Science Fiction?*

What fannish energy we had then, Jim, Lynn, and me. Carolyn. Anyone care to put out a one-shot?

Advent:(ing with Ed, George, Jim, Jon, and Sid) began as a fanac (fan-activity) idea and a rented IBM typewriter on my kitchen table. It lives! Year after year growing stronger and better, leaving in its wake an unparalleled accumulation of science fiction data. Pride. Prestige.

My original prognosis that the quality of the contributions to *Who Killed Science Fiction?* and the unavailability of copies would make the book exceptionally noteworthy proved to be correct. In Seattle in 1961 I was presented with a Hugo. It felt great! I actually didn't know I had won until the announcement was made (because by that time I had become totally involved in science fiction politics, campaigning to bring the next Worldcon to "GO ChicaGO!"). There was a heart-stopping moment before the adrenalin surged through me and I held the statuette in my hands. It was especially rewarding because it meant that the people who voted for *Who Killed Science Fiction?* were, in most instances, voting for something they had to borrow even to see, as there was no chance for them to own a copy until now.

I recall making a vow that I would attempt no follow-up to the publication. Surely by waiting 20 years to do just that, I haven't broken too solemn an oath to myself, however much I try to convince myself that I've retired as God (without usurping any prerogative of Elmer Perdue's), leaving egomania to those better equipped to handle the residuals.

The replies came in to the symposium questionnaires, all 71 of them, and I began arranging the responses and abstracting the data for publication and—Christ, I was insufferable—had the audacity to hold my audience captive, forcing them to listen to my final word (often meaningless blather).

I don't do things like that any more. That's one of the things about me/then that's abhorrent to me/now. Perhaps I *needed* to do it for some long-forgotten reason; I no longer need things like that. I might be doing a bit of unconscious penance in my efforts to expand the original edition, and I do want to take this (again captive?) opportunity to apologize to everyone for having been such an insufferable ass before. A specific illustration being my comments directed toward Kurt Vonnegut, Jr., yet I discovered I had begun this Foreword by paying homage to him *without* remembering (or rereading until I had written this) what I had said or why in 1960. Hopefully time will not make such fools of us all.

Fragmented! Bits and pieces of science-fictional time/places crowding in on me and recycling. 1950. 1960. 1980. 20___. To such an extent that I can't remember when the fragments were real. If they were. They were.

Religion. Scam. Same-same. (?) Remember the Golden Era of *Astounding*, L. Ron? Broad sweeping theatrical gestures while affecting that old opera cape and chugging it out for half-a-cent a word? *Fear, Typewriter in the Sky*, and finally that eventful first article for John about something new you wanted to call Dianetics. Success *is* success. You're everywhere now (*and* secluded on the big boat at the same time)…buildings, billboards, and bumper-stickers; stacks of books in most of the stores. Your disciples (so sincere) stop me on the street to "clear" the way, only they don't even know who you were. I don't know who you are. But you made it and that's enough, you're real to enough people, and when you *believe*, as they obviously do, that's all that matters. And I still think *Final Blackout* is your best book.

In those days I wasn't even into sex and drugs and rock and roll (Ian Dury and the Blockheads). I had to get out of kindergarten first. I couldn't say "fuck" out loud (or think the word without blushing). The airbrushed (heaven forbid even a hint of pubic hair—a questionable shadow—should appear beyond the fringes of the centerfold's chaste bikini bottom) thigh-flesh in *Playboy* absolutely astounded me.

1962. Me a 33-year-old virgin with the whole Pick-Congress stuffed with 'round-the-clock hookers, waiting for the big convention. (After it was over, there were semiofficial complaints that we hadn't engaged enough of them. But even cowgirls get the blues, eh, Tom Robbins?)

Homecoming! GO ChicaGO! Chairing the 1962 World Science Fiction Convention. People coming from far-off exotic places. (I wasn't into traveling then, and that's where the fragmentation actually began. You really *can't* keep them down on the farm once they've seen Paree.) Freaks and multi-millionaires rubbing shoulders in the ballrooms. Me trying to force myself back to the podium instead of pursuing my favorite writers so they could autograph my books (Doubleday book club editions…"With cut-rate best wishes, Isaac Asimov"), frantically reassuring some of the more reticent that yes, indeed, the puff of smoke would magically happen and they could appear—

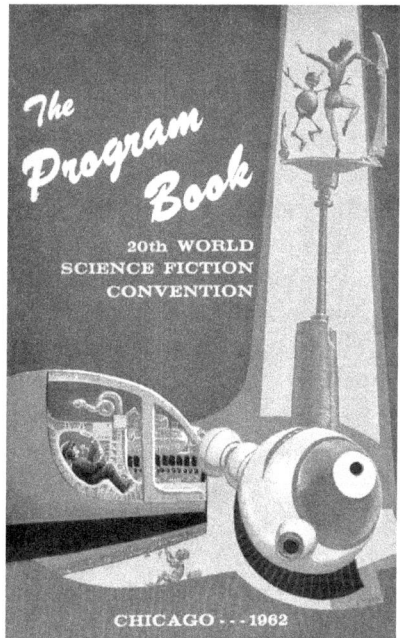

The Program Book

20th WORLD
SCIENCE FICTION
CONVENTION

CHICAGO - - - 1962

immaculately conceived yet again—in a blaze of theatrical glory or a white tuxedo, whichever they most desired.

Me (flat busted broke as usual) and old H.L. Hunt (flusher than just about anyone) sitting on soda fountain stools, having breakfast. *Money! (The Dark Side of the Moon.)* Seated at the counter because he's too cheap to tip for a table. Nibbling through long silences of dry toast and never finding out why he invited me or what he wanted to say. Watching him—incredulously—Jack Benny finger *pennies* from the deep recesses of a (well-worn and much-used) snap-closed change purse, doing his damnedest to outwait me, hoping I'd pick up the check. How're things in Alpaca?

Assembling the writers panel for the big *Playboy* symposium on science fiction for "Spec"—kind gentleman all the way—then making it over to the mansion (1313 N. State Parkway; before the California period) for a little party. "You are cordially..." A Four Fuckin' Ayem Breakfast Bash! Christ, what class! Charlie Beaumont and Shel Silverstein bullshitting and ripping off improbably impromptu tunes. Hef in the corner propped up with pillows and Pepsi, staring starry eyed, surrounded by more prominent genre writers than had ever been assembled before at one time in one room...sliding down the fire-pole to heaven, finding it stage-set with underwater bathing beauties, chastely beyond shatter-proof glass walls.

Fragmented! The wedding night...bedside, nightstand, and all...contraceptives and sterile lubricant courtesy of Blake Pharmaceutical. ("Say, Officer, does this look like a drug store to you?")

Scott & Crew trying to be very secretive, especially from each other. "For God's sake, don't ever let anyone know...just keep the checks coming." Closet pornographers; at one time, half the SFWA roster. Ripping off rent money and car payments by hacking out a novel ("whore books," the typesetter insisted) or two a month. Instant cash. The more eager writers clearing in excess of $20 grand (in *1960 dollars*) a year that way. No sweat. Hello, Don Holliday, J.X. Williams, John Dexter, etc., etc. Hope all is well with you these days...somehow your current science fiction books are much more enjoyable.

Fragmented! Nothing does it better than 2,000 miles between breakfast and lunch. Combine a business trip with a little fun and games...check out San Diego and see what it feels like, how it'd be to move there, office and all. (Percy Foreman, very much into his continuous happy hour..."I wouldn't give those FBI fuckers the time of day." Ian Ballantine to the rescue, checking out Neiman-Marcus at the same time.)

Tijuana! Unique and different. The single largest city on the west coast. The *entire* west coast, and growing like a brush fire in a drought. *Gusto mucho, gracias.*

Then the traveling began for real, meetings with foreign publishers about translation rights, attending international trade fairs in fantasylands: K/obenhavn, Frankfurt, Saó Paulo, Tokyo, Amsterdam, etc.

Nine days in Nice, sipping California (*elegamment*) sherry and talking about Martha's Vineyard and pornography with Harold Robbins but desperately wanting to talk with Gore Vidal (across the room from me every day) about *Messiah* (one of my all-time top ten), but too timid to approach him, being too much in awe of the man who gave/gives me so much over the years.

Mexicos. Plural. So many of them. So many times. Bypassing my first world-con in dozens of years for Teotihuacán and sitting atop the pyramid of the sun where the beating hearts were harvested, looking down the processional street of the dead toward *Palacia Mariposa* (the Butterfly Palace). So science fictional, every bit as genuine as *2001: A Space Odyssey* (with Arthur all the way to hell and gone, playing Columbus in Columbo and scuba-ing through acres and acres of smooth brown firm boy flesh). Sitting on the steps of the observatory at Chichen Itza, a commonplace, functioning landmark before Mary's virginity ever came into question. So many real/imaginary fantasies—too much science fiction for one planet. (*Planet* and lovely Leigh; two early loves that never faded, even for a moment.)

Fragmented! New, conflicting data began doing their share of reconstruction—less a Renaissance man and more an ambulatory paint-by-number. Absorbing. Recording. Homogenizing. Computerizing.

And at each stop, looking for home. That very special paradise. Papeete. Montego Bay. Cancun. Santo Domingo.

Rejecting most and eagerly rushing toward the next, knowing paradise was surely just ahead if I could only be patient long enough to get there.

Paradise is different things/places to different people, until it changes even for them. L. Frank Baum lived in paradise for a while during the early 1900s—San Diego, at the Hotel del Coronado, inspiring the set for "Fantasy Island." ("Tattoo in Munchkin-land?" Hervé Villechaize and Margaret Hamilton. Ricardo Montalban and his Cordova commercials were actually filmed there.) Inside the cool, protective gingerbread, Baum recorded some of Oz's best histories. Later, he designed the radical "Crown Room" as it remains to this date. "Paradise" was the word he used to describe his retreat, not mine.

I *know* paradise, for a time at least, is/was/will be Camelot.

Camelot is Ajijic.

La casa de mi Corazon—the subconscious residence of my dreams.

A 100-year-old adobe shack right in the middle of a native Indian village a block and a half from the shore of Laguna Chapala, Mexico's largest inland lake, where Ken Kesey parked his Kool-Aid acid bus for a while. The science fiction Mexico (A science fiction film festival in nearby Guadalajara) five and a half years of houseguests—fans and writers alike. Books in the library or scattered around the rooftop sundeck; bare bodies burning at Jalisco midday…the sun directly overhead. Sweat rolling from the tips of firm nipples and trickling across the pages of Heinlein. Margaritas overturned onto Clement.

Horseback riding in the hills. Boating down to San Juan Cosalá to the hot mineral springs baths, jammed with a dozen visiting writers/fans, naked and satiated, eating fresh Oaxacan mushrooms and acid-laced hashish brownies (frosted), washing them down with Santa Maria Reserva.

Tetsu Yano and Nori Ito and the League of Professional Translators getting me drunk on Sapporo and showing me paradise Geisha style. Naked and satiated 30 floors above the Ginza in a high-rise bathhouse, finding out about delicacy and strength and listening to the sibilant slapping of tiny feet running up and down my back. Same-same.

A fannish trek southward, making regular pilgrimage to San Miguel de Allende to dip into Mack's bottomless imperial gallon of tequila—shot by shot. Ted and George Cogswell and the kid-glove wedding—fresh sangria all around. Lunching with two tables and thirteen high-visibility secret service agents separating me from Lady Bird at La Casa de Sierra Nevada, Jeanette's very best.

Everyone naked into the pool at midnight, con-time. Anywhere. *Everywhere.*

Fragmented! Some color beginning to be visible in the background. Things starting to look a bit alive as the paint-by-number continued to absorb data stored for use in alternate reconstructions. A little balling. A little hallucinogenics. A little loud music.

Approaching a separately real Mexico through the separate reality of Carlos Castaneda. Don Juan also taught me (only my Yaqui was a brujo named Bill). He prepared the smoke and power plants and choreographed a scenario to move me, comprehendingly, through the unknown recesses within in my head. Weeks, years, moving together between the cracks in the world. Me don Genaroing—or Sancho Panzaing—gliding over the silent desert like a huge silver crow. Acapulco Gold in the spectacular Sonoran sunset or looking through dayglow windowpane, finding bits of myself—reflected everywhere.

Fragmented! Mescaline in the desert during a full moon. Gagging down peyote buttons in the infinite sand dunes then playing Morrison's lizard, crawling belly down naked through the vastness of my altered imagination.

Sitting in a lush green plaza in Cuzco just getting high on rarefied air, determined to remember the special thrill of breathing two-mile-high oxygen while watching the Indians peddle fresh-dried *Truxillo coca* leaves. Green cocaine tea, pumpernickel toast, and roast guinea pig. Walking through streets and into buildings in continuous use since before Columbus (*discover!* My ass…) was born. Machu Picchu—strolling with the alpacas, wondering how any city so magnificent could have remained unknown for so many years in modern civilization as we know it today courtesy of the Firesign Theatre and George Leroy Tirebiter (*Don't Crush That Dwarf, Hand Me the Pliers*).

Fragmented! The paint-by-number outline is definite, the flesh tones coming in stronger, stopping just at the beltline with nothing visible beneath. Space—sex, the ultimate frontier—the border separating the things you're expected to believe and the things that are.

Jojo left his home in Tucson, Arizona, bought some California grass (*Let It Be.* I never had the chance to tell you I love you, John). Philip and *Flesh; The Lovers* and "your place or mine?" Opening minds and removing fetters. Furtive midnight skinnydippers at Stopa's ski lodge (Cheers, Fritz!) to hundreds of fans in convention-hotel pool(s), year after year and growing bigger/stronger. Don't dream it; *be* it (from *The Rocky Horror Picture Show* soundtrack album)!

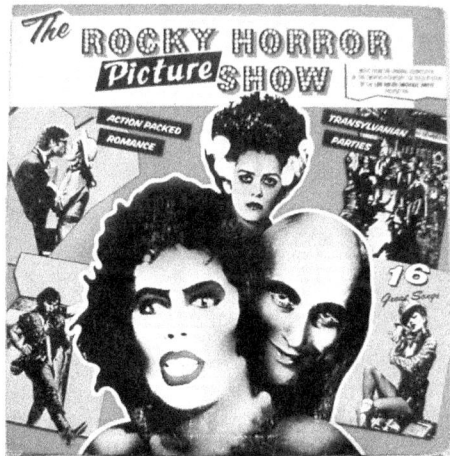

Take the limits of your imagination and push onward, starting from there. Grab your *Titanic* doughnut and jump into Michelangelo's *Creation of Adam—*In Just Seven Days *I Can Make You* A Man—with Frank N. Furter and the rest of the chorus line from the floor show while watching the late-night "science fiction double-feature movie show"(in the back row). I'm not much to look at by the light of day, but by night I'm one hell of a lover. Do the Time Warp again all the way back to the beloved planet of Transsexual in the galaxy of Transylvania, you unconventional conventioneers in ego-matching costumes and black fishnet hose.

Oh, God! I *am* the American dream (from the *Sheik Yerbouti* album)…
Dreams die quick in America. FBI locking you in a room and bad-coping
you relentlessly. "Here's your script, just the way it happened. Memorize your
part and don't forget it. We want you to say it just the way we wrote it." Customs
locking you in airport slammers, naked—jeering, meticulously searching, finding nothing… "Turn around and bend over. Spread them just a bit wider so I
can…" Postal Inspectors jumping out of the shadows and giggling…"Gonna
get your ass, man. Gonna get it good!" Military Police—a major, wow!—in Viet
Nam…"don't give a fuck what it says on these papers, sign them okaying what I
said we did yesterday. Or else…it's a *long* way back to California…"
Oh, God! I *am* the American dream (reprise)…

Social nudity. Thousands of people on Black's Beach on good days. One
small strip for person, one giant orgasm for personkind. Sex. Reaching the limits of my quite-active imagination and continuing onward, gently led by softly
enticing muses. There are confidences to be found *menage a trios*-ing that exist
nowhere else, take my word for it…and about multiple balling and recreational
sex and sex as spectator sport and hello there, Michael Valentine Smith—you
finger-lickin' good devil—why don't we do it in the road (*White*)?

Mickey Mouse and me. Annette and rat-eared beanies (a very far cry
from Boomtown Rats…"Billy, take a walk; take a walk with me…" Pilgriming
again…from the *Boomtown Rats* album). 50 years old!
Bob Bloch wrote a fascinating article (see *The Eighth Stage of Fandom*;
Advent:) about his feelings upon turning 40, and here I am, writing a fragmented reconstruction of myself to commemorate turning 50. We're the
same age, Mickey and me, and we each act about the same.
Mickey Mouse and me (and the CIA looking over our shoulder) in the
Sheraton as this fantastic speed-freak hands me the phone so her brother,
Peron's physician (the old man wasn't quite dead yet; "syphilis, you know"),
could prescribe for my head cold…then trading me half a lid for Mickey
("You can't imagine what this is worth in Argentina…" *Arr-hen-tee-neah*)
right off my wrist (shades of Hirohito). Good shit, too, but alas not Buenos
Aires weed. (Her stash was flown in periodically from a dealer just off the
University of Chicago campus. The University of Chicago Science Fiction
Club, *home* for many wonderful years.) Fantasy worlds and bad-ass weed.
Bogotá and white crystals, clearing out the cobwebs in the head… " 'so-
kay, mahn, *no problemas*. We deliver right to your hotel room…."
Ali Baba and the 40 Thieves in caftans and burnooses, 1001 Nights in
one week in a fourth-floor walk-up in Tangier. Walls draped with thick tap-
estries and hookahs strategically placed, ganja burning continuously. Kef…
three-year-old kids building houses with their toy blocks (compact kilos of

finest Moroccan hashish). Another toke from Aladdin's lantern and off we go, Sabu and me, on the Caliph's magic carpet, dodging the minarets at prayer time, our heads bowed reverently toward Mecca.

Enterprise—flying rug. Same-same.

Rabidly antiwar, anti-Nixon, anti-administration. Positions that too many assumed were downright un-American, but which were in fact just the opposite. Too many speeches, too many editorials, and too much personal attention from the wrong sources. But there are repayments. I don't have words enough to describe the satisfaction of watching John Mitchell and Richard Nixon live through their finest hours.

"Who is Adam Hart?" (Pink Floyd? *Atom Heart Mother*?) You remind me of the man...Frank; his cap and ever-present white socks. The rogue of Sherman Street, 31 Flavors ("More ramsberry sherhoo, Algis?"), and the Dark Place. Frank and his painfully sunburned ass...flashing German tourists on a secluded Mexican beach long before Irwin Allen fired his retros, jet-propelling Frank into upward mobility. Dove. Sharing a byline on *The Truth About Vietnam* and learning what it is to gut-twist hate what we were doing over there. Me determined to help make sure we never did it again.

Visiting Richard Eney at his apartment in Saigon quite by accident. A tourist, for God's sake. Flying in first class via commercial and flipping the military off. Arrogantly, ugly-Americanishly pulling press credentials strong enough to priority-bump my way via military transport to PhuBi, ChuLi, Da-Nang, etc. Checking the "Six O'clock News" out firsthand. Being checked out in return. Finding, even there...in Saigon—bidets and superb gourmet French cuisine, helicopters overhead incessantly and war all around—that science fiction endures, *whoever's* in charge. *While* they are. Writing "War is hell!" postcards as a lark and sending them via military frank to the fans back home before Air Cathaying over to Phnom Penh, picking up my first injury—dysentery, from first-class French champagne and Russian caviar (war *is* hell).

Limping back to Hong Kong ("Bartender, will you settle an argument for us? Is this the Hong Kong Hilton or the Tokyo Hilton?") and locking myself in the john for a week, sending the bellboy out for Simak and van Vogt ("The only 'space stuff' I could find!"), rereading some old friends and moaning, "Oh, God! Oh, God..." while shitting my life away.

A day in the life (*Sgt. Pepper's*)....

Busted. On the beach at San Blas. Half a dozen of us playing soccer on the sand after skinnydipping—temperature *and* humidity hovering around 100°. Locked up. Slow, endless hours of nothing but solicitations from pimps trying to convince us they should bring their girls *into* the *carcel* for us. The shock of the reality of locks and barred exits; the poor conditions and humor of it all.

Busted. (Watergated?) Half a world away; lecturing on "Sex as Political Protest" at the Vincennes campus of the University of Paris, built on the site that was once Donatin de Sade's palatial summer *chateau*.

The final appeal denied—three trips through the Supreme Court and four and a half years later—picking up the current issue of *Time* and discovering that impossible happening for myself—*shock!*—then going out among the strings and mulattos of Copacabana in a fog of disbelief. Ah, Rio ("by the seao, on a summer night..." Bette Grable, Don Ameche, Carmen Miranda, Phil Silvers), the most spectacularly beautiful city in the world, from Jesus Christo to Sugarloaf with Ipanema in between—and I have to convince myself to come back to...*that?*

Locked up. Slow, endless hours of nothing beyond the calculated-but-assuredly-nonexistent sadism of a very few, working overtime to prove there are *no* political prisoners...certainly not in Terminal Island. The shock of the reality of locks and barred exits; the inhumanity and irony of it all. Warner Brothers. Firs*t* *National* 1940 with Edward G. Robinson (cigar in corner of mouth) and George Raft (one-two-three-kick, four-five and dip) in the adjoining cell, plotting the B*I*G Break.

Pushing aside needles and boringly omnipresent heroin and watching guards turn away so they wouldn't have to witness six people shooting up with the same unclean needle. Smoking high-quality weed (deliberately exhaling smoke toward the guards so they'd have to pretend not to smell it) and snorting kick-ass coke almost daily...wondering if there wasn't something a little fucked up with the system. Rapping with Sarah Jane Moore (everyone calls her Sally) about politics and secret code messages and official orders to which blind obedience must be given...with Sandra Goode, one of Charlie Manson's chicks, discussing the philosophy of mass mind control. "I've got some friends inside (*L.A. Woman*)...."

Buying absolutely *any*thing for a price—carbon copies of the warden's letters concerning me *before* he got them to sign; two packs of coffin nails per. Packages of six pre-rolled high-grade Colombian numbers; $5 green or $10 script. Watching hundreds of dollars being rolled up regularly for the Man to take outside when his shift ended for the day. Listening to Gordo on the telephone once a week, reeling off memorized numbers and code names, talking to Culiacán (business as usual), making sure the brown sugar flowed northward. Fist fights and racial tension and the shower room scene "...just temporary, you know. I'd never think of doing *this* on the outside. Come on, man, let me play with it..." Macho man on the outside; Village People to the core.

Too many lifetimes jammed into three and a half months, absolute proof positive of the power of power. "Don't confuse me with facts, man; I got my orders."

I wouldn't have missed the experience for anything.

Fragmented! The whole dispersed into a kaleidoscope of once-and-future. Divorced. Beginning. Stumbling. Connecting. Growing. Reconstruct/ing/ed. A 20-year instant replay.

Merely to reprint *Who Killed Science Fiction?* as a 20-year-later nostalgia item is not good enough for me. I had that thought early-on, when structuring a mental reissue, and came up with the idea of including four new questions of a more current-interest/timelessness nature.

Those four additional questions are:

1. Looking backward for 20 years at the fortunate turn of events that has brought us from science fiction's low reception in 1960 to to-day—what single event (or person) do you feel contributed most to 1980's success, particularly in academic circles and visual mediums such as television, films, etc.?

2. If you found yourself in a position where you could have one only science fiction book published between 1960 and 1980, which single title would you select to own?

3. Looking forward to the year 2000 and the third edition of *Who Killed Science Fiction?*, what medium (already existing or not yet contemplated) will become, in your opinion, the largest market area for science fiction material?

4. Do you have any retrospective comments concerning the 1960 edition of *Who Killed Science Fiction?* that you would care to share?

Replies to the new questions are presented here in two sections. Persons who contributed material to the 1960 edition of *Who Killed Science Fiction?* are assembled in Appendix B, called "Twenty Years and Tomorrow." Persons whose remarks are contributed to this edition but who are not included in the original are assembled as "Other Voices," in Appendix C.

Abstracts and summarizations of the new data from Appendix B and Appendix C are included in my Afterword, "The Singer's Going to Sing a Song,"

There are a number of people who have made significant contributions to this edition of *Who Killed Science Fiction?* in real time and physical effort, and others who have encouraged the intangible. Acknowledging their kindness and helpfulness is more a pleasure than an obligation.

To Frank M. Robinson—for the Introduction, the advertising, the encouragement, and for being there whenever.

To Betsy Groban—for bringing it all together.

To Charlie Brown, Edie Buckner, Howard DeVore, Gillian Jones (for the good times), Earl Terry Kemp, Vivien Kern, George W. Price, and George Scithers—for giving *Who Killed Science Fiction?* 1980 its measure of quality and pertinence.

To all the contributors, 1960 and 1980, who wanted to share their opinions within the framework of this symposium.

I LOVE YOU ONE AND ALL!

Now please, everyone, may I have your close attention? Lock your wigs in place, let all the air out of your shoes, and prepare yourselves for a token period of simulated exhilaration. (*I Think We're All Bozos on This Bus.*) Everybody ready? Okay then, let's get in sinc for our flight to the future...

uture...
ture...
ure...
re...
e...
...
..
.

EARL KEMP
El Cajon, California
December, 1980

Introduction 1980
For Sale: One Cloudy Crystal Ball

by Frank M. Robinson

By some standards, 20 years isn't all that long a time. The events of the last two decades—that is, those events that affected me personally—are still relatively fresh in my mind. In 1960, I was editing *Rogue* magazine, a publication more than a little similar to *Playboy* but one which at least had pretensions. If you ask what I've done since then, I could cover it in a few lines: a little editing, a little writing, a brief sojourn in San Francisco, back to Chicago for three years, and then a return to San Francisco.

And if you press me, I'll insist—despite all physical evidence to the contrary—that I really haven't changed that much in 20 years. Sadly, perhaps gratefully (historians will make the final decision), that can't be said for the world at large. In the last 20 years, we've gotten into and out of Vietnam and we've seen riots in our major cities and on our college campuses. We've lived through the sit-ins and the Free Speech Movement, a president who resigned a few weeks before he would have been impeached, several wars in the Middle East, a revolution in the relations between the races, the growth of half a hundred religious/psychological cults, and dramatic changes in the rights accorded women and homosexuals. And, far from least, we've watched a total of twelve Americans walk on the surface of the Moon.

Not bad for 20 years.

On a different front, in 1960 a small furor was raised among the ranks of the science fiction faithful as to whether or not magazine science fiction was dead and if so, who—or what—had killed it. Perhaps no more than a grace note to history (though I tend to think that science fiction has vastly more significance than even its fans accord it), the question drew an in-depth response from a surprising number of the fans and science fiction writers of the period. Many of the answers, of course, reflected the ever-present longing for the "good old days," despite the fact that on close analysis the good old days seldom turned out to be all that good.

175

In the survey conducted 20 years ago, eleven of the respondents said that magazine science fiction was dead. Some 55 denied it, but of these, 38 qualified their denials. It was actually something of a curious response: the mourners were showing up for the funeral a little late. What is popularly referred to as the "golden age" of science fiction (1939-1941) had long since passed and the majority of the magazines that died later, died along with the rest of the pulp magazines in the early and middle 1950s.

Approximately 60 issues of magazines devoted solely to science fiction were published in 1960. The total for 1980 will probably be a few more than 70, though the number of peripheral publications will add substantially to that. It is of interest to note that all the major science fiction magazines published in 1960 are still with us. Yet, if you asked the average science fiction fan today if magazine science fiction was dying, the answer might still be: "No, but—"

When the question was first put forward in 1960, there was no way the respondents could look into the future and see the course science fiction would take. There was no way of knowing, for example, that John W. Campbell, Jr., the editor of *Astounding Science Fiction* (soon to become *Analog*) in 1963 would undertake his Noble Experiment of enlarging *Analog* to standard magazine size (8 ½ "x11 ½ "), printing it on high-quality book paper and making an attempt to attract *Scientific American*'s advertisers as well as its readers. The large-size *Analog* was to run for 24 issues and in the eyes of many was the most beautiful science fiction magazine ever published...

Nor was there any way of knowing, in 1960, that two of the most successful series in the history of science fiction would be featured in the pages of *Analog* during the next 20 years: the *Dune* novels by Frank Herbert and the Anne McCaffrey stories about the dragonriders of Pern. (And who would have guessed that both these series would field hardcover bestsellers?) In 1960, James Schmitz was yet to do his best work for *Analog*, Randall Garrett was yet to write *Too Many Magicians*, the pulp Bob Silverberg was still undergoing a transformation new and strange, and Larry Niven, Jerry Pournelle, and Joe Haldeman were yet to contribute their not-inconsiderable best. Hal Clement would write a sequel to his popular *Mission of Gravity*, and a number of outstanding women writers (among them Vonda McIntyre, Joan D. Vinge, and "James Tiptree, Jr.") would become part of *Analog*'s stable.

A *Galaxy* which had fallen upon hard times would, nevertheless, publish a string of stunning stories by Cordwainer Smith, *I Will Fear No Evil* by Robert Heinlein, *Rendezvous with Rama* by Arthur C. Clarke (another hardcover bestseller), Fred Pohl's *Gateway*, and a number of superb stories by Theodore Sturgeon, James White, and others.

If, a relatively minor magazine in the late 1950s, was to be nominated as "Best Science Fiction Magazine of the Year" three times in the 1960s. And there was good reason. Under the editorship of Fred Pohl (and, later, Judy-

Lynn Benjamin and Ejler Jacobsson), it published *Podkayne of Mars, Farnham's Freehold*, and one of the very best of Robert Heinlein's novels, *The Moon Is a Harsh Mistress*. Keith Laumer's "Retief" stories would be featured, as well as tales by Alan Dean Foster and Piers Anthony. And just before *If* combined with *Galaxy* in the middle 1970s, it would publish one of the last stories by Leigh Brackett: "The Ginger Star."

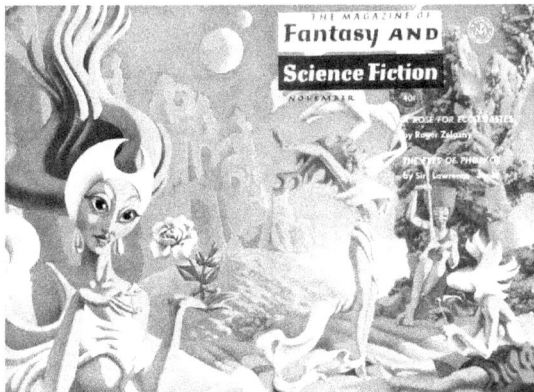

Roger Zelazny was to publish heavily in *Amazing* and *Fantastic*, as well as in the *Magazine of Fantasy and Science Fiction*. The latter magazine would also publish Heinlein's *Glory Road*, Zelazny's *The Doors of His Face, the Lamps of His Mouth*, *Man Plus* by Pohl, A.J. Budrys's *Michelmas*, and stories by talented new authors Tom Reamy and John Varley.

There were, of course, the lights that failed. *Vertex*, a slick-paper magazine out of Los Angeles, applied modern layout and art techniques to science fiction and featured interviews with writers and reviews of books and films along with its fiction. An ambitious magazine ahead of its time, it published fifteen issues starting in 1973. Its final two were printed on the same paper and in the same size as the underground newspapers of the period.

In the 1960s and 1970s, science fiction would appear with increasing frequency in the better men's magazines. *Playboy* and *Rogue* would consistently publish Ray Bradbury, Arthur C. Clarke, Charles Beaumont, Harlan Ellison, Robert Sheckley, and others. The question of whether or not science fiction would be accepted by a mass-magazine audience would be answered with a definite *yes*.

During this same period, science fiction in hardcover and paperback climbed in popularity to the point where it eventually accounted for almost 10 percent of *all* fiction titles published. (It shouldn't be forgotten, of course, that a sizable percentage of the titles were stories and novels that had originally appeared in the magazines, or were based on concepts and characters first popularized by the magazines.)

Academia, which had warned generations of school children not to read that "trash," finally decided it couldn't beat back the flood and launched its own boat. High schools and universities started giving courses in science fiction and, by the late 1970s, these courses numbered in the hundreds. It was a novel experience for writers to run across their stories in textbooks, complete with quizzes at the end....

The burgeoning popularity of science fiction reflected into the conventions as well. From one annual get-together and several regional ones, conventions proliferated to the point where it was difficult to find a weekend when some convention wasn't going on some place. The 1979 Westercon, held in San Francisco, even found it necessary to ask the local newspapers and television stations *not* to popularize the event for fear it couldn't handle the crowds.

And then there were the Apollo missions which, more than anything else, legitimatised science fiction. No longer were the authors wild-eyed dreamers. A proud and sometimes bitter Robert Heinlein considered the landing on the Moon as his personal vindication. A lifetime devoted to popularizing the idea of travel to other planets, of encouraging the interest of boys and young men in the sciences, had finally paid off in magnificent fashion: Robert Heinlein and his fellow authors were as responsible for the success of the landings on the Moon as the engineers who built the rockets that carried the astronauts there. Most of the engineers owed their interest in the project in the first place to Heinlein and his compatriots…

Other events contributed to the popularity of science fiction during the 1960s and 1970s, not the least of which was the growing interest in science fiction and fantasy graphics: the publication of calendars, science fiction "encyclopedias," and unabashed collections of the artwork that had contributed so much to the success of the early magazines. Frank R. Paul, Howard Brown, Hans Wessolowski, Leo Morey, and Virgil Finlay finally came into their own—as did newcomers Frank Kelly Freas, Vincent di Fate, and Chris Foss, among others.

It was on the television tube and the silver screen, however, that science fiction had perhaps its finest triumph. On September 8, 1966, *Star Trek* began its first season. It was canceled after the fall season of 1969, but by that time Captain Kirk, Spock, Doc, Scotty, and Uhura had become household names—and not just in the homes of science fiction buffs. In 1968, MGM released the Stanley Kubrick version of Arthur C. Clarke's *2001*. The most ambitious science fiction film made up to that point, *2001* boasted an overlay of Kubrick's mysticism along with spectacular special effects by Doug Trumbull. The critics loved it, the critics hated it, the critics didn't understand it… Surprisingly enough, some science fiction writers didn't care for it either, claiming a lack of plot. But the film remains Arthur C. Clarke's crowning achievement (as well as Kubrick's) and its special effects became the mark at which other filmmakers were to aim.

Silent Running and *Soylent Green* were lesser efforts, though the latter was a stunning realization of Harry Harrison's book, *Make Room, Make Room*, and provided a great vehicle for actors Edward G. Robinson and Charlton Heston (Robinson died soon after the film was made).

Star Wars, released in the late 1970s, became the highest-grossing film of all time. Some science fiction writers, again, gave it mixed reviews but the general public loved it. George Lucas had made it with the mind of a professional filmmaker and the soul of a child... The rush was now on to cash in on the box-office appeal of science fiction. *Battlestar Galactica* played one season on television before being canceled (great but repetitious special effects and a discouraging lack of imaginative stories). *Alien*, with a story line similar to A.E. van Vogt's "Discord in Scarlet" (first published in *Astounding* for December 1939) and set designs by H.R. Giger, was another smash success. Waiting for release at this writing is Disney's *Black Hole* and *Star Trek—The Movie* (which may top *Apocalypse Now* as the most expensive film ever made).

The effect of the films and television series on the science fiction field isn't difficult to calculate. The number of readers has increased vastly and the hardcover and paperback book fields have benefited tremendously. The blockbusters in the book field haven't been limited to the movie tie-in editions of *Star Wars* and *Alien*, however. Other titles have also done very well and advances paid to writers have increased in direct proportion. It's no longer unheard of for a science fiction author to receive a $100,000 advance for a book—a figure usually restricted to mainstream novels. Science fiction is no longer the ghetto of the publishing world.

Detailing the growth of science fiction from 1960 to its present popularity doesn't answer the question of whether magazine science fiction is dead, dying, or more popular than it's ever been.

But, then, the premise was wrong in the first place: magazine science fiction never died. Its nadir was the mid-1930s, when there were three titles in the field, only one of them a monthly. Titles began to proliferate in 1938 to 1939 and reached their peak in the early 1950s. Most of the titles that died in the 1950s died because the pulp magazines themselves died. (Street and Smith killed off *Doc Savage, The Shadow, Western Story*, and its other pulps in 1948-49; the collapse of the remaining pulp magazine chain and the demise of the American News Company in the mid-1950s completed the carnage.)

Magazine science fiction in 1960 played a vital role in the field and still does today, perhaps even more so. The field has seen a remarkable newcomer, *Omni*. Promotion and advertising have been heavy, especially on television, while the magazine itself features topnotch graphics, four-color reproduction, and slick paper. *Omni* has the type of production job usually associated with magazines such as *Playboy* and *Penthouse* (the publishers of *Omni*). The editorial mix is an enormously successful one of fact and fiction: the first issue of the magazine sold close to a million copies.

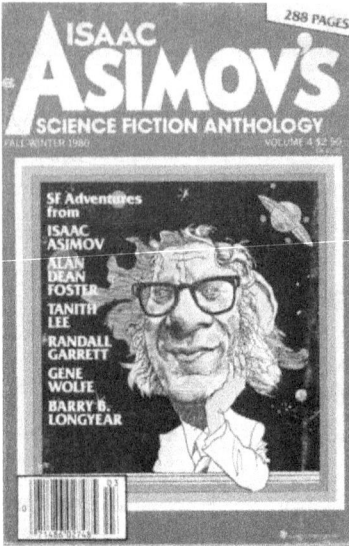

Galileo is a magazine that started as a semiprofessional publication and then switched to regular newsstand publication. In addition to its fiction selections, it offers articles about the field and numerous reviews. *Analog, The Magazine of Fantasy and Science Fiction, Galaxy,* and even *Amazing* and *Fantastic Adventures* are still with us. Davis Publications, under the more-than-capable editorship of George Scithers, has introduced *Isaac Asimov's Science Fiction Magazine* and *Asimov's SF Adventure Magazine.* Peripheral publications include *Starlog, Future, Heavy Metal,* and a soupcon of others, both professional and semiprofessional. In 1980, the science fiction magazines are alive and well.

To some critics, the success and vitality of the science fiction magazines is astonishing. Magazines devoted solely to science fiction have outlasted all other branches of genre fiction, with the exception of mystery stories (and of a few remaining mystery story magazines, none approaches the age of either *Amazing* or *Astounding/Analog*).

The reasons for the success of the magazines aren't hard to discover. A sense of continuity is one obvious sales advantage, as is familiarity. You see the same title month after month and, unlike a book by a new author, you know what to expect. Price is another inducement to purchase. The average magazine costs a little more than a dollar; the average paperback a little more than two; the average hardback, ten. For the reader who's fond of short stories, the competition narrows considerably to the magazines versus anthologies. And, like an anthology, the magazine can serve as a "sampler," letting the reader familiarize himself with a number of different writers.

There's another major advantage to magazines: in addition to the fiction, there are the graphics, editorials, letter columns where the reader can express his opinions on the magazine in particular or the world in general, book, movie, and television reviews, articles about science or about the science fiction field itself, information about upcoming conventions and similar events that might interest the reader, and ads for new science fiction books, games, and other related products.

In short, the science fiction magazine is far more than just a fiction magazine—it's also a service magazine on a scale that the original editors and readers never dreamed of. It represents a complete hobby, prepackaged with fiction, games, conventions, and social contacts all for $1.25 a throw. It was in 1960, and is now, one of the biggest entertainment bargains available at the newsstand or bookstore.

For the writer—and for the science fiction field in general—the magazines serve a function that's been grossly underestimated by their critics. They represent a ready market for beginning writers who are hesitant about investing the time and effort to attempt a major novel. Any author will tell you the difficulty of writing without any feedback on your work. Writing short stories allows a writer to build confidence in his own abilities. To sustain a novel requires that one have faith in one's self. It's no accident that most science fiction authors, from Asimov to Zelazny, started by writing short stories.

Once seasoned in the magazines, many authors graduate to the longer lengths. It's this constant flow of fresh talent and new ideas, first nourished by the magazines, that keeps the field as alive and vital as it is. If and when the magazines should vanish, we won't be talking about just *their* death—we'll be bemoaning the death of science fiction, period.

FRANK M. ROBINSON
San Francisco, California
December, 1979

Foreword 1980

Twenty Years and Tomorrow

Seventy-one people contributed their thoughts to the 1960 edition of *Who Killed Science Fiction?* The basic point of discussion at that time was the steady decline of magazine science fiction, and in trying to find other market areas that could take up the slack and be an economic factor within the genre. The comments were quite varied and pertinent. Of those original contributors, several of the very best have died within the 20-year span separating these two editions. It is indeed unfortunate that we do not have a full house once again, as they are definitely missed this time around.

There were additional problems with this reissue as well. I had lost contact with many of the writers who made *Who Killed Science Fiction?* such a success in 1960, and it was a near-impossible task even to reassemble their addresses. Time, too, took its toll, in the form of an abrupt deadline that denied the opportunity for patient research.

However, many of the original contributors are back again, giving us their thoughts on four new questions. These are the people who make up "Twenty Years and Tomorrow."

The questions asked for this edition were:

1. Looking backward for 20 years at the fortunate turn of events that has brought us from science fiction's low reception in 1960 to today—what single event (or person) do you feel contributed most to 1980's success, particularly in academic circles and visual mediums such as television, films, etc.?

2. If you found yourself in a position where you could have one only science fiction book published between 1960 and 1980, which single title would you select to own?

183

3. Looking forward to the year 2000 and the third edition of *Who Killed Science Fiction?*, what medium (already existing or not yet contemplated) will become, in your opinion, the largest market area for science fiction material?

4. Do you have any retrospective comments concerning the 1960 edition of *Who Killed Science Fiction?* that you would care to share?

Other Voices

BRADLEY, MARION ZIMMER

Hindsight, they say, invariably has 20/20 vision. For that reason I hadn't intended to issue any corrections or afterthoughts on my 1960 (!!!) commentary in *Who Killed Science Fiction?* It's easy to second-guess and say that we knew it all along. Because it seems that I was right; science fiction was far from dead, and in the years since then we have seen a most miraculous renascence of the whole genre.

But I've always been a sucker for people with nice soft voices who call me "luv" on the telephone, and when my old friend Earl Kemp called me up and specially asked me, so nicely, for a few afterthoughts, I told him, "Earl, flattery will get you almost everywhere," and sat down to the typewriter to gloat about the fact that I was right all along and that I told you so.

Science fiction has been alive and well all along; it was the mainstream that was dead, and the shortlived "New Wave"—an effort to bring the most trivial mannerisms of the mainstream into science fiction, with an eye on that will-o'-the-wisp known as "Academic Respectability" or "literary quality"— proved, by its rapid demise, that science fiction would not follow the sterile mainstream whose emphasis was on form, rather than content, into the trashbins of criticism. (Those who can, write; those who can't, become critics. It is easier to attack than to emulate.)

I think what saved science fiction was (and I fully expect to be thrashed, again, by those people who are secretly ashamed of writing science fiction instead of Literary Little Novels) the same surging force which sent the whole country's young people into long lines to see *Star Wars*; the desire, the *need*, if you will, for a sense of wonder. No, I don't think *Star Wars* was a "great

185

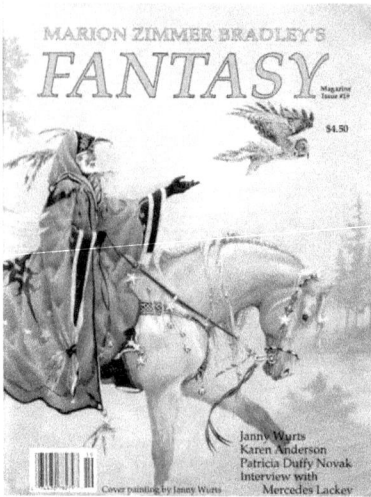

film," or even a good film. But it was bad in ways that did not matter to the audience—in fact, that did not matter in any way except to intellectuals and critics, who make up such an infinitesimal part of the audience that *they can, and should, be ignored.*

And, being bad in all the ways that mattered to the critics, it was good in all the ways that mattered to the audience. It had characters with whom the kids could identify—whole generations of fans and young kids flocked to conventions in Luke Skywalker or Princess Leia costumes. It had so many Jungian archetypes that it would take a psychological treatise to explain them all. It had a good story, and it had a happy ending where genuine human values triumphed after much struggle. It gave happiness and it gave catharsis, and that, I say, is worth all the damned good reviews in the world! So, to hell with the critics; what people want is the sense of wonder and the consolation of the happy ending—now, in the world of 1980, we need it a lot more than we did in 1945!

Because, ever since the days of the Greeks, what we need is a good story, and catharsis, and inspiration. And, damnit, that's what science fiction still has, if the critics will stop analyzing it to death and trying to find literary values in it! Let the critics dig around, 400 years from now, and bore everybody in their classrooms to death with analyzing *Dune* and *The Left Hand of Darkness* and *The Forgotten Beasts of Eld* and *A Spell for Chameleon* and works by C.J. Cherryh and Tanith Lee and John Brunner and Marion Zimmer Bradley, until future generations hate our names the way kids now hate Nathaniel Hawthorne and Herman Melville and William Shakespeare. By then, the young people will find something else they like, and it will be time for our works to be turned over to the critics, as dead as the works of Horace, Catullus, and Philip Marlowe…and as alive forever. (People are still reading Euripides—because he told damned good stories—not for his "literary merit.")

What trends do I like? Well, Don Wollheim says that about 70% of the good new writers are women, and that pleases me. I like the rebirth of fantasy, but that's personal—I never cared about "technology fiction." I like the franker handling of sex, because that's something I have fought for, tooth and nail, and laid my reputation and my income on the line in order to get that freedom.

I like the way in which science fiction is expanding to cover other races, women's interests, and while we did not lead the way (I don't think any artform ever does, despite the claims of the avant garde—you cannot force things down people's throats until the time is ripe), we are at least solidly reflecting the social changes, and trying very hard to design new ones and make them acceptable to the slower half of the intellectual climate, the ones who don't have a chance to see social change at their Aunt Minnie's dinner table, but can imagine it, through science fiction, and accept it when they do meet it in the world outside.

And, of course, I like the higher rates and the way in which people no longer stare and grimace when I tell them *what* I write. But I can live without that. Because science fiction is no longer my recreation and my delight, it's my profession, and that's what life is all about—finding out what you love, and doing it, and getting someone to pay you enough so you don't absolutely starve while you're doing it.

Unlike other writers who are proud of "not writing science fiction," or having "graduated honorably from my beginnings in the genre," I am proud and happy to be a science fiction writer. It was, in an old cliché, "a proud and lonely thing to be a fan," and it's still a proud thing, but not half so lonely, to be a fan and a writer. I hope I am still doing it at 86. Agatha Christie clung to *her* chosen profession that long, and I intend to follow her splendid example.

DE CAMP, L. SPRAGUE *

1) I don't think any *one* event caused the revival of science fiction during the 1970s. As far as there was a revival (and the sales of science fiction publications continued with a gradual rise throughout the decade, I believe) it can be attributed to several factors: the public's tiring of antiheroes, sociological tracts thinly disguised as fiction, experimental narrative techniques that leave the reader wondering who did what with what to whom, and tediously literal, tape-recorded realism; to the revival of fantasy sparked by publication of J.R.R. Tolkien's *Lord of the Rings* and republication of Robert E. Howard's *Conan* stories; and to the dizzy rate of technological progress, e.g., nuclear power and space exploration, both long favorite subjects of science fiction speculation.

2) Not sure, but it would probably be one of the Krishna novels.

3) Don't know.

4) Can't answer because I do not have a copy of *Who Killed Science Fiction?*

DEVORE, HOWARD

1) It's my opinion that man's landing on the moon was the major event as far as science fiction is concerned. With few exceptions, the U.S. population approved of the event and they believed that man had a destiny in space.

Suddenly those with the capability talked of space and were even convinced that it wasn't wild-eyed dreams; they might pick up a book that followed through on the general ideas. Many of them really didn't understand what they were reading but, since it was the "in thing," they would talk of the bits that they did understand and, if necessary, they would fake the rest. No longer could they dismiss the idea of space travel as being some sort of fairy tale.

There was the general feeling that now we could do anything we really wanted to. The American public has little interest in how things are accomplished by science; they just want to see the results, and suddenly the scientists had beaten the Russians. There's been a feeling of disillusionment since World War II. Each generation looks back to the good old days, not forward to the future, but finally there was something coming up. Perhaps we hadn't found life on the moon, but there was always Mars and Venus—surely something existed out there, and if necessary we'd go to the stars to find it. Luckily, this same population had no idea of the costs and time involved in future space flight.

When they learned, of course, they started whining about spending all that money on silly rocketships when it could be spent to feed "the poor"; they are still whining about social programs and the huge amounts wasted on space flight, but they continue to make use of the technology that was at least partially developed as side effects of the space program.

The moon landing has not tripled the readership of *Analog,* but it appears to have persuaded millions to see *Star Wars* at the movies and to watch *Battlestar Galactica* on television. A much smaller portion of the population is reading *Omni,* a much later version of Hugo Gernsback's *Science Wonder Stories;* they're being fed science and science fiction in doses they can tolerate. Hopefully they will become addicted, rather than allergic, to it.

2) Limited to a single science fiction book, I think I would immediately choose *The Science Fiction Hall of Fame.* Forced to choose a single story/novel, I might well make another choice, but for sheer quality and enjoyment, I would find more good reading in that single book. Perhaps it contains some rather dated/crude writing, but the ideas simply leap forth from the pages.

Many readers cling to the tales of their childhoods, fans apparently more than the general population. There seems little doubt that the stories that impressed you as a child cling stronger than more recent material. Oh,

I suppose that LeGuin and Haldeman are better writers than Weinbaum, but I can still recall the thrills I felt when I read Stanley's *Martian Odyssey* or Campbell's *Who Goes There?* As I read them I tried to think of a test that would separate the aliens from the men. I had no technical knowledge but I could follow the plots as the writers came up with something… and I could do the same with much of the material being published in that period. It didn't matter that their science was sketchy or nonexistent. I took things on faith in those days—I didn't know how to question it, nor did I want to.

Sometime in the coming weeks I'm going to meet with a local science fiction teacher. She tells me that she uses "traditional" material, and while I can admire and respect H.G. Well's *Time Traveler*, I'm going to do my best to change her curriculum. I'm going to force a copy of *The Hall of Fame* on her and, one way or another, I'll talk her into reading "First Contact," then I'll go on to Tom Godwin's "Cold Equations." It's time that these kids learned to *think* and solve problems, and if we can get them hooked, as I was 40 years ago, they'll continue to read science fiction. A portion of them will stay with it and, hopefully, they'll learn some discrimination.

3) Sense of Wonder? *The Hall of Fame* is loaded with it; good fiction should always stir the emotions. You can love the heroine, hiss the villain, and admire the man that chose the words to make this possible.

I would suppose that the standard paperback will remain the principal source of income for science fiction material, the magazines appear to be a marginal market at best, whereas people are accustomed to picking up books at almost any location. I assume that television specials will play a much larger part, but doubt that any television series can last over an extended period of time—they just simply wear themselves out in a matter of months or years. Oh, I suppose they'll have a flurry, but then cop stories did that, and before that, westerns played the same role. The public becomes jaded quickly and looks for a new medium; there's no reason to think that science fiction will fare any better than other genres.

However, what I'd like to see, and it's entirely possible, is the appearance of some form of animated game (perhaps using a television screen) that the public can participate in—something along the lines of the puppet show theater in *Star Wars*. The technology either exists or is almost here. Science fiction is primarily an interest of the young, and eventually someone will come up with a device that operates the figures or images by radio control or some such gadget. Can't you see your kids playing "Skylark" and moving Kimball Kinnison and Worsel the Venetian through their paces as they fight Boskone? Then, after supper, Pop will send them off to bed and switch figures while he decides how he will help rescue "The Golden Amazons of Venus" (*Planet Stories*, Vol. 1, No. 1); "Hey, look at the tits on that doll!"

4) When *Who Killed Science Fiction?* appeared in 1960, I felt quite strongly about the future of science fiction. I'd spent half of my lifetime then reading and enjoying it, and it certainly appeared that it was dying. Indications were that soon the magazines would all be gone, and while paperbacks were already a good portion of the market, I just couldn't get the feel of them as I had the old-time magazines. I could still remember the joy of opening a copy of *The Spider, Astounding, Doc Savage,* or *Flynn's Detective Fiction Weekly.*

I spent a deprived childhood; there were available to me two bimonthly science fiction magazines and one monthly, plus the borderline material, and whatever could be scraped up at the local public library. The appearance of a new issue of a magazine didn't really mean much since I had to wait until it showed up at the local used bookstore for 7 to 10 cents a copy or until I could beg two old magazines from someone and trade them in for the issue I desired. To the best of my knowledge, I didn't buy a magazine new, off the newsstand, until 1938 (and those were rare indeed, usually *Doc Savage*—if I could scrape up a dime), until I started earning my own money in 1941.

I must confess that I don't worry much about the future of science fiction now, and doubt that the new publication of *Who Killed Science Fiction?* will have the same effect it did 20 years ago. The market is strong enough now that most writers, artists, editors, etc., probably won't worry about it, and neither will I. I own a private library of some 20,000 books and magazines; they've taken me 40 years to accumulate and, if necessary, I can start with *Amazing Stories* No. 1 and reread them. I strongly suspect that they will last longer than I will.

Mostly what I recall about *Who Killed Science Fiction?* was the wild, wonderful feeling of being part of 1950s fandom, when even little events seemed important and, in those days, there were the friendships that developed as well, the small, intimate feeling of fandom when we had a common cause and interest.

I still attend conventions regularly, but it's just not the same; I don't know the people and their interests, families, etc. "Now, in the old days—the snow came way up to here"—no, that's Campbell's line, but there was a feeling of involvement. I can recall getting postcards from Chicago announcing a weekend party and deciding that I just couldn't make it, then a phone call from Cleveland and when I said that the tires on the car were bad, they'd announce that, after all it was only 100 miles out of the way, and they'd pick me up at 9 A.M. I'd turn to Sybil and tell her that I was going to Earl's party after all. There was the worry over attending the Midwestcon some years, but never really any doubt that I would attend…including 1954, when I'd been out of work for about six months and only had $2 in cash I could dare try to spare!

They were wild, adventuresome times, and we won't see their likes again, but sometimes it's better to remember the past than to regret the present and deplore the future.

EDMONDSON, G.C.

Who Killed Science Fiction? Well…it's alive and well in Argentina. I can't remember what opinion I had 20 years ago, but I'm sure I had one. Used to have lots of them. But I recall John W. Campbell, Jr., thought any reports of its demise were greatly exaggerated. Hard to tell what he'd have to say about the current crop.

Memory is selective, with an inverse Gresham's Law built in. Were it not so, the steady and inexorable accumulation of crap would render life beyond 40 unbearable. But even in a golden age, 99-44/100% of everything is crud. I've done over 50 volumes of it. Only two, maybe three, that I willingly hang my own name onto. The main virtue of the other 47-plus operas was that they paid off a couple of mortgages.

Do I enjoy writing? Well, there's a certain satisfaction in putting my name across the back of a publisher's check.

So who killed science fiction? Certainly not the scientists. I think the literacy explosion had a lot to do with it. Had I been born a century earlier, my writing would have been limited to letters and possibly a diary during winter months when the work was not too exhausting. But I was born into an era when every blacksmith knows how to spell and every housewife has a husband to subsidize her, plus clothes and dishwashers to give her the necessary time.

It's really a leisure explosion. Biologists assure us that no organism can exist in an atmosphere of its own waste products. To put it bluntly, science fiction is drowning in its own shit.

There enters an element of semantics into question No. two which is ambiguously phrased. My own choice would be the obvious one: a novel of my own—the only science fiction novel published in two decades. I could still use the money.

So let's say that, like any fiction, science fiction has undergone a number of changes in the past 20 or 30 years for various reasons—perhaps some writers and readers were no longer enchanted with the "gadgets" of the earlier magazines or the types of stories identified with A. Merritt and H.P. Lovecraft. (This is not to say that such stories and authors do not still have a following.) But for three or four generations science fiction has dealt perhaps more directly than any other fiction with the dreams and nightmares which have been a part of the twentieth century. That gives it strength, not a coffin.

1) I personally do not think science fiction had a "low reception" in 1960. After all, the Modern Language Association had already held three consecutive seminars (those dirty killers, I suppose some would say) on the genre. Nevertheless, it was undoubtedly the MLA Seminar and then the Popular Culture Association which brought academic attention to science fiction. And one must remember that many of those early teachers had been reading science fiction since the 1930s at least. Check with Jack Williamson for specific detail. In the visual medium, of course, it was *Star Trek* that captured the imagination as Buck Rogers and Flash Gordon had done a generation earlier. But *Star Trek* had a technical (visual) sophistication that not even the earlier movies had had. Notice, too, that during the 1960s there were both the so-called "New Wave" and *Star Trek*: the impact of both expanded the science fiction audience.

2) Details must be glossed over in such an instance as this; so to move on to the next question. To choose a single title published between 1960 and 1980 is one of those impossible tasks; however, if I had to choose the single title, my preference would be for one of Robert Silverberg's novels. If it were a short story, "Sundance" would have no competitor. Novel? I keep changing my mind as I reread them or try to work with various ones in class. Okay. *Tower of Glass,* because it illustrates so well how many significant themes can be treated well at one time.

3) I think the printed page, whether short story or novel, will remain the strength of science fiction by the year 2000. Primarily, the printed page allows one the greatest freedom of the imagination. *At present*, too, it permits subtleties that the picture does not allow. Of course there are exceptions; for example, if all films could match Harlan Ellison's *A Boy and His Dog* (all right, some people didn't like its story), then I might be convinced that the film will become science fiction's strongest medium. But film is too susceptible to formulas that are basically if not entirely visual in their effects. I think of *Prophecy* and, yes, *Alien*. Perhaps, however, if the writers were to do the films....

Science fiction will be alive and well in 2000, as it was in 1960 and 1900, as well as 1980. And there will be sufficient variety so that many readers will find authors and titles they like.

GERROLD, DAVID

1) *Star Trek.*
I believe that the *Star Trek* television series
(Gene Roddenberry) has been a first exposure to
science fiction for millions, perhaps hundreds of
millions of viewers. As a result, their basic science
fiction vocabulary has been taught to them, their
sense of wonder has been tickled, and their imaginations have been stretched to include the rest
of the universe. Their appetites for science fiction
have been whetted, and overall, I think it was *Star Trek* that established the
science fiction context for a mass audience.

A secondary event was the US Space Program, which lent science fiction
(and *Star Trek*) an air of legitimacy through implied government approval.

2) Which single book would I choose? This is an impossible question
for a science fiction writer to answer. I very much like *Ringworld, The Left
Hand of Darkness, Starship Troopers, The Moon Is a Harsh Mistress, Nova,
Triton, Imperial Earth, Rendezvous with Rama, The Fountains of Paradise,
The Gods Themselves,* and a couple of my own works. If it were a movie that
I had to choose, I'd choose *Star Wars* because it's so much fun. If a television
show, I'd probably take *Steambath.* But a book? I don't know. There are too
many good ones.

3) I think the next big science fiction market will involve a home computer environmental simulation/role-playing game in which the reader/con-
sumer will act out the part of the hero and have to make the appropriate
decisions in order to move through a structured environment. While many
of these environments will be adapted from various subcultures and mythol-
ogy, a major—perhaps *the* major—function of science fiction will be to provide new environments for this ultimate kind of escapist medium, the one in
which the consumer is the hero.

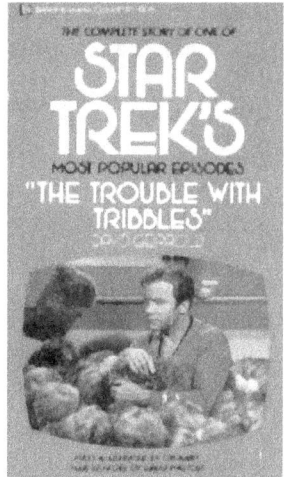

GOTTLIEB, SHERRY M.

1) Man's landing on the moon (1969).
2) *Dune,* by Frank Herbert.
3) Movies and/or holograms.
4) (I never saw a copy of it.)

HICKMAN, LYNN A.

You ask such tough questions.

I ran two different fanzines for you while I was living in Dixon, Illinois; *Why is a Fan?* and *Who Killed Science Fiction?* If I remember right, we did *Who Killed Science Fiction?* in the basement on Dement Avenue. That's when the bats got in and we were chasing them with tennis rackets. We got six of them, but the seventh got away and we never did find it.

As a young man, I see that science fiction has stood the hard test of time. It has rebounded from my sound drubbing. Beaten and smashed by a stick, killed by the force of a child's imagination, it has rebounded, filled with a dynamic, unquenchable spirit. Beautiful words and weird visions have coaxed me and persuaded me to follow it. The calm breeze of science fiction wafts me forever gently over smooth seas to the farthest shores and the limitless horizons of the intellect.

Who killed science fiction? I did. And, like the phoenix, it has burst forth more brilliant and dazzling than ever before. My children will take slingshots in hand and prepare to kill this great beast again. Their tomorrows will then be filled and amazed by the wonder and power of this phenomenon called science fiction.

LEIBER, FRITZ

1980: Retrospect and Prospect

Looking back from my present vantage point at 1960, I can understand why I was then in a mood to examine pessimistic questions about science fiction. Although I'd been writing strongly (for me) for the past two and a half years, I had to depend for income almost solely on pulp magazine publication of new material. My novel *The Big Time*, which as a serial in *Galaxy* had won the Hugo for best novel of 1958, still had not been published as a book, even a paperback. For that matter, I'd not had a new book published since 1957 and hardly a paperback reprint during the interim. About the only bright note was that at long last I'd found a low-paying market (*Fantastic*) for my Fafhrd-Mouser sword-and-sorcery stories, which had gone begging since the early 1940s, when they'd gotten started in the shortlived *Unknown*.

The general situation seemed no better. Fantasy wasn't selling while science fiction seemed no more than a qualified minor success. The fulfillment of the field's predictions of atomic energy, space flight, and electronic brains seemed to have led only to article leads such as, "Unlike the childish dreams of science fiction writers, space flight is now a hard-headed reality." Our individual successes (such as, say, Bob Heinleins sales to *The Saturday Evening Post*) were conspicuous because they were so rare. Also, they seemed fugitive; they didn't endure, lead anywhere. Really, the prospect was bleak.

What's most responsible for the changes 20 years have wrought? I'd simply say, the continuing output of good science fiction by popular writers such as Arthur C. Clarke, Isaac Asimov, Robert Heinlein (*The Moon Is a Harsh Mistress* is the book I'd save from the two decades), and their many successors and colleagues: Poul Anderson, Hal Clement, James Blish, Gordon Dickson, Robert Silverberg—I only give a sampling. All the rest flows from that—perceptive publishers such as Ian Ballantine and Donald Wollheim, television programs like *Star Trek*, increasingly workmanlike science fiction films, increased income from translations, better and more entertaining critical writing leading toward academic acceptance of science fiction, etc.

And I truly believe that A.D. 2000 will find book publication the largest as well as the most significant market area for science fiction material.

LUPOFF, RICHARD A.

1) The credit for science fiction's modern success can be traced to two events. The first of these, ironically, was the crash of the pulp magazine field that precipitated the 1960 edition of *Who Killed Science Fiction?* As long as science fiction was associated with cheap and lurid media—pulp magazines and comic books, especially the former—it could not be taken seriously by academics, librarians, etc. Philip K. Dick mentioned (in a piece in the early 1950s) that someday science fiction would be accepted in schools and libraries. He was absolutely correct, and what it took for that acceptance to begin was the ending of science fiction's association with pulp magazines.

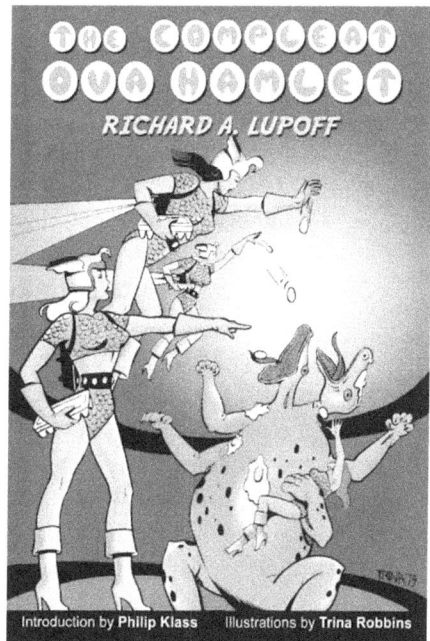

THE COMPLEAT OVA HAMLET

RICHARD A. LUPOFF

Introduction by **Philip Klass**   Illustrations by **Trina Robbins**

Once the dominant medium for publishing science fiction switched over to books—even paperbacks—it became possible for reviewers, scholars, and bibliographers to start paying attention to it. It also became possible for librarians to begin to stock science fiction.

As this process advanced, Sturgeon's Law came into play. The 90% of published science fiction that was crud fell by the wayside and the 10% that was *not* crud remained on library shelves and academic reading lists.

It was all uphill from there.

The second event that made science fiction successful—especially in film and television form—was President Kennedy's decision to send astronauts to the moon. The actuality of spaceships and interplanetary travelers made science fiction real and acceptable to the masses, showed Hollywood what could be done, and brought images of rocketships to the front page of every newspaper and to the screen of every television set in the land.

For all that science fiction had successfully predicted atomic weapons, peaceful uses of atomic power, television itself, computers, high-speed, long-range aircraft, etc., it was *still* identified in the public mind with "that crazy Buck Rogers stuff." And *that* was identified with spaceships.

Once spaceships became real, serious, acceptable—so did science fiction.

2) Looking over the science fiction books published in the past 20 years, it seems to have been an incredibly rich and rewarding period for the genre. Dozens, scores, perhaps even hundreds of candidates suggest themselves as "the one book" to be retained.

A lengthy winnowing process brings me down to the following novels, listed in no particular order:

The Dispossessed, by Ursula K. LeGuin
The Crystal World, by J.G. Ballard
Dhalgren, by Samuel R. Delany
Gravity's Rainbow, by Thomas Pynchon
Lord Valentine's Castle, by Robert Silverberg

All are rich and can be read over and over without exhausting their store of ideas, images, and pleasures. Most, you will notice, are long books. Only the Ballard is of average or shorter length for modern genre novels, and the Ballard is a work of extreme density and numerous layers of meaning.

Of the five, I think I would settle finally on the Pynchon, however, because of its great length, complexity, ingenuity, and humor.

But since you use the phrase "one only science fiction book" rather than "one only science fiction novel," you leave the gate ajar for consideration of collections and anthologies. Two of the latter deserve consideration, in my opinion.

The first is *The Science Fiction Hall of Fame*, the original volume, edited by Silverberg on the basis of a poll of SFWA members. It contains dozens of truly splendid science fiction stories by as many authors, with wildly varying themes, styles, etc. For picking around in, reading, and rereading, it would offer a constant variety that no novel could match.

In the same vein, I have recently been in the enviable position of assembling an anthology called *What If: Stories That Should Have Won the Hugo*. While one aspect of this book is a lot of second-guessing of the fan electorate of the past 20-odd years, in another sense it is my opportunity to assemble my own favorite stories, two-dozen-plus of them, under one cover. Think of having a book with all your own favorites in it—and not a single story that you don't love!

I'd be sorely tempted to take *What If* with me, instead of *Hall of Fame*. Especially since *What If* covers a more modern era. (There is some overlap, but not very much.) It would take a lot of thought, a lot of wavering among *Gravity's Rainbow, Hall of Fame*, and *What If*. But in the end I think...I think...I think I would still take *Gravity's Rainbow*.

3) Books!

4) It seems to me that the original edition of *Who Killed Science Fiction?* was based on a false premise. Odd that this should be the case, and that the symposium should still have become such a landmark!

The premise was that science fiction had died (or was dying) when in fact it wasn't science fiction but the pulp magazine industry that was dead or dying. This was both too large and too small a fact to be accurately observed.

On the one hand, much more than the science fiction pulps were dying. *All* the pulps were dying—westerns, romances, mysteries, war pulps, pirate story pulps, aviation pulps, superhero pulps—*everything!* To look at this picture and see only that science fiction was dying was far too narrow a view.

On the other hand, science fiction was *not* dying in books: it was about to enter the greatest period of growth in its history. Nor was it dying in motion pictures, on television, in comics, in popular music, or in any other medium. In this sense, to say that science fiction was dying was to claim far too much.

As I recall, in the original *Who Killed Science Fiction?* Kurt Vonnegut noted this point quite acerbically. I notice that science fiction has done very well for Mr. Vonnegut in the past 20 years, even if the opposite has been less the case.

If anything, the pulp magazines were the chrysalis of the new science fiction, the cocoon in which science fiction turned from caterpillar to butterfly. In crawled Hugo Gernsback, T. O'Conner Sloane, F. Orlin Tremaine, Raymond A. Palmer, John W. Campbell, etc. Out flew Kurt Vonnegut, Thomas M. Disch, Ursula K. LeGuin, John Varley, etc.

This is the best time in the history of science fiction...up to now. But it's nothing at all compared to what we will see and enjoy from now on!

McLAUGHLIN, DEAN

1) To finger a single factor more responsible than any other for science fiction's current commercial success is about as reasonable as identifying which snowflake in the avalanche started it all. But I've a hunch it might be demographic. Between 1960 and 1965, the postwar (World War II, that is) baby boom came of age. And, for the most part, science fiction appeals to a more youthful (or youthful-spirited) audience than does, say, shuffleboard.

Some other significant threads do show themselves in the warp and woof. Earliest perhaps was the slowly explosive growth of Tolkien's *Ring* "underground classic," which has now become a million-dollar industry. A second breakthrough into the general audience was made by Heinlein's *Stranger in a Strange Land*, which struck a responsive chord in the youthful bohemians of the time (because it lent endorsement to what they wanted to do anyway). Frank Herbert's *Dune* took similar advantage of outside-the-ghetto concerns, though I suspect no one was more surprised than the author. *Star Trek*—which put science fiction on prime-time television came later, and capitalized upon a trend already underway but also carried the trend forward. And *2001: A Space Odyssey*, one of the few nonmonster flicks, gave us more of the same.

Any media will continue to exploit a genre as long as the hope of gain exists, just as a bad horseman will kill his mount trying to win an endurance race. I would hazard a guess that no more high-quality science fiction is being written now than 20 years ago, although there's a lot more being published; but on the commercial side, conditions are much more comfortable now for the average run-of-the-mill science fiction writer than they were when H. Beam Piper put a gun to his head because he couldn't pay the rent.

2) Given the choice of only one book from the past 20 years, I'd have to settle on *Dune*. Mind you, I don't say it's the best book from that breadth of time, and there are several books—and a lot of writers—I have enjoyed more. But for multifarious and provocative content, it's the one which, I think, could stand the most rereading. And what could be more appropriate for the desert island lurking between the lines of that question?

3) It's always easier to look backward than forward, and science fiction writers are no more adept at predicting than the tea-leaf reader on the corner. But to make a guess, I suspect the largest "market area" for science fiction in A.D. 2000 will remain print media, with books dominant. Television (or its unforeseen successor, as television was radio's) will be the biggest-paying (with the possible exception of cinema, if cinema survives). But that medium's purchases will be at most a few dozen "buys" a year. In the same interval, several hundred science fiction books will be published. Individuals, the writers of such books, won't receive a fraction of the reward a t'feely writer might earn (unless t'feely rights to his book are sold) but there will be dozens of print media writers for every t'feely writer.

When I say "book" though, I don't necessarily mean the familiar object we call a book today. If/when some clever technician or consortium of technicians can develop an inexpensive (both to purchase and operate) battery-powered microfiche reader no bigger than a one-pound candy box and weighing no more than that, the typesetters' union will be looking for new jobs *en masse*, and the pressmen's union won't be far behind. But they'll be awfully happy at Eastman Kodak.

4) Looking back over what I've written here so far, I see that I might be misunderstood to confuse science fiction and fantasy. Normally I don't; I believe they are two fundamentally different genres. There is, of course, endless argument on the question, sometimes as acrimonious as that between the big-enders and the little-enders. And, to the uncritical eye, there are points of resemblance which mask the differences.

That's why. The science fiction/fantasy audience frequently fails to distinguish clearly, which is not its fault because many writers nowadays also fail to distinguish. Witness most recently Orson Scott Card's excellent *A Planet Called Treason*, which invokes the name of science but which nevertheless is pure fantasy. Quite a few "modern" writers appear, to my view, innocent of what science is truly about. Such innocence is, of course, quite liberating in one sense; the "hard" science fiction writer is far more inhibited. Personally, though, I am convinced that no worthwhile achievement comes easy, and realistic science fiction is, on the whole, more satisfying.

O'MEARA, JAMES H.

1) My feeling is that the long-term success of *Star Trek* contributed most to the current recognition and reception of science fiction. Though *Star Trek* ran only three (first-run) seasons, it was tremendously successful in reruns and spawned a cult following. This following was the right age and background to move into colleges, graduate schools, and the academic community. With enough support, science fiction could come out of the "closet" and be accepted as an important branch of literature, or as in my own academic background, worthy of sociological analyses. My only regret is that my interest in science fiction was ahead of its time. Looking backward, I see a number of sociological approaches that I could have applied to science fiction if I had progressed through the graduate school hoops to a Ph.D.

2) I find that I have to break this question down. If you are talking about a nonfiction title, the single title I would select to own would be Tuck's (Yeah! Advent:!) *Encyclopedia of Science Fiction*. I find it to be my most valuable reference document when I have any question concerning the field of science fiction. If you are talking about a fiction title, I would have to say that I have no choice. I've looked back for 20 years and find that nothing stands out enough for me to choose it over anything else. I don't know if this is due to my drifting

away from the field or a general lack of anything outstanding being published within it. I suspect it may be a combination of the two. In the 20-year period before 1960, I would have picked the Heinlein "Future History" volume as being the single book I would have wanted to own.

3) My feeling is that books, and especially paperbacks, will continue to be the largest market for science fiction in terms of properties bought. However, I also feel that the big money and success will continue to be in the area of the movies. Television still seems to be a very limited market and only *Star Trek* has been a real success in the past 20 years. Even the success of *Star Trek* was limited; it managed only three seasons compared to the ten-to fifteen-plus seasons of *Gunsmoke* and other long-running television shows. *Star Trek* was good because it showed there was a market for science fiction. However, the ratings showed that the market was limited.

Your question implies that we should consider other mediums such as computer terminals, video cassettes, etc. I don't really see much chance for science fiction's developing a significant market in these areas. I may be wrong, but I feel that books have been around a long time and will continue to be around. I would personally rather read a book than watch television or a movie, and I think the people science fiction appeals to feel the same way.

4) Can it really be almost 20 years since I helped Earl Kemp put together the first *Who Killed Science Fiction?*

Age seems to sneak up on us. I look back and bits and pieces come to my memory. I still remember starting out early one Saturday morning to go to Lynn Hickman's house to do the printing. My memory of the trip was that it was sometime in the winter. I don't remember where Lynn lived then, but an examination of a map suggests that Dixon, Illinois, is the most likely candidate. It is amazing how one remembers some things and forgets others. I can't remember the town without prodding but I can remember Lynn's basement, his Multilith, and our troubles with a wandering bat. I still remember Lynn and me chasing that bat with tennis rackets around the basement and speculating that it was really Count Dracula (Lugosi, not Langella) trying to stop the publication of *Who Killed Science Fiction?* Or Reva Smiley.

The main thing that sticks in my mind about the production of *Who Killed Science Fiction?* was that it was a lot of effort, especially on Earl Kemp's part. There were a lot of Multilith masters involved, and he typed them all. There was a lot of effort in printing and there was a lot of work in collating. I remember that it took us two days at Lynn's house just to get the whole thing printed. Somehow, at the time, it seemed like too much effort for an organization like SAPS. This is not to put down SAPS, which was serving a real purpose, but that purpose was communication and comment, not the quality literary analyses approach that *Who Killed Science Fiction?* represented. *Who Killed Science Fiction?* should have been an Advent publication, rather than an amateur press association effort.

I look back on *Who Killed Science Fiction?* and its production with real fondness. It represents a simpler time in my life when I had the time, money, and energy to commit to a hobby. Twenty years later I find that I don't have the time or energy to devote to science fiction. Somehow the responsibilities of job and home seem to absorb all available time and energy. I look back now and wonder how Earl Kemp managed to get the time and energy not only for *Who Killed Science Fiction?* but for *Why Is a Fan?* and CHICON III, given his job and family responsibilities.

In any case, it was a good time, and something was produced from it of lasting value: A friendship that continues across 20 years and 3,500 miles.

PANSHIN, ALEXEI

Alexei Panshin

I've been privileged to see a copy of the rare first edition of *Who Killed Science Fiction?* only once. About the time that it was first published, I stayed overnight at the home of its editor, Earl Kemp, and in the morning, before the house awoke, I was able to pick up a copy off the end table and page through it hastily.

What did it say? I hardly remember now, my time with it was so short. I think I remember John W. Campbell, editor of the magazine that was about to change its name from *Astounding* to *Analog*, saying: "Nonsense, my good friend. Science fiction isn't dead. Science fiction is better than ever."

But I could be wrong about that.

What did *Who Killed Science Fiction?* really have to say? I'm not at all sure, but I'm very interested in finding out. I may not remember the details of ten brief minutes of reading but, for 20 years, the *fact* of that publication, *Who Killed Science Fiction?* has been of great importance to me.

At the time, I was only an uncritical science fiction fan, a bolter of raw meat. New science fiction paperbacks were published every day—and I took little notice of whether they were reprints from the magazines of 1941 or brand-new work published for the first time. As far as I knew, there was a bottomless well of science fiction. I wasn't prepared to note the weakness of contemporary work. I was not yet taking account of the fact that the *Queen's Own FBI* series of novels that John W. Campbell was currently printing in his magazine were shallow and trivial next to the SF that had first won my heart.

That science fiction was dead was a new thought to me.

How could science fiction die?

It brought me up short. It made me think.

I wanted to write science fiction. I was trying to write it.

I needed to know—was science fiction dead? Who had killed it, and why? What did it all mean?

Like a good detective, I had to get the whole picture. If I wanted to write SF, as I did and still do, I felt I needed to know what the nature of science fiction was, where it came from, and where it was going. Ever since 1960, I've wrestled with Earl Kemp's question, "Who killed science fiction?" and attempted to solve the case.

I pursued the question through the middle and late 1960s, when it seemed far stranger and less likely than it had in 1960. Science fiction apparently rose from the grave. In the hands of writers like Zelazny and Delany, science fiction seemed renewed, turned to new subjects, framed in new language. And I was part of all this action. My first novel, published in 1968, won the SFWA Nebula Award as Best Science Fiction Novel of the year.*

A strange and powerful corpse, this science fiction.

And yet, by the end of the 1960s, I came to the conclusion that, unlikely as it might seem in the midst of all this blaze of activity, Earl Kemp had been right to raise his question in 1960. I was gripped by the conviction that the science fiction I had known and loved all the years of my youth was no longer valid. That it had no more room for growth, no more spark, no more truth. And that I could not write it.

And yet I still believed in the validity of SF. I was still touched by its magic. I still wanted to write SF—as I do today.

I still wanted to write SF. And I believed that "science fiction" in the Gernsback/Campbell sense was dead.

I've spent the 1970s, with the help of my wife, Cory, in trying to get to the bottom of this. I've written little fiction. Instead, I've collected testimony, compared clues, examined facts, and written in my casebook. Through the 1970s, perhaps more than any other persons, Cory and I have written about the nature and meaning of SF, and the mortality of science fiction.

It's only appropriate, then, that Earl Kemp should have written to me now, 20 years later, invoking the name of the kid from Michigan who once slept on

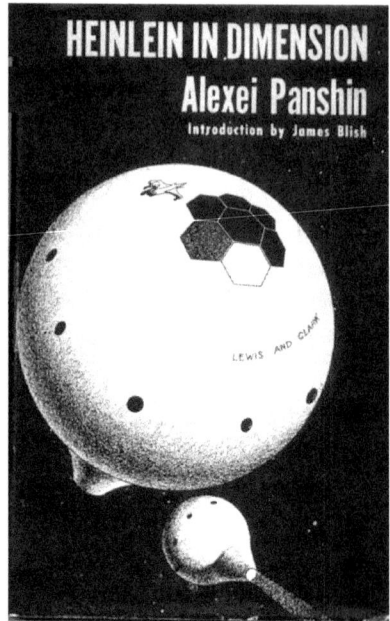

---

*Alexei is too modest. He should have named his first novel, *Rite of Passage,* and be justifiably proud of its awards as well. –E.K.

his sofa, asking me to contribute to this after-20-years edition of *Who Killed Science Fiction?* Cory and I think we know the answer to the question at last.

Our conclusion is that each era has its own SF—in the large sense—its own form of mythic literature, attuned to the needs and knowledge of that time. Each new formation of SF has its own life and death. It starts off full of beans and tricks, rife with possibility, and at the end is a tired old shuffler, a tyrant, an impediment ripe for a slit throat.

Science fiction, born in the days of Wells, recognized as itself in the days of Gernsback, came into its Golden Age in the days of Campbell—pushing the previous lost race and occult formation of SF from the stage. Science fiction had its period as the typical form of SF, its galactic venturings the mythic template for the technological expansiveness of the postwar era. Science fiction stumbled mightily at the end of the 1950s—and Earl Kemp rightly detected this first sign of mortality. Science fiction isn't quite dead yet, as I write this in 1979, but its breathing is labored.

The new form of SF is already here. It doesn't have a clearly separate name, but it might be called eco-SF. In these stories it is the environment, the web of ecology, the interaction of the whole of human consciousness that is the transcendent driving-wheel, the source of energy, and not technological inventiveness as in "science fiction." Early examples of this new SF form appeared in the 1950s. *The Space Merchants* (Pohl and Kornbluth), which based its criticisms of rampant technology in ecology, is one. More and more SF since, whether apparently "science fiction" or "New Wave experimentalism" or "neo-fantasy," has shared this same new basis, founding its wonders and marvels not in technology but in ecology.

We are now in the process of leaving the technological era for the ecological era—signaled by the so-called Energy Crisis—and the new eco-SF is about to step forward into its own Golden Age: 1938 all over again, but more so.

In fact, so fast is the revolution of thought these days, by the year 2000 it seems likely that the ecologically minded form of SF will have had its day and be showing its own first signs of impending mortality. The question of that day is likely to be "Why Has the Force Been So Wan Lately?" The successor myth, eco-SF's challenger and heir, antagonist and offspring, will already be on the stage, giving eco-SF the elbow, challenging it for its lack of centrality of vision, for its failures to acknowledge higher purpose, for its relativity and irresponsibility.

So much will have happened by the year 2000, in the sphere of daily life every bit as much as in the sphere of mythic consciousness, that all in all I can't help but wonder whether the Third Edition of *Who Killed Science Fiction?* that Earl Kemp has projected for the year 2000 will ever be published. Who killed science fiction? Too much will have happened in the meantime for anyone to care who done the old goat in. It was all so long ago, and besides, it was only the plumber.

Surely the question can be settled now, once and for all, so that it won't ever have to be brought up again.

Who killed science fiction?

You say that Heinlein didn't quite do the job? There are still a few kicks in the corpse?

All right. Hand me the knife. I'll do it.

There! (Anyone else want to have a hack?)

Hail, Death!

REYNOLDS, MACK

1) I'm of the opinion that the factor that has led most of the present boom in science fiction is the increase in pay for the writer. Before 1960 there were a few markets compared with today and the pay was fantastically low, often as little as a penny a word. And at that time there were few anthologies. In short, when you sold your story it was unlikely that you'd ever make anything more on it. Paperbacks were relatively few, and, if you sold a serial to one of the magazines, you'd have little chance of seeing it later as a book. There were very few writers who made a living writing science fiction exclusively. I doubt if there were more than half a dozen. Even such old-time favorites as Jack Williamson and Cliff Simak wrote their stories in their spare time, while Jack taught and Cliff edited a newspaper. The present writer made a living as a free-lancer but had to augment his science fiction income by doing travel articles and other things outside the field.

Today, you can make a living. In fact, some of the top pros have become comparatively rich. At this writing Arthur C. Clarke has retired in comfort. Bob Heinlein is holding out for a million for his latest book. Bob Silverberg got nearly a quarter of a million for hardcover rights alone on the strength of an outline.

For one thing, the markets are considerably more numerous. Science fiction used to be largely an American and British phenomenon. Now it's worldwide. The other day, I sold four stories to Yugoslavia. One was "The Business as Usual," which I originally wrote in 1950 and sold to *The Magazine of Fantasy and Science Fiction* for around $35. The Yugoslavians gave me over $100. And it's sold elsewhere, to anthologies, to collections, to college textbooks, in translation—perhaps 30 times. They even made it into a television show in Belgium. Then there are movie sales. Before 1960 precious few science fiction writers sold to Hollywood. The same applied to television.

When you sell a story now, you have a property, not a one-sale thing. You'll sell that same story over and over again. It means that you can afford to make science fiction your profession now. There are dozens of full-time science fiction writers in the field, and that makes for better quality. You no longer dash off a yarn in your spare time, largely out of pure affection for the genre, but devote all the hours necessary with the expectation of making quite a bit of money.

2) I think I'd probably choose Ursula K. Le Guin's *The Dispossessed* as the one book I'd want to keep. I'm a specialist in science fiction with socioeconomic themes myself and think there is much too little of political economy in our field. You'd think that science fiction would be crawling with stories about future societies. But no. More often than not, when even such masters as Asimov and van Vogt wrote their *Foundation* and *Weapon Shops* series, the governments of the future are feudalism. They don't even have capitalism. They've gone back to feudalism. Ursula, however, in her book, presents us with an anarchistic society, and a sympathetic one at that. It's a beautiful job of extrapolating in the field of socioeconomics.

3) I hate to say it, but I have a suspicion that television (and possibly Tri-Di) will continue to take over. I suspect that by the turn of the century there will be fewer books and more screens. What books we do read will probably be flashed on a screen for us from the National Data Banks. The cost of paper is skyrocketing and will continue to do so as our forests become more and more depleted. Newspapers, magazines, and even books are going to make less and less sense. Flash 'em on a screen rather than outright buy a hardcover or paperback book.

4) Sorry, I was in Europe when *Who Killed Science Fiction?* was published and, though I heard of the book, I've never seen it. I look forward to the new edition.

SCHWEITZER, DARRELL

1) It's not simple enough that one person can be singled out, but I feel a lot of credit goes to Donald Wollheim. He is responsible for both the Edgar Rice Burroughs and J.R.R. Tolkien booms, which caused fantastic literature to be more widely read than ever before. While Burroughs and Tolkien aren't directly related to the mainstream of science fiction, it did bring to the attention of publishers the fact that fantastic books *sell*. This is of enormous value, particularly after the barren period of the late 1950s when they didn't seem to have been selling much. Donald Wollheim also gets credit for publishing the first novels of writers who would become the superstars of the more prosperous late 1960s—Roger Zelazny, Ursula LeGuin, Samuel Delany, Thomas Disch, etc.

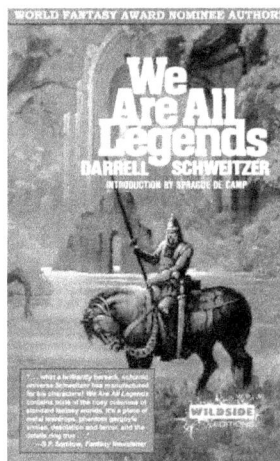

The field has gained sophistication and sensitivity since the end of the 1950s. Credit for this goes to editors who published material which might not have been understood or even recognized as science fiction in an earlier period. Cele Goldsmith, as editor of *Amazing* and *Fantastic*, certainly raised those magazines to heights not achieved before or since. John Carnell's *Science Fantasy*, even more than his *New Worlds*, helped to raise the quality of the field. The Michael Moorcock *New Worlds* and the various "new wave" anthologies published in the United States, notably *Dangerous Visions* (edited by Harlan Ellison), were important more for the publicity they generated and the change they brought about than the actual quality of the material published in them, although there was much of merit in them, particularly in *New Worlds* from 1964 to 1967. All this concern about expanding the boundaries of the field couldn't help but do exactly that. This helped to bring science fiction out of the creative paralysis it was in circa 1960. Writers began to do something more than just repeats of previous concepts. They began to pay more attention to *how* their material was written. This in turn created a market for more sophisticated material. My guess would be that many of the most distinguished works of the 1960s, including Zelazny's *The Dream Master*, Disch's *Camp Concentration*, Aldiss' *Barefoot in the Head*, and Brunner's *Stand on Zanzibar* could not have been published ten years earlier.

An increase in quality brings in new readers, and it also attracts academics, which introduce their classes to the material. It would have been absurd to teach the *Lensman* series in a classroom, since the writing fails on every level the academically trained person knows how to recognize, all the way down to grammar. An innovative idea is not enough for this audience. They demand excellence of form, too. Now there were stories worthy of adult interest published in science fiction magazines as early as the middle 1930s, and literate science fiction appeared with some regularity after John Campbell became editor of *Astounding*, but as a general rule it takes a university English department 20 to 30 years to find this sort of thing out. The universities, far from being leaders in any cultural trend, are always well to the rear. I suspect the process is one of teachers being replaced by their students. When, in the 1950s, a college teacher proclaimed science fiction to be illiterate trash, his students (who read what was then being published and were not basing their judgments on, at best, a skimpy knowledge of 1930s material) knew better. By the 1960s these people had become the professors. Jack Williamson's researches in the area of science fiction courses will bear this out. The numbers increase dramatically from the early 1960s onward. Someone entering an academic career in, say, 1965, grew up reading the science fiction of the late 1940s and of the 1950s. He knew better than his teachers.

On a broader scale, we find that a vast number of fantasy and science fiction books were published by regular publishers, and science fiction short stories were published in mass-circulation magazines. About the time of the Depression, this stopped. It did not resume until after World War II. Anyone whose literary values were formed in the schools or by what was critically fashionable from the 1920s onward would be under the impression that fantasy is for children and anything imaginative is somehow suspect as not being "serious." In my experience, this has been true of older professors I have known, but not of the younger ones. It's also true of older people in general, those who were part of a generation raised without any exposure to the fantastic. But this is a temporary aberration, since human literature has been dominated by the imaginative throughout most of history, except very recently. I suspect things are simply reverting to normal. There now exists an audience which regards science fiction/fantasy as an ordinary form of writing. The idea that it is shunned and forbidden is probably beyond the experience of most people living today who are under 35 years of age.

I do not think films have had any important impact. There is not enough evidence that the *Star Trek/Star Wars* audience is a reading audience, although *2001*, with its attempts at philosophical seriousness, perhaps did attract book readers to science fiction. But it is important to note that no significant science fiction films, marketed as science fiction, were produced during the period of recovery, roughly 1963-67. I would say that the recovery is an artistic phenomenon, in that writers learned new things to say and new ways to say them, and thus kept boredom and stagnation away, and a publishing phenomenon in that publishers began to see science fiction as a money-making category. Each science fiction bestseller, *Stranger in a Strange Land, Dune*, etc., helped to make science fiction more than an extremely marginal proposition.

2) This is really an unanswerable question, since one must choose either an anthology which contains the most representative selection of stories, or a collection by one of the best writers, or the best novel. It is a very imprecise thing to say this or that is *the* best work because something else may be just as good in another way. Disch's *Camp Concentration* attempts things never attempted in a science fiction novel before, and it is written with a polish and sophistication seldom matched, but the author found himself backed into a corner where allegorical necessity forced him to pull a rabbit out of a hat, and so he did, at the expense of plot logic. Probably the richest book of this period, for detailed imagination and ideas, is John Brunner's *Stand on Zanzibar*, which also represents a quantum leap for the science fiction field as a whole. Roger Zelazny's *The Dream Master* may be the most perfect infusion of outside literary material into science fiction, and it too is a significant advance, since one of the failings of science fiction during the failing period of the end of the 1950s was that it was too derivative of other science fiction and too little aware of the rest of human thought and culture. Samuel Delany's *Driftglass* is probably the best story collection of the decade, demonstrating

all the growth and acquired strengths of the new science fiction without any of its self-indulgent weaknesses. J.G. Ballard's *Chronopolis* is also of considerable note for its infusion of surrealism into science fiction, something which probably would have been unpublishable fifteen years earlier.

3) I think science fiction in 2000 will still be a printed medium for the most part. If one projects current publishing trends, the growth of science fiction against the shrinkage of other forms of fiction, it seems obvious that science fiction will account for all fiction being published in a decade or so. Of course curves like that never work out. They level off. The growth of science fiction is inherently limited by the available number of literate people capable of assimilating imaginative material. By the end of the century the old prejudice against science fiction should have died completely, although there may be a reaction in the sense it may seem old hat to some readers, the same way the medieval romance seemed exhausted by 1600 and the gothic novel (real gothics like Hugh Walpole and Mrs. Radcliffe, not ladies' nightgown and candle epics) were pretty worn out by the middle of the nineteenth century. There is a real possibility of this if the writers and readers of today become complacent with what is being written and published. I see some indications that the science fiction market is presently expanded, the demand exceeding the supply of top-grade material. As a result some mediocre writers, who scarcely would have attracted any attention at all in the late 1960s, are now superstars. But excellent science fiction continues to be published, and new writers are entering the field at an unprecedented rate, so I don't see stagnation in the immediate future. Probably in the year 2000 there will be science fiction novels as conventional and formula-ridden as a contemporary bestseller, serving the same needs, selling the same way, and being forgotten just as quickly, while the best material, which may not sell as much at the outset, will remain in print as long as there are discriminating readers. This has been going on already, which is why a 40-year-old book like de Camp's *Lest Darkness Fall* remains in print while many more popular but inferior works of the intervening years are dust.

4) I can't answer this since I know the original *Who Killed Science Fiction?* only by reputation and have never seen a copy. The 1980 reprint of it is most welcome.

SCORTIA, THOMAS N.

Earl Kemp's questions proved to be more difficult to answer than I had anticipated. However, with the help of my ever-trusty Horizon II, I submit the following deathless observations:

1) By "1980's success" I presume Earl means science fiction's wide acceptance rather than its literary or prognosticative success.

The "event" was the relentless intrusion of sophisticated technology into daily life to the point where even "mainstream" popular novels become increasingly based on essentially science fiction themes. (Witness: *FailSafe, The Child Buyer, Kalki, The Pidgeon Project, Marooned*, and a dozen other bestsellers of the recent two decades. Even the Scortia-Robinson books are basically science fiction.) The rapid development of space travel, information processing machines, advanced surgery, molecular biology, and early genetic tailoring, the frightening development of military devices—all of these have become the stuff of our morning front page.

Such rapid growth has thrown the average man into what Alvin Toffler calls "future shock." Science fiction was the one fictional form that routinely dealt with such matters. Although the theme of a story might be downbeat, the average science fiction story tried to describe the world into which we were evolving and the physical aspects (at least) of that science fiction world worked.

In that sense even the downbeat story carries a note of optimism. (Bad as the future is, we survived and got there. For all the political dangers of *Star Wars*, the gadgets are beautiful and the future exciting.) The promises and the problems and the hazards of today are those explored in science fiction. In a phrase, science fiction is popular because we are day-to-day living in a science fiction world.

2) Assuming that I would be allowed to keep only one science fiction book published after 1960, which one would I elect to keep?

I have not been that impressed with recent science fiction novels. Many are enjoyable and thoughtful books, but there is no single *sui generis* book I could name that would stand out among the books published after 1960. I am very fond of Robert Silverberg's *Dying Inside*, but the science fiction content is only incidental to the novel. If you offered me "The Collected Works of Robert A. Heinlein," I'd probably settle for that. I am much impressed with George Zebrowski's *Macrolife* (Harper and Row, 1979); it is a sprawling book of giant intent. It fails on several levels, but abounds with ideas for future novels in the series.

3) What will dominate science fiction in the year 2000?

I suspect that the major theme will be related to the biological sciences coupled with space travel. The advent of relatively low orbital costs with the development of a second-generation space shuttle together with the rapid growth of molecular biology should focus our interests on what is becoming known as "exo-biology." I expect that the major themes will center around genetic tailoring of animals, plants, and *man* for both space colonies (see the previously cited Zebrowski novel, *Macrolife*) and for planetary colonies. Terraforming of alien planets by biological techniques (probably the only practical approach because of the chain-reaction effect) is, of course, a part of the larger themes of exo-biology.

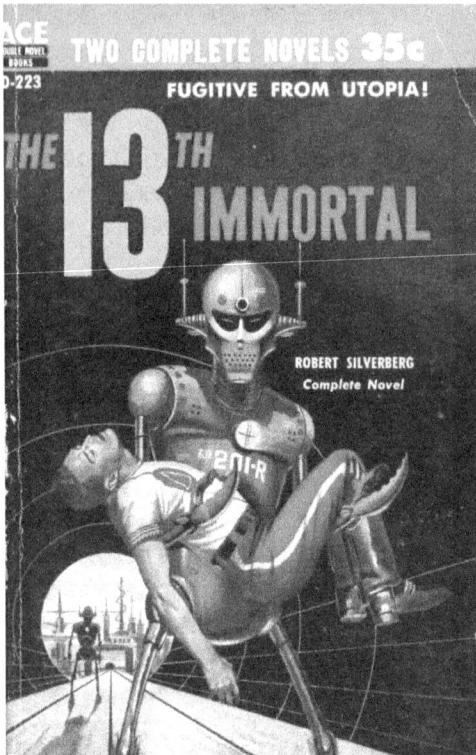

SILVERBERG, ROBERT

Alas, a search of the archives here does not reveal my copy of the original *Who Killed Science Fiction?* Whether it was a victim of the fire I had in 1968, of my move to California a couple of years later, or simple misfiling, I can't say, but at any rate I can't find it and, with the summer moving along, I see I'll have to contribute to the 1980 updating without knowledge of whatever it was I said in 1960. Anyway:

In fact, those new movies and occasional books that have had unprecedented popular successes in recent times have not been "science fiction" but rather the new eco-SF. *Star Wars*, however much it may have borrowed from science fiction, as science fiction borrowed from the lost race novel, does not rely upon a science-fictional superweapon constructed out of toothpicks and chicken wire to smash the *Deathstar*. Rather, it is the universal mind-power, The Force, that is called upon.

Before long, the popularity of the new eco-SF will be so overwhelming and general that science fiction will be completely shoved into the background. A curiosity. A strange prototype. A who cares? Before the end of the century, the new SF will be the mainstream, the commonplace mode of expression. "Science fiction" will look like the work of plumbers. The new SF will be subtle and flexible, its paramount means of expression the video disc circulating by subscription, mail order, and clandestine means.

No Grand Sachem should be picked as the paramount figure in the emergence of eco-SF. No Gernsback. No Campbell. Instead, the combined work of many persons in a variety of areas will be recognized—academics, critics, editors, writers, directors. Such will be the scope and power of the new SF that many persons will be recognized for many reasons. In fact, such will be the ecological frame of mind that no one particular person will be singled out for unique honor. Rather, it will quite properly seem that the efforts of a wide variety of particular persons, the drift of events, luck, and this and that, all contributed to a field effect, a sudden great synergetic alteration explainable in the current fashionable and persuasive languages of Catastrophe Theory and the Theory of Dissipative Structures—and suddenly, lo!, SF emerged into prominence and became the mode of the day.

From the perspective of the year 2000, if one is concerned with the fate of science fiction, the most important book of the period 1960 to 1980 may well be Robert Heinlein's *Number of the Beast*, for Heinlein's deliberate undermining of the metaphysical centrality and veracity of the *Future History* series, Heinlein's fundamental contribution to modern science fiction.

AAEEEIii!

The Singer's Going
To Sing a Song

"...Twenty years ago today, Sgt. Pepper taught the band to play...
may I introduce to you the act you've known for all these years..."
(Sgt. Pepper's Lonely Hearts Club Band).

I want to thank you all again, you're such a lovely audience.
Flipping through the pages of my memory, the pages of *Who Killed Science Fiction?*, and letting my thoughts wander over the names as they pop out of the pages and grab at me...

They are gone now, so many dear old friends, or disappeared or altered into some unrecognizable other. Hugo Gernsback, the modern-day father of us all. *Astounding* and John. *Astonishing* and Ted Carnell. *Weird* and Seabury Quinn ("Bon Voyage, Michele"). *Star Trek* and James Blish/Atherton. *Famous Fantastic Mysteries* and Hannes Bok. Convention standbys Tony Boucher and Willy Ley. The ever-present Midwesterners Auggie Derleth, Rog Phillips, Ray Palmer, and Mr. Wonderful himself, Doc Smith.

Startling, Planet, and *Thrilling Wonder Stories.*

All of our yesteryears; the people/things who/that made up *Who Killed Science Fiction?* 20 years ago. I am almost overwhelmed by the magnitude of it all. Who could have foreseen, 20 years ago, that anyone would be sitting here celebrating the absence of so much that is so dear to all of us, as I am doing at the moment I write these words? I am not aware that so many well-loved science fiction people have ever been assembled together in one such effort before.

It is fitting then that *Who Killed Science Fiction?* should be a monument to the era.

The results:
Rendezvous with Rama
Ringworld

Stand on Zanzibar
Starship Troopers
Tower of Glass
Triton
What If: Stories That Should Have Won
the Hugo

and two "pretend" books, both by Robert A. Heinlein:

"The Collected Works of Robert A.
Heinlein"
"The Future History Series"

In addition, one movie (*Star Wars*), one television show (*Steambath*), and one short story ("Sundance") received honorable mention.

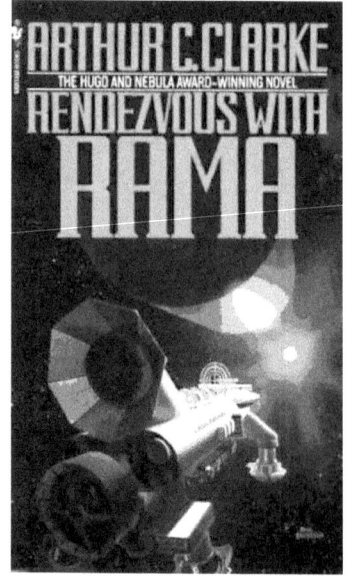

For item Number 3:
Looking forward to the year 2002 and the third edition of Who Killed Science Fiction?, *what medium (already existing or not yet contemplated) will become, in your opinion, the largest market area for science fiction material?*

*These data not available for 1979 as of this writing, which would bring these totals upward somewhat. Statistics courtesy Donald Franson and Howard DeVore: *A History of the Hugo, Nebula and International Fantasy Awards* (Detroit: Misfit, 1978).

The definite and loud response was: BOOK PUBLICATION (in some still-recognizable form) for four mentions, with an additional two mentions of science fiction in paperbound formats.

The significant runner-up, with two and one-half mentions, is television, advanced considerably and incorporating three-dimensional, sensurround, and/or plug-in t'feelyvision.

There was additional speculation regarding:

1. Subscription video-discs and/or tape cassettes.

2. Movies incorporating holograms.

3. A home computer environmental simulation role-playing game.

Of all these, I personally prefer the latter. There is an empty spot in my living room waiting for just such a strange device.

Who Killed Science Fiction? 1980: The other voices have spoken and 20 years and tomorrow have come and gone and the singer is finishing up the song he felt like singing. It is time for us to move on toward our next reunion, our third edition.

Hurry, 2002!

– **EARL KEMP**

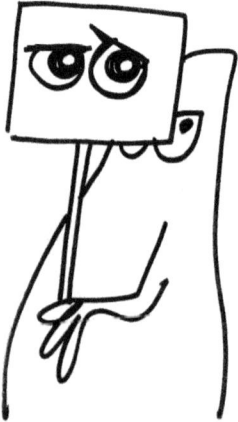

Index

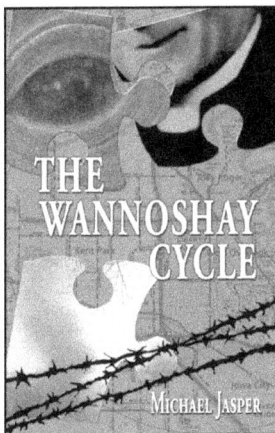

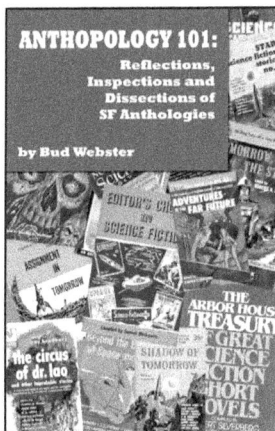

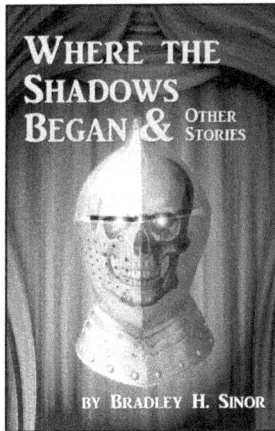